Other Books by Paul Hellyer

Agenda: A Plan for Action (1971)

Exit Inflation (1981)

Jobs for All: Capitalism on Trial (1984)

Canada at the Crossroads: A Liberal Agenda for the 90's and Beyond
(1990)

Damn the Torpedoes: My Fight to Unify Canada's Armed Forces
(1990)

Funny Money: A Common Sense Alternative to Mainline Economics
(1994)

Surviving the Global Financial Crisis: The Economics of Hope for
Generation X (1996)

Arundel Lodge: A Little Bit of Old Muskoka (1996)

The Evil Empire: Globalization's Darker Side (1997)

Stop: Think (1999)

Goodbye Canada (2001)

One Big Party: To Keep Canada Independent (2003)

A Miracle in Waiting: Economics that Make Sense (2010)

LIGHT AT THE END OF THE TUNNEL

A SURVIVAL PLAN FOR THE HUMAN SPECIES

PAUL HELLYER

authorHOUSE®

AuthorHouse™
1663 Liberty Drive, Suite 200
Bloomington, IN 47403
www.authorhouse.com
Phone: 1-800-839-8640

First published by AuthorHouse 4/12/2010

ISBN: 978-1-4490-7614-6 (e)
ISBN: 978-1-4490-7612-2 (sc)
ISBN: 978-1-4490-7613-9 (hc)

Library of Congress Control Number: 2010900756

Printed in the United States of America
Bloomington, Indiana

This book is printed on acid-free paper.

CONTENTS

For

My late wife Ellen

and

All God's Children on Earth and in the Cosmos

ACKNOWLEDGMENTS

As always, I am deeply grateful to a number of individuals for their assistance in the preparation of this book. In am indebted to Dr. Donald Anderson, Noel Cooper, Paola Harris, Kathy Hellyer, Kent Hotaling, James Maclean, Dr. Edgar Mitchell, Dr. Douglas Peters, Anne Turcot, Warren Ralph and Victor Viggiani for reading part or all of the manuscript and making suggestions as to how it might be improved.

Three of them deserve special mention for help and advice well beyond what one might expect. Jim Maclean for getting me back on track when I got off on a tangent; Kent Hotaling for a painstaking review and a multitude of useful amendments; and, especially Noel Cooper for a line by line review of both some of the major issues and the inevitable errors and omissions. At the end of the day responsibility for those that slipped through the net, and for the positions taken, rest with me alone.

Beatrice Orchard and my executive assistant Nina Moskaliuk contributed many hours of research, as did the Parliamentary Library in Ottawa that was marvelously helpful. Nina also prepared the extensive notes.

I am indebted to Sarah Reid for preparing the index in a professional manner and also for noting a number of errors in need of correction.

My thanks, also, to all the people who briefed me and those that I interviewed at length – especially Travis Walton and Jim Sparks.

Finally, I would like to thank my wife Sandra for her rare insights, and for putting up with me these many long months when I have been pre-occupied with "the book" at the expense of more congenial pursuits.

INTRODUCTION

An infuriating revolutionary, is the way Jack Granatstein, former York University historian describes me. Let me deal with that charge at once by pleading guilty. I am a revolutionary – not the kind that take up arms against his fellow man, but one who sees a policy or practice he considers to be dreadfully wrong and who feels driven to try to do something about it. The revolution I seek, therefore, is a revolution of the mind and heart. And sometimes I can be a bit infuriating because I have found that you can't change anything of significance without upsetting someone.

This book began as an autobiography of the second half of my career beginning in 1968 immediately after the Liberal Party of Canada convention where I was defeated by Pierre Elliot Trudeau, who became prime minister. Before it was finished, however, my heart and mind were flooded with concerns a thousand times more important than the political games that were the center of my life for more than half-a-century. I am profoundly concerned about the future of the human species, and want to ring the alarm bell. So I have eliminated the historical section to make space for more urgent concerns.

Before I continue, however, I should let you know this much about me. My God is the God of Abraham, Isaac, Jacob and Ishmael, and my role model is Jesus of Nazareth. I would like to make it clear that I am no saint. Far from it! But every ship needs a star to steer by – a beacon by which a moral compass can be recalibrated when it goes askew.

In politics I have been branded as everything from far left to far right. I put myself in the radical center – one who seeks solutions to problems based on first principles without regard to ideology. I believe that it is the kind of solution the world desperately needs at a time when niggling change or fine tuning is not good enough. My philosophy can be summed up in three words: The Golden Rule.

I favor neither big government nor small government. I seek effective government that creates a climate of opportunity where individuals can live and work creatively seeking novel solutions to seemingly intractable problems without suffocation by entrenched bureaucracies. At the same time governments have a solemn obligation to guarantee that every citizen has access to certain basic services including health insurance. This is not socialism it is just human decency – treating others the way we would want to be treated if we were in their circumstances.

Governments must also ensure that our cars, planes, trains and ships are of sound design and that public transportation vehicles of all kinds are well maintained and safely operated. We expect them to protect us from contaminated foods and unsafe products including new drugs that should be tested under their supervision without relying on private test results that may downplay negative side effects of which consumers should be aware. In a word, we expect our elected representatives to undertake those measures on our behalf that we are unable to do for ourselves, or in concert with small collectivities.

Finally, our governments should be brave enough to take the long view on our behalf – even when that results in measures that are unpopular with some classes of voters and financial supporters. The way we are headed we are going to make the planet unfit for habitation by man or beast. No special gift of prophecy is required to validate this prediction. All one has to do is project the trend lines to know that it is true – an uncanny gift that I have proven on more than one occasion.

Consequently the book has been reworked as an unusual mix of religion, economics and politics because they are the keys to our salvation as a species. And to those who say that religion and politics don't mix, read your history. Religion has been and continues to be the source of more wars and conflicts than any of us who call ourselves believers want to admit.

Similarly the art of politics is influenced by ideology – good, bad, and indifferent. In recent years we have found that the United States, our world leader and a country that claims to Trust in God, has been leading us along the path to extinction. This is because its richest, most powerful elite who have been running the country, seem committed to policies that line their own pockets with short-term profits with little heed to the long-term consequences for all humankind.

To regain the moral high ground, and restore hope for Americans, along with the rest of us, the new U.S. administration will have to totally reverse most of the initiatives of the last eight years, and some that go back much further – its imperial pretensions, its emphasis on preparing for war rather than establishing peace, and its apparent indifference to climatic trends that threaten the future existence of the species.

In addition, it must disclose everything it knows about the extraterrestrial presence and technology, and the extent to which it has been replicated in the last half century or so. The time has come to accept the "broader reality" as I call it, and make plans that embrace cosmic concerns as well as our own. What is called for, then, is a spiritual and intellectual revolution unprecedented in our written history.

This book, that discusses life and death issues, will pull no punches. Consequently it will upset many of my friends regardless of their faith and nationality. I will try to temper my language as much as possible in the hope of encouraging cooperation rather than rousing resistance. There is light at the end of the tunnel if we all move in unison toward the light.

In my youth, as a British subject, I was taught to sing "God save the Queen." Now my prayer is "God save us all." Will the answer be positive or negative? That depends on us. God gave us the power of choice – to do good or do evil. So the choice is ours and He is waiting anxiously to see our response.

CHAPTER 1

WE ARE HELL BENT TOWARD THE EXTINCTION OF THE HUMAN SPECIES

*"We're all doomed! 40 years from global catastrophe –
and there's NOTHING we can do about it."*

James Lovelock

Put another way, we have about ten years to turn the situation around and invalidate the above prediction that is based on our present trajectory. The possibility of saving the planet as a hospitable place for human life is real. But the probability, based on our track record to date, is not good.

James Lovelock is a maverick to some but his views are increasingly gaining credence in respectable circles. He has been proclaiming his Gaia Theory for a generation. This states that the Earth is a living, self-regulating system and that by filling its atmosphere with CO_2 (carbon dioxide emissions) we have destroyed the balance and overheated the planet. We are in the phase when the thermometer suddenly shoots up.[1]

The scientist's predictions of what this means in real terms are so dramatic that I am reluctant to repeat them here. Two or three examples will suffice to give the magnitude of the pending catastrophe. Over-industrialization will make it impossible to grow food in China. Consequently the Chinese will relocate in Africa. They are already there preparing a new continent. "The Chinese industrialists who claim to be out there mining minerals are just there on a pretext of preparing for the big move."[2] Central London would be inundated by water and the Parliament Buildings would have to be moved to higher ground. Many, if not most, Americans would move to Canada and not much of a rise in the sea level is required to wipe out Bangladesh from the face of the earth.

"Crackpot or visionary, the fact is that more and more people are paying attention to Lovelock, and that he, himself, supports the Intergovernmental Panel on Climate Change (IPCC) – the influential group who shared the Nobel Peace Prize with former American vice president Al Gore for their campaigns on global warming."[3]

A full-page article in the *Toronto Star* entitled "Grim prognosis for Earth: The World in 2050," almost echoes James Lovelock's grim predictions. 'It's a useful year to focus on,' Matthew Bramley, director of climate change at the Pembina Institute, which does environmental policy research, said in an interview from Ottawa. 'It's far enough away to be a year when real change is both necessary and possible.'[4]

A subject that should be close to America's heart is **BREEDING PERFECT STORMS: A Canadian researcher has demonstrated how global warming has widened the spawning grounds for hurricanes by hundreds of square kilometres since 1970, explaining for the first time why recent storm seasons have shattered one record after another.** "Canadian researcher Robert Scott is the first to offer a physical explanation – backed up by statistics and measurements spanning decades – linking the Earth's warming to increased hurricane activity and intensity. Hurricanes are not entirely natural disasters. Humanity has had a discernible impact on hurricanes, Scott, a 40-year-old oceanographer at the University of Texas, said in an interview."[5]

The sky-high cost of global warming witnessed following Hurricane Katrina in 2005, is just the tip of the global cost iceberg.

A lead editorial in the Toronto *Globe and Mail* had this to say about conclusions reached by Sir Nicholas Stern, the World Bank's former chief economist.

"A comprehensive study by Britain's top government economist has helped to fill that gap. It provides some hard truths about the enormous costs to the global economy if governments worldwide fail to take drastic measures to tackle the problem. It also provides an important counter-weight to those who argue that such action would carry too high a price tag and pose too big an economic risk for an uncertain result.

"In fact, Stern argues that the opposite is true. It is doing too little too late that would have by far the more devastating impact on the global economy. He says that a weak global response to climate change in the next few decades could cause economic and social disruptions on a scale similar to those triggered by the world wars and the Great Depression, but at a far higher cost than all of them combined. He calculates that the cost in lost output could reach $7-trillion. What's worse, it will be hard, if not impossible, to reverse such changes."[6]

The evidence of the effects of global warming are often dramatic and quite overwhelming. An article by Jessica Leeder in the *Globe and Mail* reported the reality of why the Inuit people are so concerned about their traditional habitat and hunting ground.

"A four-square-kilometre chunk has broken off Ward Hunt Ice Shelf – the largest remaining ice shelf in the Arctic – threatening the future of the giant frozen mass that northern explorers have used for years as the starting point for their treks.

"Scientists say the break, the largest on record since 2005, is the latest indication that climate change is forcing the drastic reshaping of the Arctic coastline, where 9,000 square kilometres of ice have been whittled down to less than 1,000 over the past century, and are only showing signs of decreasing further."[7]

It appears that Antarctica is not immune from the global trend even though some weather stations, including the one at the South Pole, have recorded a cooling trend. This anomaly provided some comfort to the skeptics and contrarians. An article by Kenneth Chang entitled "Study Finds New Evidence Of Warming in Antarctica" gives a more comprehensive view.

"In the new study, scientists took into account satellite measurements to interpolate temperatures in the vast areas between the sparse weather stations.

" 'We now see warming is taking place on all seven of the earth's continents in accord with what models predict as a response to greenhouses gases, said Eric J. Steig, a professor of earth and space sciences at the University of Washington in Seattle,' the lead author of the paper published in the journal Nature, January 22, 2009."[8]

One note of dissent comes from a Russian scientist, Dr. Habibullo Abdussamatov, who has been tracking the temperature on Mars and has noted an increase there. He attributes this to a long-term change in solar irradiance that is affecting both Earth and Mars. The implication, of course, is that the whole change is beyond our control and therefore there is no point in doing anything.

He may be correct that there is a natural increase that is beyond our control, but that is no excuse for ignoring the proven global warming effects that are due to our human lifestyles and the burning of fossil fuels in particular. The consensus of our best scientists is that we have a very significant measurable effect and that we could do something about it if we cared about the future habitability of our planet.

This "Let's take a chance and see what happens" attitude really bugs me. It reminds me of a time many years ago when I was bitten by a bat. I went to the doctor for advice. He said there was a probability that the bat did not have rabies, but on the other hand it might have. "How many people who have contracted rabies have lived?" I asked. "None yet," was his reply. Needless to say I was not wildly enthusiastic about playing Russian roulette with my life, so I took the shots.

An example that is more relevant for many people is the warning that increasing intensity of ultra violet radiation from the sun will certainly result in more skin cancer for those who allow themselves to get burned. Yet young people, in particular, pay no heed because the unhappy consequences may be decades away. This same generation routinely ignores the warning that listening to a lot of rock music is very likely to cause significant loss of hearing at an early age. But why worry because all that is somewhere in the distant future.

I was particularly incensed when I read "Enemy of the planet" by Paul Krugman. "Lee Raymond, the former chief executive officer of Exxon Mobil, was paid $686 million over 13 years. But that's not a reason to single him out for special excoriation. Executive compensation is out of control in corporate America as a whole, and unlike other grossly overpaid business leaders, Raymond can at least claim to have made money for his stockholders. There's a better reason to excoriate Raymond: For the sake of his company's bottom line, and perhaps his own personal enrichment, he turned Exxon Mobil into an enemy of the planet."[9]

Though the company denies the allegations – naturally – Al Gore agrees with the critics. In an article headlined "Public misled, Gore says." "There has been an organized campaign, financed to the tune of about $10 million (U.S.) a year from some of the largest carbon polluters, to create the impression that there is disagreement in the scientific community (about global warming)," Gore warned at a forum in Singapore. "In actuality, there is very little disagreement.

"This is one of the strongest of scientific consensus views in the history of science," he said. "We live in a world where what used to be called propaganda now has a major role to play in shaping public opinion."[10]

The propaganda continues. In March 2009 Andrew C. Revkin wrote that 600 self-professed climate skeptics were meeting in a Times Square hotel to challenge the widely held scientific and political consensus that humans <u>are</u> over-heating the planet. The sponsoring organization, according to the article that appeared in *The New York Times*, was the Heartland Institute.

A later article by Andrew Revkin headed "On Climate Issue, Industry Ignored Its Scientists" states that:

"For more than a decade the Global Climate Coalition, a group representing industries with profits tied to fossil fuels, led an aggressive lobbying and public relations campaign against the idea that emissions of heat-trapping gases could lead to global warming …

"Environmentalists have long maintained that industry knew early on that the scientific evidence supported a human influence on rising temperatures, but that the evidence was ignored for the sake of companies' fight against curbs on greenhouse gas emissions. Some environmentalists have compared the tactic to that once used by tobacco companies, which for decades insisted that the science linking cigarette smoking to lung cancer was uncertain. By questioning the science on global warming, these environmentalists say, groups like the Global Climate Coalition were able to sow enough doubt to blunt public concern about a consequential issue and delay government action.

"George Monbiot, a British environmental activist and writer, said that by promoting doubt, the industry had taken advantage of news media norms requiring neutral coverage of issues, just as the tobacco industry once had.

" 'They didn't have to win the argument to succeed, Mr. Monbiot said, only to cause as much confusion as possible.' "[11]

A few days before going to press the following Associated Press article appeared on the front page of the *Toronto Star*, "**Greenhouse gases rise to record levels.** Greenhouse gases in the atmosphere reached record highs in 2008, the UN weather agency says. 'Concentration of greenhouse gases continued to increase, even a bit faster' than in previous years, Michel Jarraud, World Meteorological Organization chief, said Monday. Carbon dioxide was 385.2 parts per million, up 2 parts from 2007. Nitrous oxide increased by 0.9 parts per billion to 321.8. Methane was 1,797 parts per billion, up 7."[12]

The facts are irrefutable and should convince anyone who is not in total denial. So I am obliged to come down heavily on the side of the environmentalists. I can understand the attitude of industries that profit from fossil fuels wanting to make as much money as they can for as long as they can, but they must not be allowed to get away with it. When the worship of mammon is weighed against the destruction of the planet as a friendly habitable biosphere it is "no contest." Life itself is more precious than any amount of money so no industry, no matter how paramount and profitable, can be allowed to continue as a prescription for certain death.

This is a message that had not yet gripped world leaders when they met in Copenhagen in December 2009. Most of the people I talked to were both sad and disillusioned by the bickering and my mind drifted to the story of the Roman Emperor Nero who fiddled on his violin while Rome burned. There was an alarming similarity between that story and an accord that is voluntary and non-binding in the face of great danger.

I was especially upset by the foot dragging of the Canadian delegation in a callous effort to put the interests of the oil industry ahead of global sustainability. Shame on us!

One can argue that the Copenhagen accord was a small step forward. The fact that so many world leaders actually met to consider and discuss what must be done to save our planet can be interpreted as positive. But as President Obama correctly observed, the accord was only a tentative step down a long road.

The poorer countries, in particular, felt let down and abandoned. The *New York Times* reported the summation of their spokesman as follows:

"Lumumba Stanislaus Di-Aping, a Sudanese diplomat who has been representing the Group of 77 developing countries, denounced the accord. 'The developed countries have decided that damage to developing countries is acceptable,' he told reporters, noting that the 2-degree target 'will result in massive devastation to Africa and small island states.' He said many other vulnerable countries wanted a 1.5 degree target. Today's events, which really are a continuation of the history of the negotiations for the last two years, represent the worst development in climate change negotiations in history,' Mr. Lumumba said."[13]

The inference is that the industrialized countries are willing to stand by and let the low-lying countries sink ignominiously into the sea. That doesn't have to happen. Mr. Lumumba's preferred 1.5 degree target is possible if the leaders of the industrialized countries would vigorously pursue the radical reforms necessary to make the miracle happen.

Three Essentials for Change

I have been giving considerable thought to the breadth and depth of change required to salvage a seemingly hopeless situation, and put planet earth on the road to recovery and its diverse inhabitants on a path of undeniable hope. It is a massive change that is required, an intellectual and moral revolution without precedent, leading to major action on many fronts.

There are three principal elements that come to mind. The first, and probably most urgent in some respects, is the availability of reliable sources of energy to replace the fossil fuels on which we have been relying for too long. There are, of course, some immediate steps that can be taken to reduce consumption. These include new skins on old high rise buildings that can dramatically reduce power consumption, better insulation for houses and low rise buildings, more fuel efficient cars and trucks and a drastic reduction in the use of military aircraft that are major contributors to carbon dioxide pollution. All of these things are good, and deserve urgent attention. But they pale in significance compared to the need for an exotic alternative to fossil fuels.

The second necessity is a world culture of cooperation in contrast with the traditional desire to dominate and rule supreme. This can only happen through leadership at all levels of government and industry that is more concerned about the welfare of all mankind and the future habitability of the planet than they are about accumulating power or wealth. In effect, men and women of high morality and unquestioned personal integrity.

The third requirement is a monetary and banking system that gives governments the financial flexibility to facilitate the transition from an oil economy to something quite different without undue hardship. I truly believe that such a system is possible because this is a subject that has engaged me all my adult life. I lament, therefore, that emerging from the worst financial crisis in decades, caused, once again, by an inherently unstable monetary and banking system, that there is not one government in the G20 group of countries that appears to have an inkling of what has to be done to prevent a recurrence. So this is a subject I will be addressing forcefully in a later chapter.

On the question of alternative fuels I claim no expertise. I have strong reason to believe, however, that exotic sources already exist, and remain secret. If this is the case, it would not be necessary to establish farms of unsightly and noisy windmills and install other systems that may be more expensive and less satisfactory. At least these alternatives should not be pursued until all the facts are known.

The facts I refer to include what governments have learned from visitors from other planets and their technology that is so much more advanced than ours. This subject is one that held little interest for me until 2005, when I was first introduced to it in a serious way. Until then I was an agnostic – neither believing nor disbelieving. Now I know that visitors from other planets are real and that significant aspects of their technology have been adapted to our every day uses. This whole area was, for me, an uncharted road and I propose to discuss some of the things that I have learned to date, as well as some of the questions that remain unanswered.

Another uncharted road became an avenue of discovery in the realm of religion. Like most of us I had a lot of beliefs that I had learned from childhood, and that I had never questioned. Suddenly, without warning, I was exposed to thoughts that challenged some of my assumptions and I would like to share the discoveries that I have made along the way.

Some of these may disturb you, but in all conscience I feel compelled to say what I believe because I think the major religions must abandon their centuries old antagonisms and rivalries for conquest and domination, and start working together to build the Kingdom of God on Earth, defined as a world where all His children regardless of race, creed or color have access to healthy food, potable water, appropriate clothing and shelter, and sufficient education to give them opportunity to use their talents creatively.

All of this is a tall order, but it is not impossible. We earthlings have all the tools required to achieve the miracle. The missing link is the moral integrity and character to set the right priorities. This is the reason that I doubt the uncharted roads were mere serendipity. I sense they were part of a broader and grander plan.

The First Uncharted Road

In the spring of 2004, my wife Ellen, took ill and died from cancer of unknown origin. I was devastated because we had been so interconnected during my long political career, and I felt her loss most keenly.

The adjustment was not easy. On the surface I was eating well, swimming regularly and going about the responsibilities that were mine in this major transition of my life. But I was desperately lonely, and after a few months I decided that I didn't want to live alone for long. So I asked Sandra Bussiere, widow of my closest friend Bill, who had died ten years earlier, if she would consider marrying me, and she agreed. So we decided on October 1, 2005, as the big day.

In the months leading up to our marriage I found my feet on a road I had never known before. It was a road leading to the stars. The subject of Unidentified Flying Objects, and whether or not they were fact or fiction, had never been on my radar screen of priorities.

It is true that when I had been Canadian Minister of National Defence I had received reports of sightings of diverse sorts, most of them natural phenomena, and a few that were unexplained. At the time I was much too involved in the battle to unify the armed forces to consider asking the kind of follow up question that I would ask today. So I fell into the general category of skeptic. Someone who was basically uninformed.

In late 2002, however, a chap by the name of Pierre Juneau began to send me material on the subject with some regularity. Regrettably, due to my lifestyle and the fact that I was usually so preoccupied with one or more projects that filled every available moment of my time, I didn't read what he sent. He was so patient, however, that I made a mental note that I would like to do a quick read of some of it if I could ever take the necessary time out.

Most of the material comprised memoranda, reports and copies of relevant e-mails that were not too eye-catching. Then one day a book arrived that caught my eye immediately. It was titled, *The Day After Roswell*, by Colonel Philip J. Corso (Ret.)[14] and I decided it would be a good holiday read at an appropriate time. On a couple of occasions I looked for it, but it was elusive and always escaped my eyes. In the summer of 2005, however, when I was searching for another book to take on vacation, there it was staring me in the face. I decided it would be the perfect substitute.

My interest in the subject of UFOs had been piqued by a two-hour documentary the late Peter Jennings had put together for ABC News. Juneau had insisted that I watch it when it was aired on February 24, 2005. Jennings had assembled such an array of credible eyewitnesses that I found their reports impossible to dismiss.

So I took Corso's book with me to my cottage at Arundel Lodge, the small tourist resort that Ellen and I had operated for 45 years before her death. The book became my constant companion for the next few days as I relaxed in what is called a "Muskoka Chair," only raising my eyes briefly from time to time to survey the lake and the exquisite cloud formations on the horizon. I found the story told by the former U.S. Army Intelligence Officer, who had been a member of President Eisenhower's National Security Council and, later, head of the Foreign Technology Desk at the U.S. Army's Research and Development Department, totally compelling.

The text was so fascinating that I had to ask myself if it could be a beautifully constructed fiction. I read very little fiction, but a year earlier I had read *The Life of Pi*, a best-selling thriller that kept me wondering until the last few pages whether or not it was fact or fiction. In comparing the two books I concluded that Corso's book was the kind of exposé that no one could fake. It included too many real names, real places and real dates that were quite familiar to me to be contrived.

The former intelligence officer confirmed, beyond any shadow of doubt, the long-circulated rumor that on or about July 4, 1947, an Unidentified Flying Object had crashed not far from Roswell, New Mexico.

Corso was not personally present at the crash site, but subsequently saw one of the alien bodies while it was being transported for autopsy.

Even more convincing was the Colonel's personal involvement ten years later when he found himself in charge of the army's Foreign Technology Division of Research and Development. In this top secret job, his boss Lt. Gen. Arthur Trudeau turned over a filing cabinet full of scrap collected at the Roswell crash site. It had been collecting dust until Corso was given Trudeau's mandate to sort it, and then feed it to U.S. industry for the benefit of the U.S. military. This was done without any reference to the source, but the well-screened recipients, who were tops in their respective fields, would recognize at once that what they received was technologically decades or centuries ahead of our own.

As I sat on the lawn reading Corso's book I shared some of its mind-stretching secrets with my curious nephew Philip. He was incredulous, and highly skeptical, as many people are. He left for home and a couple of days later phoned to say that he had called a retired United States Air Force general of his acquaintance to ask him about Corso's book. "Every word of it is true, and more," the general had told him. That was enough to convince Philip who wanted to know where he could get his hands on a copy of the book.

It was also the confirmation I needed to change my mind about an invitation I had received from Victor Viggiani and Mike Bird, two of Canada's more active ufologists, to address their Exopolitics Toronto Symposium on September 25, 2005. I had fully intended to decline with thanks, because I didn't know enough about the subject, and I had nothing to say. All that had changed, however, as I had contemplated the enormous policy implications of the extraterrestrial presence and technology, and concluded that issues of earth-shaking consequences were not being discussed or debated because the official position of the U.S. government was that UFOs do not exist. As a lifelong policy wonk I knew that someone had to speak out.

Before going public, however, I took the precaution of getting the message from the general personally. I had met him at an aviation exhibition so I asked Philip for his phone number and to give him a "heads up" that I would like to talk to him. When I called he seemed pleased to hear from me, so I asked about Corso's book. "Every word of it is true, and more," he repeated for my benefit. We then spent twenty minutes discussing the "and more," to the extent that he could without revealing classified material. He told me that there had been, in fact, face-to-face discussions between the visitors and U.S. officials. What he said was even more fascinating and compelling than the book. So with that assurance, I was ready to say my piece.

There was one significant complication, however. The symposium was being held exactly one week before I was to be married. So I had to ask Sandra if she had any objection. I assured her that it would be a "one off" shot, but that I thought what I was proposing to say should be in the public domain. If I recall correctly she was a bit reluctant, and she certainly would have been much more so if she had realized what would happen to my well-intentioned promise. But neither of us was blessed with a crystal ball, and I got the green light.

So on September 25, at the very end of the program, most of which I had missed due to preparation of what I intended to say, I mounted the podium and told the assembly that "UFOs are as real as the airplanes flying overhead," and that "The time has come to lift the veil of secrecy and let the truth emerge so there can be a real and informed debate about one of the most important issues facing our planet. Forgive me for stating the obvious; but it is quite impossible to have that kind of an informed debate about a problem that doesn't officially exist."

Having said that, I earned the dubious distinction of becoming the first person of cabinet rank from the G8 group of countries to say un-equivocally that UFOs are real, we are not alone in the cosmos, and we had better get used to it and make any adjustments necessary to benefit from what I call the "broader reality." Making the short speech was not too different, in a way, than hundreds I had made before. In another, more profound way, I set my feet on an unfamiliar road leading to the cosmos – a road that I had been quite comfortable not to know about.

Later, after I began to write this book, I asked Pierre Juneau why he had picked me to inform on the subject of the extraterrestrial presence. His much too generous response follows.

"Ultimately, I began sending you information about the UFO issue in late 2002, early 2003, because I felt that you were a wise open minded man who could make sense of the complex connections between this enigmatic subject, spirituality (consciousness), religion, and its potential to trigger a new paradigm of cooperation on our planet. In other words, I felt this was the most important revelation in the history of humanity and that you would see that it could provide solutions to our human condition; that it could provide the leverage to become a global unifying force to lead policy-makers and people of all walks of life to put aside their differences and focus on new solutions to create a positive action plan for the future of humanity."[15]

Another Uncharted Road

Following our marriage, and Sandra's relocation to Toronto, she began to search for the kind of spiritual involvement that she had been familiar with in Ottawa. There, she had been a member of various prayer and study groups in which she participated fully. She volunteered to work in the "Out of the Cold" at Metropolitan United Church and was accepted enthusiastically. That led her to consider Metropolitan as her regular church and to become fully occupied leading to our eventual membership.

She also wanted to find a small group for weekly prayer and Bible study. She asked about my Wednesday morning fellowship group. She had joined us once or twice when she was in charge of the wider Fellowship on Parliament Hill, and it was her duty to report from time to time. I am sure she was a bit disappointed to learn that some time ago, after giving the matter some thought, we had decided to maintain our male only rule. With that door closed, she decided to launch another one with male and female participants mostly from Metropolitan. Still in its infancy, it appears destined to fill an important need for her and others.

In the meantime, someone at my group suggested that we get Noel Cooper, a former priest who had written the excellent book, *Language of the Heart: How to Read the Bible*,[16] to lead us in a series of evening meetings to study the gospel of John, and wives would be included. The idea was that half a dozen regulars would provide, one after the other, a simple dinner following which Noel would comment and lead a discussion in which everyone participated.

As a matter of happenstance, our turn to host was the last on the list. Noel, who had a long distance to come, arrived early. So we sat in the living room chatting until the others began to arrive. At one point Noel said: "The gospel of John was written just after the 'people of the way' (as Jesus' followers were called in those early days) had been excommunicated by the Jewish Rabbis and religious leaders, resulting in the loss of their protection under the Roman law." "That means it is a political document," I blurted out with less than a second's hesitation.

I had always wondered why the gospel of John was so different from the synoptic gospels, Matthew, Mark and Luke. For any of you who may be less than totally familiar with the books of the New Testament, the story line is different, and it is considerably more anti-Semitic than the others. It also contains those long, long dissertations in direct quotations from Jesus' mouth I had wondered about because I considered them to be far beyond anything that would be possible based on an oral tradition.

I felt inexplicably drawn to this fascinating issue. What were the circumstances at the time of writing? What were the reasons why the writer or writers of the gospel decided to say what was said? I knew that I must do a lot of research and try to put my mind in the mind of the writer, whoever he may have been.

So there I was, my feet set on two new roads that led I knew not where. I felt strongly that they were roads of the Lord's choice, and that I would be led to discover some things that He wanted to be said. I have never wavered from that belief, though I sometimes think how much simpler the balance of my life might have been if I had never heard of them. It would have been a simpler and more comfortable life, no doubt, but not nearly as challenging and ultimately enriching. Even more exciting is the sense that, in some mysterious way, the two roads may converge toward the eternal.

CHAPTER 2

EXPLORING THE MIDDLE EAST – 2006

*"The further backward you can look the farther
forward you are likely to see."*

Winston Churchill

It had been my intention for some time to travel to the Middle East for a first hand look at the area before commenting on matters of such extraordinary complexity. I had long been convinced that there will be no peace in the world until there is peace between Israel and its Palestinian neighbors. To read about the seemingly intractable problems is one thing, but it is only exposure to the sights, sounds and smells of the region that give life and meaning to the words.

When we got to the planning stage, Sandra got the bright idea of inviting Kent and Kay Hotaling, an Oregon couple who had introduced the Prayer Breakfast Movement to Canada and had become very dear friends, to accompany us. It was an inspired suggestion. Not only were Kent and Kay fun to travel with, it was their friends, and friends of their friends, who made the journey one of the most educational we had ever experienced.

Sandra and I planned to visit London for a few days enroute to Tel Aviv where we would join up with the Hotalings. My daughter, Mary Elizabeth, lives in London and there were several others we wanted to visit. In addition, I had been corresponding with Nick Pope, the ministry of defence officer in charge of the UFO desk, who had read my Toronto speech on the Internet and who wanted to meet me. After we got together Nick did give me two unclassified U.K. files that he thought I might be interested in, including the well-known Bentwaters Forest case.

After several good visits, a play and other sightseeing we left for Tel Aviv. The flight was quite long – somehow I had not managed to wrap my mind around the route that was very similar to the one I had taken to Beirut on the way to Cyprus to visit Canadian peacekeeping troops in 1964. The Hotalings were taking a different route but, as events unfolded, we all arrived at Israeli immigration at the same time.

Getting through immigration and customs was a formidable challenge. Eventually, however, we were cleared for entry and took cabs to the Continental Hotel to rest overnight. If we had been more familiar with the geography of the country we would have proceeded to Jerusalem, but that was part of the learning experience. In any event, I had planned to see the Canadian Ambassador at his Tel Aviv office for an early morning briefing, but he hadn't received my telegram and was out of the city on business.

Consequently, there was no reason to hang around after breakfast so we rented a van to take us to Jerusalem, and our home away from home at the very comfortable Dan Panorama Hotel, just a long field away from the old walled city that Kay, Sandra and I went to explore after lunch. We entered through the Jaffa Gate and found ourselves in a labyrinth of very narrow streets lined on both sides with shops displaying their colorful and varied wares. The remainder of the afternoon was spent quietly in preparation for a trip to Bethlehem and dinner with Zahi Khouri and his friend Professor Albert Aghazarian.

Mr. Khouri picked us up at the hotel and drove us toward Bethlehem. We had no problem at the Palestinian checkpoint because they obviously knew Khouri, and waved us on. Bethlehem was not the small silent town of my imagination formed from singing the well-known Christmas carol for so many years. It was a city in ruins behind a high wall and surrounded with barbed wire. Once inside we got the impression of a ghost town, effectively cut off from the sources of commerce.

The sense of desolation was accentuated by the atmosphere in the beautiful Continental Hotel. It was virtually deserted, and we noted with some dismay that we were the only people in the grand dining room. During dinner, the professor gave us a thorough review of the history of the Middle East in what appeared to be an attempt to be factual. It is, of course, one of the most fascinating histories of any part of the planet. We were also briefed on some of the immediate problems.

A few of the most important points, from a Palestinian point of view, are the following as copied from Kent's notes. Kent agreed to be our *rapporteur* for the trip but each of us kept journals and the following pages are a collage of our collective observations, except where specifically noted.

* Gaza is a place of 1.3 million people, with 80% of them living in poverty. It is the most densely populated place in the world.

* The primary issue is access. The Israelis have closed the gates so goods and services cannot move easily, and thus economic stagnation has taken over. There has been a huge decline in economic activity since 2000.

* Now that the Hamas has been elected in Gaza, foreign aid from the western powers is being cut off. The Palestinian need for humanitarian aid will double, or triple, in the coming year.[1]

The most anxious moments of the whole trip for me occurred when we exited the West Bank and stopped at the checkpoint to re-enter Israel. A teenage Israeli girl with her machine gun at the ready, ordered us to produce identification including passports. A teenage boy followed her out to provide cover during the interrogation. He, too, had his machine gun pointed loosely in our direction. It was the girl's nervousness that unnerved me. I imagined what might happen if one of us were to cough loudly and moved to put a hand over our mouth or reached for a handkerchief. Eventually all was well and we were able to move on.

We had three objectives for our time in Israel. The first was to get a first-hand experience of the issues dividing Israelis and the Palestinians living in the occupied territories. The second was to experience together this part of the world where we had spent so little time. And the third was to have a spiritual pilgrimage as each of us reflected on our faith in this place where it all began.

The next day was our tourist day in Jerusalem when we visited the holy sites that we had long read about in our Bibles. We began by driving to the top of the Mount of Olives that provided a panoramic view of the old city and its environs. Especially interesting for me were the vast Israeli, Christian and Arab burial grounds – the latter directly in front of the gate through which Jewish tradition prophesied that the Messiah would enter the temple, but presumably will be prevented from doing so because walking through a graveyard renders one ritually unclean and therefore unable to enter the temple.

The traditional site of the Garden of Gethsemane, with its gnarled, millennium old olive trees, was particularly moving. As I sat nearby, I could imagine Jesus sweating blood as he prayed about the sacrifice he knew in his heart could not be avoided. The nearby Franciscan Church of the Pater Noster and the Church of the Holy Sepulchre, which houses traditional sites of both Calvary and Jesus' burial place, were also meaningful as I compared in my mind the reality of what I saw with the Bible images that had been with me since childhood.

The whole scene was, of course, highly commercialized, but I learned to close my eyes to that and just concentrate on the likelihood that I was walking on the ground where Jesus walked and where, eventually, he was crucified.

Friday, April 7 was a truly incredible day. Friends who had confirmed many of the things we had learned in Bethlehem, and added statistics and impressions from their own experience, picked us up right after breakfast. Our first stop was the Lazarus Home for Girls in Bethany, a refuge for orphaned or abandoned Palestinian girls. My first impression was incredulity that they were all girls because they were dressed in slacks and their hair was worn extremely short – presumably for sanitary reasons. We were introduced to each one personally, after which we played games and tried to demonstrate the kind of universal love that surpasses language.

The question of the Wall being built by the Israelis came up as it was very much on everyone's mind at the time. It would cut off the girls' access to services like health care and future choice of schools. It would also pose an impediment for the wonderfully dedicated school director who commuted to and from Jerusalem daily.

After saying goodbye to the girls, we headed out on a long journey to Tuwani, a remote Palestinian village of less than a hundred people. By then the ever-present Israeli checkpoints, with the youthful guards and their machine guns, had become routine. They were a stressful and time-consuming fact of Palestinian life. Eventually we were flagged down by a lady standing at the intersection of the highway and an unmarked lane of a road that lead to Tuwani, a tiny enclave at the top of the hill a few hundred yards distant. At that point the lady, a Mennonite peace worker, introduced us to the village elders and two or three of her colleagues who had a tiny outpost there.

Some of the stories we were told were disturbing, and some hair-raising. Two of the village elders had built new houses that the Israelis had bulldozed to the ground because they didn't have building permits. Building permits were required even though it was Palestinian territory, and they were almost impossible to get due to the difficulty in establishing title to a specific building lot on land that had been passed down from generation to generation for centuries. Even worse, the small infirmary, that had been for some time the only health care provider for the district, was subject to a demolition order because it, too, had been built without a permit from the Israeli authorities.

We were curious, of course, as to why there was a Christian Peacemaker team from Canada and the United Kingdom in such a remote place. The answer was not reassuring. Just across the valley from the village was one of the new Israeli settlements, built on Palestinian land. The young people from the settlement harassed the Palestinian children on their way to school and we were told that the teenagers were given this assignment because they were not subject to prosecution. The peace workers came to escort the Palestinian children past the Israeli settlement to their school.

When news of the need for the foreign escorts was publicized the Israeli government became embarrassed to the point of assigning Israeli troops to provide the protection. But, on occasion, they were late. And once, at least, they showed up at the wrong place – the after-school rendez-vous point in the morning, and the pre-school site in the afternoon, so the peace workers continued to act as backup in case anything went wrong.

A village elder alleged even worse intimidation by the Israeli settlers. He said they had poisoned the Palestinians' sheep. On one occasion he had recruited his aged mother to try to rescue some sheep and she was harassed. When he dashed to the rescue, he was shot at. It would appear that the only possible motive would be the desire of the settlers to annex some or all of the land occupied by the village. Of course I can't verify that story, but I am inclined to believe it after tasting some of the bitterness that exists between the two peoples.

We had brought lunch that we ate with the village elders and the peace workers. Then, all too soon, because the stories were just beginning to flow, we headed back to Jerusalem to be briefed by the United Nations Office for Humanitarian Assistance. Our host, David Shearer, documented with maps, statistics, and personal observations all that we had been hearing from the Palestinians as they spoke of the oppression by the Israeli government. We were given lots of material but one item that struck me most forcibly was a map of the Israeli checkpoints that effectively prevent Palestinians from traveling from anywhere to anywhere else without being stopped, searched, and maybe, or maybe not, allowed to proceed.

That evening the four of us splurged on a delightful dinner at the American Colony Hotel, just enjoying each other's company. We were very much aware, however, of the contrast between the good things we could enjoy, and what the people we had been with that day – and a couple of million others – were not able to enjoy. At one point in the discussion I waved my arm across the horizon toward the Wall and the checkpoints, and said: "Apartheid revisited."

Even though Saturday was "*Shabbat*" we were able to hire an Israeli guide to take us sightseeing with our first stop to be Masada, where the last remnant of opposition to the Roman destruction of the Jewish nation took place in the first century CE. This eye-popping experience ended one of my long-standing myths. I knew that the Jewish Zealots had survived for seven years in what I had always assumed, in my ignorance, to be caves in the mountains.

The reality was quite different. We came to a huge outcrop of rock in the middle of the desert and took a special Scandinavian cable car to the top where we discovered King Herod the Great's northern fortress that he had built with slave labor, and furnished to be available should he ever need it as a kind of final refuge. It was this mountain top fortress, fully stocked with food and water, that the Zealots had used for the seven years they withstood the Roman siege.

We were told the poignant story of how the end came for the Zealots. As the Romans gradually built a ramp to allow them to reach the top of what had proved to be impenetrable, it became increasingly obvious that God was not going to save the defenders, as they had been expecting, and they decided never to be taken captive. So the night before the final Roman assault, they drew lots and killed each other in turn, with only the last remaining man committing suicide because suicide was considered to be a sin.

If the ascent to the ancient fortress had been eye-popping, the descent from the mountain height and drive to the Dead Sea was ear-popping as the air pressure increased on approach to the lowest point on earth. Our group had decided that a trip to the Middle East would not be complete without a dip in the famous terminus of the Jordan River. So Kent, Kay and Sandra donned bathing suits at one of the beaches set aside for tourists. I was nursing the sniffles so decided to pass and act as group photographer.

Getting to and from the water was the biggest challenge. Unfortunately Kent and Kay left their sandals at the changing room and burned their feet negotiating the hot stony slope leading quite a distance to the water's edge. Because the Dead Sea is about eight times saltier than the oceans, once they entered the water they experienced the weird sense of buoyancy finding that they couldn't do much more than recline on their backs in a semi-sitting position and bob around like corks. Sandra made an effort to swim but yielded to the power of the environment. Soon they came out having accomplished their purpose of being able to say that they had "swum" in the Dead Sea.

Later we were informed that the Dead Sea is truly dying. This is due to the fact that most of the water in the Jordan River is taken out for irrigation purposes both by those living in Israel and the occupied territories, and the Jordanians. Only a trickle of about three percent of the river's flow actually reaches the Dead Sea. In addition, a major industry has developed to extract salt and other minerals for therapeutic procedures and much of the salt water is evaporated for that purpose.

That evening was spent having dinner with two senior editors of the *Jerusalem Post*. We had to wait until after sunset, and the end of *Shabbat*, which suited our schedule perfectly. We ordered the famous St. Peter's fish, a Mediterranean delicacy, which seemed perfect for the occasion.

The conversation couldn't have been more different than those we had enjoyed with the Palestinians. Kent remarked later that it reminded him of the book about English and French-speaking Canadians, entitled *Two Solitudes* – two people each with its own history and perspective. One of the questions the ladies posed was, "We have given them so much. What more do they want?" and later the plea, "If only they would just leave us alone."

Our hearts ached for them, partly because of their sense of insecurity, and partly because they had absolutely no understanding of what their government was doing to the Palestinian people. It was all so sad – hate and disinformation on both sides. Before we left Israel we wondered if our journalist friends might have been influenced by reading their own newspaper, one that presents a very biased slant on the news. This was very clear when we compared its coverage of events with that of its competitor, *Ha'aretz*, which at least made an effort to present both sides of a story.

Sunday morning we had breakfast at the Hotel with Gavriel Gefen, a friend who Kent, Kay and Sandra had met at the National Prayer Breakfast in Washington. In Kay's words. "Gavriel is an astonishingly sweet committed follower of *Yeshua* who also happens to be a Zionist and a sympathizer of the displaced Palestinians."[2] He was one of the rare Israelis with sufficient insight to be able to put his feet in the shoes of others. Gavriel, who also considers himself a modern Orthodox Jew, told us a story that was as insightful as it was educational. It was a story he later confirmed in writing.

"In June 2002, Israel began building a wall of separation from the Palestinian Authority which was to follow roughly the green-line of Israel's pre-1967 border. The wall was officially in response to a wave of suicide bombings carried out against Israelis by Palestinians. The Israeli name for the wall was initially the *separation fence*. It is now called the *security fence*. Palestinians call it the apartheid wall.

"The Israeli government's announcements about the building of the wall stated that it would be a fence along much of the green line as a buffer of separation between Israelis and Palestinians. Only where passing through highly populated areas with histories of violence against Israel would the otherwise fence be a concrete wall. As the wall began to be constructed, it quickly became clear to many of us watching closely that this was not the case. There was a calculated campaign of misinformation about the wall in order to slowly placate both Israelis and Palestinians about it over a long period of time. In the north, where the wall first began to be built, it did not simply pass by Palestinian areas in order to separate them from Israelis. Rather, two of the first Palestinian cities by which it was constructed were literally encircled by it. This turned these cities into virtual prisons with only one single highly guarded point of entrance and exit from each entire city."

Gavriel continued: "As the wall began going up in the Jerusalem area, I went one day to see for myself the various sites where it was being erected. It was a great surprise to discover where some of the locations were. As I then climbed up to some high vantage points, such as hilltops and the roofs of tall buildings, I saw what was to me a clear trajectory along which all these sections would be connected. It was suddenly evident that the wall was not about keeping out suicide bombers. The Palestinians of East Jerusalem are peaceful people. No suicide bomber has ever come from East Jerusalem. Bombings in Jerusalem have only been carried out by Palestinians from other places, and never from here. (Author's Note: They were usually from the fetid refugee camps to which Palestinians were exiled more than fifty years earlier.) The location of the wall, at least in East Jerusalem, was being chosen based not on keeping out militants but on severing some of the peripheral Arabic-speaking neighborhoods of Jerusalem from the city. It was being done with the goal of artificially raising the Jewish demographics of Jerusalem.

"In the months that followed, I spoke up in various social circles in central Jerusalem where we live. I spoke out about what I had seen of the wall that day, and what was obvious to me about the trajectory of these sections of wall being connected. Many people said I was crazy and that it would never happen.

"Over the course of two years, the different sections of wall I had seen that day were indeed gradually connected right through the heart of those neighborhoods. By 2005, the outer neighborhoods of East Jerusalem had a 28-foot high concrete wall running through the middle of them. This has left tens of thousands of families with a high wall on one side of their village or neighborhood, and bare open desert on the other three sides. They are cut off from jobs, schools, hospitals, municipal services, places of worship, and family and friends.

"In 2005, there was one opening left in a vast section of the wall passing through East Jerusalem. I decided one day to take my four children to see it for themselves. I wanted them to walk on both sides of the wall and meet people who live there, before it became completely sealed and separate. I wanted them to witness this history firsthand. When the kids got home from school, I told them we were going to the east side of town to see the wall. Our teenage son said he didn't want to go. I told him it was important to see it for himself. He said he'd already seen it, and it wasn't that big a deal. 'Really, where'd you see it?' I asked. 'On television.' 'No,' I said, 'that doesn't count. You need to see firsthand what we're doing to these people.' 'They're all a bunch of terrorists anyway,' he said. 'Who told you that?' I asked. 'We learned all about it at school,' he said. I insisted that he needed to see it for himself, and meet the people there face-to-face. I gave him no choice, and made him come with the rest of us.

"When we got to the opening in the wall, the kids walked up to it, stood in the gap, and looked up to the top of it. Its presence and size were overwhelming. As we stood there, a woman came up to us and asked how old our youngest daughter was. 'Four,' we said. 'Really? My daughter's the same age. What's her name?' As we talked to her, we learned about her and her family. She lived on one side of the wall, but her parents lived on the other. Her husband had a job on one side of the wall, but she had one on the other. One of her children went to school on one side of the wall, but another child went to school on the other side. She didn't know how they would manage in the future once the wall closed. This was exactly the personal encounter we were hoping our children would have.

"Shortly after we got home, I went to my son's room to call him for dinner. He was sitting on his bed with his back to the door, and didn't respond. I walked further into the room to make sure he heard me, and saw him crying. I asked if he was okay, and what was wrong. He responded, 'Why are we doing this to them?'

"Before this wall began to be built, we (Israel) already had a great deal of experience with another wall we had built between Gaza and Egypt. In a few short years, literally more than a hundred tunnels were dug under the wall between Egypt and Gaza for smuggling weapons, other contraband, and blacklisted people. These tunnels were very deep and very long. In some cases, they went down more than a hundred feet and were more than a mile long. Many of them went down through the floor of a house on one side, and up through the floor of a house on the other side. The lesson was that the worst militants get through anyway. On the outskirts of East Jerusalem, the wall passes through the midst of some heavily populated neighborhoods, with houses only 10-15 feet on either side of the wall. Tunnels between these houses could be dug up literally overnight. If there really were dangerous militants in East Jerusalem, the wall would not keep them out. The worst ones would get through anyway. In the meantime, the wall places an unbearable hardship upon peaceful people, regrettably likely inspiring new militants. The wall is an immoral short-term solution to a long-term problem which creates more problems than it solves."[3]

This one story pretty well sums up the difficulty of establishing peace between the two peoples. There is very, very little real authentic communication, and the educational systems on both sides are slanted in such a way that they incubate hate rather than understanding and compassion.

Gavriel was so compelling that we kept talking and virtually had to run to attend Palm Sunday service at the Evangelical Lutheran Church. We arrived just as the bells stopped ringing, and were ushered into seats in the back row because the chapel of the old Arabic speaking church, where the English language service was held, was filled to capacity. The sermon and singing were great; a moving rendition of "Were you there when they crucified my Lord?" was especially poignant. The service ended by reading the relevant part of the gospel of Mark that we thought gained much power from the realization that we were in the city where the story had unfolded almost two millennia ago.

We missed the annual Palm Sunday procession because we had made a deal with our loquacious guide, Birte, to drive us to Tiberias on the Sea of Galilee soon after lunch. It was a long drive with a couple of stops enroute. The first was at Beth Shean, one of the major archeological digs in that part of the ancient world.

The next interlude was a visit to the bank of the Jordan River. This was my second culture shock, even greater than Masada. The world famous river was approximately the same width as the creek that ran through the farm where I was born and raised. All of a sudden Joshua's problem in leading the Children of Israel across to the Promised Land didn't seem nearly as formidable as the "word picture" I had conjured up in my mind from reading the Bible.

We parked by a spot, near the place where Jesus had been baptized, where there were riverside parks that charge admission for the privilege of donning a white garment and descending concrete steps to the water's edge to get dunked. There seemed to be plenty of willing customers but we declined to join the crowd. We had our pictures taken with the Jordan in the background, and proceeded on our way.

Our hotel in Tiberias was quite perfect for tourists, but disappointing for Sandra. She had toured the Holy Land several years earlier and had stayed at a simple kibbutz guesthouse on the other side of the Sea of Galilee where she could walk along the shore and imagine how it was in Jesus' time. Tiberias has become a very busy commercial resort town, and our hotel was very shiny with a big pool area that covered the beach completely, with railings to protect us from all that water.

"Monday morning," as Kay wrote, "things looked much better. I took my Bible and sat as near as possible to the water, early, while the mist was still lying on the lake, fish were occasionally jumping, birds were calling and a fishing boat was moving slowly in the near distance. I was aware that the unique smell of fresh lake water, the feel of the breeze, and the sounds of the birds were the same for Jesus as they were for me. Later the four of us read the Scripture together and shared thoughts, as we have done every day since. So our spirits were restored."[4]

After a late breakfast, Birte came to pick us up for a day of tourism. We went to see an old fishing boat, or what was left of it, that had been unearthed from the lake and carbon dated back to Jesus' time. There was a wonderful moment in the film about the discovery when the archeologists got it up to the surface and "sailed" it to shore for the first time in 2,000 years, cheering and celebrating as they went.

Then on we went to the Mount of Beatitudes where there is a church overlooking the Sea. The setting is peaceful, with green hills all around and beautiful flowers both wild and cultivated. The next stop, Capernaum, brought mixed reactions, but was very special for all of us because Jesus spent so much of his time there. We saw the ruins of what is said to be the Apostle Peter's house and wandered around looking at the remains of the tiny village.

Lunch had a unique significance for me. I remembered Jesus saying to his disciples: "Let us cross over to the other side."[5] So I recommended that we go around to the other shore of the Sea of Galilee as that much was permissible without any extra cost. We drove to a very large kibbutz where we had a fabulous lunch of fish fresh from the Sea. It was directly opposite Tiberias, and near the more rustic place where Sandra had stayed on her previous visit. There was a place in front of the eating area where you could go down and put your feet and hands in the water – an opportunity that we all took advantage of.

Tuesday was a long day driving from Tiberias to Tel Aviv with several important stops enroute. The first was Nazareth, which is now a very large Arab town. It was home to the Basilica of the Annunciation, the largest in the Middle East. It is said to be built over Mary's house where the angel Gabriel told her that she would be the mother of a boy child that she should call Jesus. The large and beautiful church was lined with twenty-five or so huge mosaics – one from each country depicting the culture of that country. To see so many varied depictions of Mary and Joseph underlined the universality of the event which took place in one small seemingly insignificant village.

The compound included another, smaller, St. Joseph's Church built over the shop of St. Joseph the *tekton* – one who works in stone, metal or wood. The smaller church was perfect for meditation and we took advantage of the opportunity to reflect on the part that Nazareth had played in the life of Jesus and, consequently, in our own lives as we try to live in accordance with his teaching and example.

Our next stop was Megiddo, site of many fortresses and battles. It was where Solomon kept some of his horses and chariots. The book of Revelation says this place, or the valley below, will be the site of the final battle – Armageddon. I was sufficiently incredulous that I recorded "I somehow doubt it," in my diary.[6]

The final stop was Caesarea where Herod the Great built a palace at the waterfront, and where the Crusaders had built a fortress and church on top of the ruins in the 12th century. It was all very fascinating, especially for people like me whose interest in history developed very late in life. When our physical endurance reached the stage where the "let's go" light came on, we headed for the airport city only to find a traffic jam that was reminiscent of home so we were treated to an extra hour of history from our intrepid Birte, before bidding her adieu at the Intercontinental Hotel in Tel Aviv.

Egypt, Lebanon and Jordan

We rose at the crack of dawn, 4:00 a.m., to allow ample time at the airport. We needed it. Security was tough. Where had we been? Who had we talked to? One of my bags was singled out for special attention.

When my interrogator finally appeared I was asked how many pairs of shoes I had, an item that was not on my mental list of possible questions. The truth sufficed, and I was allowed to proceed. Soon it would be *au revoir*, Israel, to which we would return briefly after Easter when the flood of tourists had subsided.

A long layover in Amman gave us time for coffee, reading and journaling. I read a few pages from *Alien Encounters*, which I noted was "Really fascinating stuff." Kent, who had just finished reading several books on the background to the conflict in the Middle East, had some especially poignant inner thoughts that he is willing to share.

"As I was finishing the last book, one of my thoughts was: 'I don't want to enter into the pain and suffering of another part of the world. Isn't Africa enough?' But my heart has been touched by the injustice on all sides and the suffering this has caused to so many. And, of course, as a nation [the U.S.] our refusal to raise the quota on Jews during and after the Second World War, made us complicit in giving the land of the Palestinians to the Zionists. [Canada's record was equally bad.]

"All of the attempts of the 'God-fearing' to fight over legislation to keep us a Christian nation seem so self-centered and non-involved in the real issue of love and justice in our world. It reminds me of the conversation with Garth and Gad, in Kigali, when Gad talked about the great difficulty the strong and dominant have to understand the emotions and responses of those who are weak and dominated. Americans find it almost impossible to understand the suffering and helplessness of most of the people of the world."[7]

Our entrance into Egypt was fairly smooth, and then we had the experience of Cairo traffic. We took separate cabs, and our young but skillful drivers decided to make a race of it. The sprawling city was bursting with vehicles – cars, buses, vans and donkey-drawn carts – all vying for position on the impossibly crowded streets. Honking was a regular part of driving and lanes, which are not marked, are totally disregarded. In the absence of traffic lights, people drive as fast as they can, edging each other out whenever possible. It took about an hour to reach the Four Seasons Hotel.

Never in our lives had any of us seen such opulence. We were worn out from our time in Israel/Palestine and really needed some R&R so this was the perfect place for it. Immaculate marble floors, spotless mirrored walls, exquisite mammoth flower arrangements, impressive artwork of all kinds, beautifully presented sumptuous food, a gorgeous pool deck, and incredibly attentive personnel everywhere. It was totally seducing!

The next day was one of quiet relaxation. We did venture out in the afternoon long enough to visit the Egyptian Museum. It was a real treat, especially the contents of King Tutankhamun's tomb. The incredible beauty and delicacy of the ornaments, and the ingenuity and creativity that birthed them were awesome indeed. Some exhibits in other areas were poorly labeled and the impressive building itself was in much need of repair. We were wishing that some rich American or Canadian would make a sizable gift to facilitate restoration and care of the priceless exhibits.

Friday, April 14 – Good Friday – was Kent's birthday. In the morning we met with Paul Gordon Chandler, a young Episcopalian minister who was working to help Muslims and Christians get to know each other, in the spirit of the Jesus of the Gospels. Jesus is accepted as one of the Muslim prophets, and consequently his teachings can have a profound influence on their lives without the necessity of abandoning their traditions.

In the evening we went to the Sound and Light show at the pyramids. To get there we had to drive past many scenes of urban squalor – trash everywhere, and people living in near-derelict buildings. It was all a vivid reminder of how most of the world lives. We asked about the flocks of sheep and goats moving through the streets and were told that they were sold to commemorate the sacrifice that Abraham was asked to make of his son Isaac, and God's provision of the ram in substitute.

The show itself was quite fantastic. It was a multimedia presentation with diverse colored lights flashing on and off the several pyramids at appropriate times, while a voice, seeming to come from the mouth of the Sphinx, related the fascinating history of the successive Egyptian dynasties. I kept wondering about the technology used to build the pyramids and whether or not they had some help from someone familiar with the miracle of levitation. It was a great way to celebrate Kent's big day, and he kept wondering what he would do for an encore next year.

On to Beirut

Saturday was moving day as we left Cairo for Beirut. The trip was uneventful, although both Kent and Kay were asked a few tough questions by Lebanese immigration as to why they had visited Israel.

When we arrived at the beautiful Phoenecia Continental Hotel we found that it was right across the street from the bombed-out site where Prime Minister Harari had been assassinated in February. On another side was a shell-riddled ruin of a Holiday Inn, now a crater hole. These were stark reminders of Lebanon's civil war that had left the city devastated only fifteen or so years ago, and the fact that it had been invaded by both Syria and Israel.

These few sites, however, were the only visible tokens of what had been. When we arrived, by way of contrast, the boulevard along the ocean side was lined with stalls and cafes filled with people. The city was alive, and moving on. Most of the downtown area had been rebuilt under the inspired direction of the late prime minister who had solved the impossible riddle of land titles in the city core with an ingenious "fresh start."

Easter Sunday we looked for a church to attend and finally found the Church of St. Francis where mass was said in several languages. We arrived too early for the English service so we attended the one in French.

A small hitch in our plans occurred when our host for the five days in Lebanon hadn't shown up when we arrived. After all else failed, Kay suggested sending an e-mail, a stroke of genius that worked. A couple of hours later Samir Kreidie phoned. He had been told that we were not coming. The message must have referred to someone else, so he was blithely unaware of our presence in his backyard.

Within minutes he was on the way to our hotel and about to show us what Eastern hospitality was like. As we were getting ready to leave the hotel, Samir introduced us to Abdullah bin Laden, one of the almost fifty brothers of Osama. Abdullah is Harvard educated, totally committed to peace, and very charming.

Samir took us on a tour of the downtown area much of which had been destroyed in the civil war of 1975 to 1989. They had begun rebuilding about ten years before our visit and it was absolutely amazing what they had accomplished in that short time. There were huge walking areas where cars were not allowed; so it was pedestrian-friendly to walk amidst the shops and tall buildings that had been restored to their former luster, but with improved materials and furnishings. We took a peek at the beautiful new mosque that the prime minister had planned to dedicate before his life had been snuffed out. The visual images here are always contradictory – vibrant life side by side with reminders of death and destruction and, everywhere, young soldiers patrolling the streets.

When we had walked enough, Samir took us to his home to meet his glamorous wife Sophie, and other members of the family and extended family. In the course of getting acquainted, we spent some time talking about all of the major issues facing the Middle East and the World, as well as plans for the next three days. There was no doubt that we had a jam-packed itinerary including some heavy evening sessions to discuss these seemingly intractable problems and what, if anything, might be done about them.

In the morning, one of "Samir's men," Robert Pelgrim, picked us up and took us to the Palestinian Refugee Camp where he oversees the work of the Inma Community Center, a development resulting from the efforts of Americans Doug Coe, Frank Wolf and Tony Hall, working in concert with Samir. These were people of various faiths who joined hands in common cause to provide some care and hope to refugees living in wretched conditions.

I had no idea what to expect, but Kay thought she would find a sprawling tent or hut city. What we found was a concrete jungle comprised of one concrete unit piled on top of the next because the camp was limited to a defined area; and as the population increased there was nowhere to go except to build new apartments on top of the existing ones. The inevitable consequence was water pipes and hoses and electrical wires swinging in great bunches between the buildings across the tiny alleyways that threaded throughout the place.

The camp had been in existence since 1948 so there was a pathetic permanence about it, and our friends were doing their best to keep hope alive by assisting with small improvements like a stove, or a refrigerator. The people seemed so wonderfully pleased at any improvement and were grateful. We were able to walk about in safety, but we were told that a year earlier that would not have been the case. My reflection was that if this is the best of the twelve camps in Lebanon, housing about 400,000 refugees, God help the inhabitants of the others.

In the afternoon Robert took us to Baalbeck, the famous Roman ruins about two and a half hours drive from Beirut. The ruins were absolutely breathtaking in their ancient grandeur. We wandered around for more than an hour looking at the massive structures. Our guide pointed out that the temple had been built by 300,000 slaves working non-stop for fifteen years. In addition, there were hundreds of elephants to help lug the immense columns inland.

Tuesday, April 18. This morning's newspaper reported the bombing in Tel Aviv in which nine people were tragically killed and many others wounded. The article pointed out that Hamas had not condemned the bombing, and Israeli officials were holding them responsible. Near the end of the article, there was one small paragraph mentioning that over a dozen Palestinians (several of them small children) had been killed by the Israelis in Gaza the previous day. The news is always weighted to blame the Palestinians, and although the suicide bomber cannot be excused for the violence, there is not a balanced picture in the reporting – even here in the Middle East.

Sandra felt ill the next morning, so the rest of us left with our driver Ghassan Hussami, who proved to be a marvelous host. Our first stop was the Jeita Grotto. We had never, ever, seen anything quite like it. The huge cavern, extending about half a mile, resembled a mammoth cathedral with the centuries-old stalactites and stalagmites providing formations of incredible beauty. Kay's notes summed it up in one word: "Indescribable!"

We had lunch in Byblos – probably the oldest continually-inhabited city in the western world. This is where the Bible got its name. We were joined at lunch by Mounzer Fatfat, Ph.D., an American of Lebanese origin who had served in Iraq as the Minister of Youth and Sports until the transfer of power to the Iraqis in June 2004. In Dr. Fatfat's opinion the transfer had been much too soon and was driven entirely by the political necessity of supporting the Bush Administration in the presidential election of that year.

It was also interesting to note that our friend had been the only Arabic-speaking member of the U.S. occupying authority and, consequently, probably the only one who had a real sense of what was going on. At the end of the meal I asked him to pray, and he willingly did. The owner of the restaurant then opened up his private museum laden with Roman, Phoenician, and other artifacts that had been recovered from the Mediterranean Sea bed. It was unusually comprehensive for a private collection.

Later, we went to Samir's place for a couple of hours' discussion. Sophie, who had undergone surgery a couple of days earlier, was considerably recovered, and able to participate. There were three other men in attendance while Samir explained how Islam and Jesus, and the Bible and the Koran were similar in so many essential ways. He had the gist of his message transcribed so there was no need for us to take notes.

Our guide and mentor on Wednesday was Dr. Fouad Mrad, an engineering professor at the American University at Beirut. He took us south of the city for the first time to show us the Hariri Canadian College, which he had helped create eleven years earlier. This modern business and engineering school bore the name of the assassinated prime minister who had played such a key role in rebuilding the country.

We drove on to Sidon which, we were told, was as far south as we should go without exposing ourselves to unnecessary risk. We enjoyed a relaxed luncheon at a seaside restaurant looking out on a Crusader fort originally built by the Phoenicians. After lunch we returned early to the hotel in anticipation of our most serious discussion in depth with Samir and his friends for which we would be picked up at 4:45 p.m.

There were about a dozen people waiting for us when we arrived at Samir's home. All were Muslim except for one Christian who was in charge of promoting Muslim/ Christian dialogue. He was there with his Islamic opposite number, a prominent Muslim lawyer. Samir introduced me to the group and asked me to explain the purpose of our visit. I said that it was primarily a fact-finding tour. We wanted to know what steps could be taken in order to move things along toward the resolution of conflicts in the area. Many strong statements were made in response, some of which were painful for Kent and Kay to hear – not because they were new to us, but because the things we had been hearing were said with such passion. The following is Kent's summary, in brief:

* Lebanon is the Middle East in microcosm. It is rife with sectarianism, promoted by the various outside influences, French, U.S., Syrian, etc.

* We are to appreciate the broad areas of agreement between Christians and Palestinians – one God, honoring Jesus, people of the Book, etc, but at the same time we move forward when we recognize the differences in our beliefs, and give each other the freedom to practice their own religion fully.

* The establishment in 1948 of the Israeli nation changed everything in the Middle East, and has been at the root of the conflicts that have ensued since that time.

* Since 1967 the Arab world has known that no one can stop Israel in the Middle East because we (the U.S.) have made them the super power here.

* The primary cause of 9/11 has been U.S. support of Israel, and our complicity in the oppression of the Palestinians.

* When the U.S invaded Iraq, we created thousands of new recruits for those who are willing to die for Allah.

* The parallels between the apartheid of South Africa and what Israel is doing to the Palestinians is striking. A major difference is that the Western powers eventually aligned themselves against the system of apartheid. There was no lobby for the Afrikaaners in America. The Western powers have aligned themselves with the Zionists because there is a powerful lobby for the Israelis in America.

* The only possible way through is the love of Jesus working through sensible Muslims, Christians and Jews in ways that will bring forgiveness and reconciliation, and moderate the extremists in all the different factions.[8]

After such a powerful sermon from the penthouse, Samir took us out for coffee at a seaside café to give us a break before we went back to his house for dinner – our only meal in a Lebanese home. Meanwhile the discussion went on and on all evening with Samir, Sophie and their family. Needless to say a sumptuous Muslim dinner was a unique and treasured treat.

To Amman

Thursday we headed for the airport and enjoyed an uneventful flight to Amman. It was my first opportunity, thanks to a window seat, to get a look at the Jordanian landscape and its relationship to Israel and the occupied territories; also the East Bank of the Jordan River where two and a half of the twelve tribes of Israel had settled in the days of Moses/Joshua. I enjoyed my brief historical reverie.

When we arrived at the hotel in Amman, Kent phoned our contact person who said he would call back, but that this was their Easter weekend and it would be difficult for him due to his many commitments. We decided that rather than add to his pressure we would just have a quiet dinner at the hotel and book a day trip to the world famous Petra for the morning.

What we found was almost beyond belief. Solid rock walls riddled with a honeycomb of tombs and dwellings all adorned on the outside by coded statuary and pilasters. This spectacular rock enclave had been occupied by 20,000 or more Nabataeans, who lived there from the sixth century BCE, until conquered by the Romans in 106 CE. It then lay dormant until it was rediscovered in 1812. As we enjoyed the beauty of the twelve different colors of rocks in the towering walls we could understand why Petra had been dubbed the eighth wonder of the world.

We were all exhausted from the day, but had to revive quickly to go to dinner as guests of Taglib and Sawson Alsaraf, two Iraqi friends who once lived in Montréal. Sandra met Sawson when she attended the Montréal Prayer Breakfast group, where Muslims had been welcome. We found that the Alsarafs had made a reservation at a local restaurant that served excellent Mediterranean food. The only drawbacks were the large table and the noisy diners who made it difficult for Kent and me, with our restricted hearing, to follow the conversation. Still, we did learn a few things.

Taglib had favored the American invasion of Iraq because seventeen members of his family had been killed by Saddam Hussein. However after living in Baghdad for a year they had to move to Amman because the Iraqi capital was unsafe. Sawson's brother had been kidnapped and it cost the family lots of money to pay the ransom for his release. The desire of some Americans to do good in this part of the world is usually frustrated by the unexpected creation of new problems that didn't occur to them. The more we saw and heard the more aware we became of just how naïve U.S. foreign policy in the Middle East really is.

Homeward Bound via Israel

A morning of quiet rest was a godsend because Sunday turned out to be a wild day of transit through the gauntlet of passport controls and security checks. We had decided to drive from Amman, Jordan, across the bridge over the Jordan River – called the King Hussein bridge on one side of the river, and the Allenby bridge on the other side – which is the border with Israel, and on to Jerusalem, our last stop before flying home. It turned out to be an ordeal, though funny, in retrospect.

We spent $85 U.S. each for the VIP Service, plus taxi fares on both sides, plus tips, so it wasn't cheap, but still less than flying. Also, I wanted to see the famous bridge mentioned in so much literature. We barely had enough cash left between us to cover the costs that seemed to pile up as we went. Security on the Israeli side is a complex web of electronic gates, baggage examinations, questions and, in Kay's case, thorough frisking, because her artificial hip kept setting off the scanner. By the time we emerged, ruffled but successful, our taxi driver (pre-arranged) had been waiting for us for an hour and a half. When we finally collapsed at our old hotel, the Dan Panorama, we realized that it had taken us four and a half hours to complete the sixty-mile drive.

Our last day in Jerusalem was rainy and cool. We decided to wander in the Old City, so got a taxi to the Jaffa Gate (our cash having been replenished by the god ATM). We found our way through the narrow lanes to the Christian Quarter and the Lutheran Church where we had attended Palm Sunday service. This time we entered the main sanctuary where Arabic services are held and just sat quietly for a while listening to a group of Koreans singing "I'd rather have Jesus," in Korean, of course. The voices rose sweetly in the vaulted space, and we felt the fellowship of believers that transcends culture.

As we meandered back to the hotel we enjoyed the commerce, too, especially the ladies. They were shopping for gifts to take home for family and friends, and a tiny icon, a diptych, for Kay. We were pretty well exhausted as we approached the Jaffa Gate, and some of us, at least, were getting hungry. So Kent and I were less than amused when, within sight of the Gate, the women decided to stop and look around the Franciscan bookstore that caught their eye.

We thought of going on without them but decided that would be a mite crass, and expose the weaker side of our nature. So we reluctantly trundled into the store behind them. The range of books was excellent, so it was not too much of a hardship spending a few minutes looking at the variety of titles. All of a sudden I saw Sandra heading my way with a small book in her hand. It was titled *John and Jamnia: How the Break Occurred Between Jews and Christians c. 80-100 A.D.* "This was not a coincidence! Wow, just what I need," I recorded in my diary. I knew it was a discovery that would save me weeks of research! The prediction was correct as it was most helpful in writing Chapter 4.

After lunch and a short nap, for me at least, we got together for a while to study John 17, followed by a very early snack dinner so we could get at least a little sleep before the alarm sounded at 1:40 a.m. for Kent and Kay, and 2:30 a.m. for Sandra and me, as we headed for Tel Aviv Airport and home, for three of us – Sandra went on to Crete to spend a few days with her daughters.

We had all learned so much in such a short time that it was difficult to digest, and one of our fears was how we could share our knowledge when we got home without undue incredulity from friends who had been programmed to think differently.

CHAPTER 3

WE ARE NOT ALONE IN THE COSMOS

*"I didn't know how much I didn't know because
I didn't know how much there was to know."*

Paul Hellyer

On Tuesday, July 8, 1947, at 11:00 a.m. Mountain Time (MT), Roswell Army Air Field commanding officer Colonel William Blanchard announced (in a press release) the recovery of a flying disc.[1] <u>THAT WAS THE TRUTH!</u>

Later that same day, at approximately 4:30 p.m. Central Standard Time (CST), Brigadier General Roger Ramey, the commander of the Eighth Air Force, and Blanchard's supervising officer, presented to the press an alternate story. He claimed the army had recovered a rawin target device suspended by a Neoprene rubber balloon.[2] (Rawin is a method of determining wind speed and direction using a radar-sensitive target or radio transponder.) <u>THAT WAS A LIE!</u>

The information provided by Brig. Ramey was not only a lie, it became the cornerstone lie on which has been built a monstrous skyscraper of lies and deceit spanning more than sixty years during which the American public, press and Congress have been deliberately uninformed and systematically misinformed about the subject of the Extraterrestrial presence on and around our planet, and the extent to which some of their vastly superior technology has been replicated for military and industrial use.

The time has long since passed when there can be any justification for secrecy in respect of matters that are so important to the lives of Americans, future Americans and all other Earthlings. The issues, that I will discuss later, include the question as to whether or not we will continue on the path of making our planet uninhabitable, as the Extraterrestrials fear, or whether we will heed their warning, take advantage of their technology and save our planet for the future benefit of Earthlings and Visitors alike.

For now, however, I would like to provide a sample of the kind of evidence that became available to me as I set out on my journey in search of the truth, and that may be helpful to you as you ponder the implications. As soon as news of my categorical statement of September 2005 was in the public domain, corroborating material of all kinds began to flow in like a mighty river. I received more than a dozen books and countless memos, magazines and documents of all kinds, including many that had been highly classified.

I soon found – and I don't know why it should have been a surprise to me – that whereas I had been disinterested and consequently uninformed, there was a small army of dedicated ufologists who had been painstakingly researching the subject for years, and in some cases decades, who had already discovered relevant information and documentation of diverse sorts, and recorded much of it in book form. So they have been the pioneers paving the path of discovery for the much larger army of skeptics and naysayers who have yet to be exposed to what I like to call "the broader reality."

As I began to contemplate the "broader reality" a humorous story that I had read in Chuckles, by Lee Vass, came to mind.

"Sherlock Holmes and Dr. Watson went on a camping trip. After a good meal and a bottle of wine they lay down for the night and went to sleep. Some hours later Holmes awoke and nudged his faithful friend. 'Watson, look up at the sky and tell me what you see?' 'I see millions and millions of stars,' Watson replied. 'What does that tell you?' asked Holmes.

"Watson pondered for a minute and replied, 'Astronomically, it tells me that there are millions of galaxies and potentially billions of planets. Astrologically, I observe that Saturn is in Leo. Horologically, I deduce that the time is approximately a quarter past three. Theologically, I can see that God is all powerful and that we are small and insignificant. Meteorologically, I suspect that we will have a clear and sunny day tomorrow. What does it tell you Holmes?'

"Holmes was silent for a minute, then spoke: 'Watson, you idiot. Somebody has stolen our tent.'"

This demonstrates, I might add as one who was born under the sign of Leo, that it is often a matter of perspective!

Supplementary Evidence

In addition to the acknowledged experts, there were people with first hand experience who wanted to share it with someone who would listen respectfully. Their stories were a helpful supplement to my expanding knowledge. My first encounter was with an aviation buff, Leo Pearce, a long-time resident of the condominium I moved into in 1981. He read about my speech and wanted to share his experience with me.

"I was driving from Port Hope to Cobourg (two small towns about two hours drive east of Toronto) at about 2:30 on a Saturday afternoon in 1956 when I heard this buzzing sound. I was driving my father's car and had a girl friend with me. We stopped and got out to look, and there is this big, huge, size of a football field object hovering directly above. It was a dual saucer, inverted, and had portholes on both top and bottom. It had a glowing blue flame around the outside of it but there wasn't any sound of motors; it was more like generators – a humming sound.

"I was enthralled with my aviation background, but this thing was unlike anything I had ever seen. I watched it for about fifteen minutes: then all of a sudden it started to glow on the outside and then accelerated over the lake (Ontario) and just disappeared. I knew that nothing in the world could go that fast – it must have accelerated to about 3,000 miles an hour. A number of other people saw it, including the girl with me, but most of them didn't talk about it. There was nothing in the paper."[3]

**

A Canadian World War II veteran also tracked me down to relate his wartime and subsequent experience with UFOs. Flight Lieutenant (Captain) Stan Fulham, of Winnipeg, Manitoba, tells the stories of his wartime and post-war experiences. I have condensed the former due to space restrictions.

In July 1944 Fulham was in a German prisoner of war camp in Poland. One hot afternoon he and his fellow prisoners observed what appeared to be a German rocket flying at incredible speed and great height over the prison camp. As they were all well trained in aircraft recognition techniques they recognized at once that it was too large, too high and too fast for any aircraft that they were aware of. For a moment they suspected it was a German rocket but then realized that didn't make any sense because it was flying in the wrong direction. It was only after the war that they concluded that it had been a UFO.

"Later, as a fighter controller with the North American Air Defence Command (NORAD), I had the opportunity of monitoring UFOs on radar and then of scrambling fighter aircraft to investigate the alien spacecraft. One night in the early 60s, two UFOs hovered two miles off the runway at an altitude of one thousand feet. The radar returns indicated craft three to four times the size of our jet fighters. I called NORAD command and informed them of the situation and suggested that I scramble standby jets to identify the unknowns. This was agreed.

"As soon as our jets were airborne the UFOs streaked away at phenomenal speeds approaching three thousand miles per hour, with our jets in slow pursuit. The discs reappeared and hovered over the ocean near Vancouver, British Columbia, until our fighters finally caught up to them. As our jets closed in they streaked away and disappeared over the Pacific.

"Thousands of people had seen the UFOs and also our jets. They called the control tower asking for information as to these strange lights and aircraft in the sky. Several people suggested that they could be UFOs since they were not helicopters and yet hovered in the sky without sound. Some authorities (not identified) stated that it was an illusion and suggested that aircraft flying west to Japan would appear as if they were standing still in the sky. This was a phenomenon, they said, that very often confused people. The media were not happy with this explanation because they knew that aircraft flying from the west coast to Japan would fly the

Great Circle route which was actually in a north-west direction toward Alaska and not directly west which would take them to Hawaii.

"Early the next morning the media called the Base Commander for confirmation and information about the UFO sightings. The Commander called and advised me of the media interest. 'However,' he cautioned, 'since nothing unusual took place last night, I suggest that we have nothing to discuss with the media.' I understood. This was the standard response to the public and the media in NORAD under a secret United States-Canada Communications Agreement signed in 1956 relating to the control and reporting of UFO sightings."[4]

**

At that point I had not yet talked to anyone who had actually seen a flying saucer close up. My long-time friend, and former Canadian Forces Information Officer, Ray Stone sent me an e-mail from one of his friends, Nickolas Evanoff, who had seen the real thing. It reads as follows.

"In the late 1970s, or perhaps 1980 or 1981, I was visiting a certain USA Government organization in Virginia, which I cannot disclose, when I was asked if I wanted to see a real UFO. Of course, I said, so I had to go through a series of documents and had to sign them, mostly for non-disclosure. Because I was in the Emergency Preparedness Organization they said it would be of great help to me and our organization if such an incident happened in Canada. I was not allowed to inform my bosses when I got back, or anyone else.

"Next I was on board a USA Gov. aircraft and flown to the midwest of the USA which I think was either Arizona or Nevada and we landed at a US Air Force Base which I cannot disclose.

"Then we went into a humongous hangar and there was a damaged UFO. The interior size of it was about that which we saw at Local Heroes Bar side. When it crashed it had eight aliens on board and six of them died on impact and the pilot and co-pilot survived for a couple of days. The USAF doctors didn't know how to treat them because they were from another planet so they died. I didn't see the bodies but I was shown some photographs of them and they were similar to us humans but thinner, had a head and arms and legs and a torso along with five digits on their hands and feet. On board was a nuker for cooking food and a supply of water along with two bathrooms. The manuals were in hieroglyphics and no one could read them including folks from Alaska (Eskimos), India and Egypt. Berkeley University was awarded a contract to photocopy and try using their computers to read them but were unsuccessful.

"The reason this UFO crashed was no different from youngsters (18 to 22 years of age) driving cars at excessive speeds on the 400 series highways in Canada or Interstate highways in the USA. The pilot and co-pilot who were young were not aware of the earth's gravitational pull and it was too late to slow down when they reversed their thrusters so they crashed. Most of the craft was not seriously damaged but the collision caused havoc on board.

"I asked why didn't the President of the USA inform the public of this incident and I was told it was because of Religion and possible panic amongst Americans and other citizens around the world. I was also informed about a two passenger (pilot and co-pilot) UFO that crashed outside of Helsinki, Finland in 1952 and was published in newspapers around the world and the next day no more information was allowed. Bizarre!

"That is pretty much it and when we left the hanger got back on board the aircraft and flew back to Virginia. I was frustrated for years because I couldn't tell anyone what I saw, including my wife.

"Nick"[5]

I wanted to get the story from Nick personally so Ray Stone set up an interview for a Sunday afternoon in October 2007. Before the day came Ray advised that if I wanted to talk to Nick, who had Lou Gehrig's Disease, before he died I had better telephone him, which I did, at once, on October 7. He confirmed the story and identified "Virginia" as CIA Headquarters in Langley. He also told me about a UFO landing near Winnipeg, Manitoba, that had not been publicized. A few days later he passed to his reward.

**

The biggest surprise I have encountered in the course of my research for this chapter was to find a file amongst my own papers going back to my days as minister of transport. It contained a 15-page booklet, including several pages of photographs, entitled "Description and Performance of Unidentified Flying Objects from 1947-1967" as taken from newsstand sources, compiled by Malcolm McKellar, Vancouver, British Columbia. Sightings were reported from Brazil; Perth, Australia; Salem, Oregon;

Queen's, New York; Danville, Virginia; Santa Ana, California; Zanesville, Ohio; Melbourne, Australia; and Rouen, France, to mention only a few where the best photos were taken. All of the descriptions are interesting but I am including only one that paints a precise portrait of one of the early-type space ships.

In 1952, "Oscar Linke and daughter, reporting to NANA, Berlin, stated that before their escape from Russian-held Germany, they used to take frequent motorcycle rides toward the border. On one such trip, the daughter called attention to a phosphorescent object in a small forest. From a distance of one hundred feet, the object appeared to be a disc, twenty-five feet across, resembling a huge warming pan without a handle. In the center of it, there seemed to be a sort of upper works which rose out of the top of the craft. It was darker than the rest of the object, which was the color of aluminum, well polished.

"Two small figures – like tiny humans about four feet tall – were seen wearing shiny one piece garments, silver in color. On the chest of one of these creatures was a box or package about the size of three packs of cigarettes, and on the front of the package was a bright, blinking blue light. They did not seem to be using this box. Both figures were standing outside the UFO.

"Suddenly one tapped the other on the helmet (shiny, glasslike) and both climbed hurriedly into the spacecraft through a porthole on the top of the square part of the upperworks aforementioned. The object was seen to have two rows of circular portholes around the edge, about the size of portholes on a ship. As father and daughter watched, the square upper works began to retract into the dome and simultaneously the UFO started to rise from the ground slowly. It rose to a hundred feet, hovered for a moment and then sped away."[6]

Interesting Personalities with More Compelling Information

As a result of the notoriety I had gained from speaking out categorically there were many people who wanted to brief me. One of the best known of these is Dr. Steven Greer, M.D., who gave up a lucrative medical practice because he was so concerned about the secrecy surrounding the whole question of the extraterrestrial presence and technology, and the implications of what that means for all humanity.

When Dr. Greer visited Toronto in May 2006, we arranged to meet for lunch at one of Toronto's waterfront cafes where he gave me a three-hour briefing of what he had learned in the course of his research. He had talked to about four hundred former military officers, scientists, civil aviation officers, policemen, pilots and others and managed to film and record about one hundred who revealed in detail what they knew about important subjects that the U.S. government has been deliberately hiding for as far back as sixty years or more.

Not only was I struck with the depth and diversity of the testimony Dr. Greer had assembled for his "Disclosure Project," I was alarmed by some of the testimony of witnesses who confirmed my suspicions of American military plans including the militarization of space, that I consider highly questionable, and not in the best interests of either the U.S. or the world. The peaceful uses of space should be open to all humanity, a frontier as challenging and thrilling as climbing Mount Everest, and even more wondrous.

These revelations were disturbing enough, but they aren't a patch on Greer's assertion that government leaders are unaware of what is going on in their own country and that, in fact, the real power is a "Shadow Government," the composition of which is unknown to man or beast with the possible exception of a handful of insiders whose names and addresses are amongst the most closely guarded secrets of the world. As Senator Daniel K. Inouye, of Hawaii, describes them: "There exists a shadowy government with its own Air Force, its own Navy, its own fundraising mechanism, and the ability to pursue its own ideas of the national interest, and free from all checks and balances, and free from the law itself."[7]

Steven Greer has been subject to every kind of harassment including threats to life and limb. Still he persists in seeking the truth and making it known before it is too late. He will be recorded as one of the pioneer heroes of the global Disclosure movement.

The following month, in June 2006, I delivered the keynote address at the Extraterrestrial Civilizations & World Peace Conference at Kona, Hawaii, at the invitation of Dr. Michael Salla, head of the Exopolitics Institute, and his wife Angelika Whitecliff, co-organizer of the conference. In addition to the pleasure of spending a few days in such a delightful part of the planet, I had the opportunity to listen to a number of speakers all of whom knew far more about the subject than I did. My role was to expand on my concerns about the military and political implications of visitors from other planets, subjects on which my long years of experience served as a useful backdrop.

Before I left for home Michael gave me a copy of his excellent book *Exopolitics* that contains much of the political background relating to the subject, and how the U.S. government and Congress lost control of the ET file. He explains how Nelson Rockefeller, as adviser to President Eisenhower, reorganized the control mechanisms for reverse engineering and essentially placed them in the hands of the military-industrial complex. Eisenhower recognized what had happened before he left politics and this led to his classic warning.

"In the councils of Government, we must guard against the acquisition of unwarranted influence, whether sought or unsought by the Military Industrial Complex. The potential for the disastrous rise of misplaced power exists, and will persist. We must never let the weight of this combination endanger our liberties or democratic processes. We should take nothing for granted. Only an alert and knowledgeable citizenry can compel the proper meshing of the huge industrial and military machinery of defense with our peaceful methods and goals so that security and liberty may prosper together."[8]

One of Greer's witnesses, Brigadier General Stephen Lovekin, a military officer who served directly under Eisenhower, confirmed the basis of the General's concern.

"But what happened was that Eisenhower got sold out. Without him knowing it he lost control of what was going on with the entire UFO situation. In his last address to the nation I think he was telling us that the Military Industrial Complex would stick you in the back if you were not totally vigilant … And I think that he realized that all of a sudden this matter is going into the control of corporations that could very well act to the detriment of this country. This frustration, from what I can remember, went on for months. He realized that he was losing control of the UFO subject. He realized that the phenomenon, or whatever it was we were faced with, was not going to be in the best hands. As far as I can remember, that was the expression that was used, 'It is not going to be in the best hands.' "[9]

**

One of the interesting people that Sandra and I saw in Kona was Paola Harris, a well-respected ufologist who had expected to be on the platform in Toronto when I first went public, but had to cancel for health reasons. Paola subsequently flew from Rome, where she was resident, to Toronto for an interview that she managed to have aired in several languages and jurisdictions. She gave us a copy of her book *Connecting the Dots*, that I found every bit as interesting as I would expect from the exuberant Paola.

The contents included a lengthy interview with Monsignor Corrado Balducci. Two things became obvious from the clergyman's answers to Paola's questions. He was well versed in the subject and although he was speaking as an individual, and not as an official Vatican spokesman, his superiors were well aware that he was speaking with their full knowledge, at least, if not their unofficial blessing. In his own words.

"The acronym UFO is used here in a wider sense to include the existence of living beings on other planets. The aim of my intervention, and speaking out, is to underline that something real *must* exist in the phenomena, and that this does not conflict at all with the Christian religion, and is considered positive, even among theologians.

"First, something real *must* exist. Secondly, I have made some theological considerations on the habitability of other planets. Thirdly, much witness testimony favors it. Conclusion: Something real *must* exist.

"Paola Harris: Is it a grave mistake to think that you are the *official* voice of the Vatican?

"Monsignor Balducci: These ideas are mine, and I do not represent the Vatican. However, I am told that the Holy Father John Paul II has seen me on Italian TV several times and follows my radio homilies. If there were some objection, I'm sure I would know. I believe there to be no problem here."[10]

His candid comments lend credence to unofficial information to the effect that the Vatican may have had direct contact with at least one species of Visitors, and that the Holy See may have been in the know from the early days when General Eisenhower was alleged to have had direct contact with the Visitors at what is now known as Edwards Air Force Base, in the company of several witnesses including Bishop MacIntyre of Los Angeles who, despite official objections, would have reported directly to the Holy Father.[11]

Another Canadian Connection

One of the first questions that the majority of ufologists I met would ask me is if I had known, or was aware of, Wilbert Smith, a Canadian public servant, who had been a pioneer in the field. I was embarrassed to admit that I had never heard of him. Shame on me. It was just further evidence that I had not taken the time to comb my own files where there were several articles about or written by Smith that people had sent me to read but that were just put away for that day of leisure that never came.

Worse, Wilbert had been a senior employee of the Department of Transport (DOT) where I became minister not long after his retirement. In a Top Secret memorandum to the Controller of Communications, dated November 21, 1950,[12] Smith recommended that a project be set up by DOT to study certain aspects of the Saucer phenomenon, particularly those in the electromagnetic and radio wave areas. Part of the case he made reads as follows.

"While in Washington attending the NARB Conference, two books were released one titled *Behind the Flying Saucers* by Frank Scully, and the other *Flying Saucers from Outer Space* by Donald Keyhoe.

"Both books dealt mostly with the sightings of unidentified objects and both books claim that flying objects were of extra-terrestrial origin and might well be space ships from another planet. Scully claimed that the preliminary studies of one saucer which fell into the hands of the United States Government indicated that they operated on some hitherto unknown magnetic principles. It appeared to me that our own work in geo-magnetics might well be the linkage between our technology and the technology by which the saucers are designed and operated.

"If it is assumed that our geo-magnetic investigations are in the right direction, the theory of the operation of the saucers becomes quite straightforward, with all observed features explained qualitatively and quantitatively.

"I made discreet enquiries through the Canadian Embassy staff in Washington who were able to obtain for me the following information.

(a) The matter is the most highly classified subject in the United States Government, rating higher even than the H-bomb.
(b) Flying saucers exist.

(c) Their modus operandi is unknown but concentrated effort is being made by a small group, headed by Doctor Vannevar Bush.

(d) The entire matter is considered by the United States authorities to be of tremendous significance.

"I was further informed that the United States authorities are investigating along quite a number of lines which might possibly be related to the saucers such as mental phenomena, and I gather that they are not doing too well since they indicated that if Canada is doing anything at all in geo-magnetics they would welcome a discussion with suitably accredited Canadians.

"While I am not yet in a position to say that we have solved even the first problems in geo-magnetic energy release, I feel that the correlation between our basic theory and the available information on saucers checks too closely to be mere coincidence. It is my honest opinion that we are on the right track and are fairly close to at least some of the answers."

Smith apparently succeeded in persuading his superior to cooperate because early in 1951 Project Magnet was set up. Smith sought and obtained the cooperation of the Chairman of the Canadian Defence Research Board, Dr. Omond Solandt, who allowed him to use the radar facilities at Shirley's Bay, not far from Ottawa. As I indicated earlier, I was totally unaware of this activity and I doubt that my immediate predecessor, Hon. J.W. Pickersgill, knew much more.

Wilbert Smith himself summed up the government's position. In an address to the Vancouver Area UFO Club on March 14, 1961, he stated the following:

"Project Magnet was not an official Government project. It was a project that I talked the Deputy Minister into letting me carry out by making use of the extensive field organization of the Department of Transport. Unfortunately the gentlemen of the press climbed on this and made a big deal of it ... However we carried the project through officially for about four or five years and then went underground because of press interference ..."[13]

The balance of the speech was much more fascinating. Smith makes it very clear that he – and some others – obtained a lot of important information from the Extraterrestrials – presumably from contacts that were checked out for accuracy. In addition to the vast array of scientific knowledge acquired, Smith gleaned enough information concerning the nature and intent of the Visitors to develop his own personal philosophy concerning them. I am sure he would like me to share a couple of paragraphs.

"Furthermore, when the material given to us through the many channels is all assembled and analyzed, it adds up to a complete and elegant philosophy which makes our efforts sound like the beating of jungle drums. These people tell us of a magnificent Cosmic Plan, of which we are a part, which transcends the lifetime of a single person, or a nation, or a civilization, or even a planet or solar system. We are not merely told that there is something beyond our immediate experience, we are told what it is, why it is, and our relation thereto.

"Many of our most vexing problems are solved with a few words, at least we are told of the solutions if we have the understanding and fortitude to apply them. We are told of the inadequacies of our science, and we have been given the basic grounding for a new science which is at once simpler and more embracing than the mathematical monstrosity we have conjured up. We have been told of a way of life that is utopian beyond our dreams, and the means of attaining it. Can it be that such a self-consistent, magnificent philosophy is the figment of the imagination of a number of misguided morons ... ?

"We may summarize the entire flying saucer picture as follows. We have arrived at a time in our development when we must make a final choice between right and wrong. The people from elsewhere are much concerned about the choice which we will make, partly because it will have its repercussions on them and partly because they are our blood brothers and are truly concerned with our welfare. There is a cosmic law about interfering in the affairs of others, so they are not allowed to help us directly even though they could easily do so. We must make our own choice of our own free will. Present trends indicate a series of events which may require the help of these people and they stand by ready and willing to render that help. In fact, they have already helped us a great deal, along lines that do not interfere with our freedom of choice. In time, when certain events have transpired, and we are so oriented that we can accept these people from elsewhere, they will meet us freely on the common ground of mutual understanding and trust, and we will be able to learn from them

51

and bring about the Golden Age all men everywhere desire deep within their hearts."[14]

The British Police are Allowed to Tell the Truth about UFOs

British police are allowed to tell the truth about their experiences with UFOs. On February 13, 2007, Gary Heseltine, a serving police detective with eighteen years experience distributed a detailed list of 213 cases of British police officer UFO sightings from 1901-2005 involving 500 officers. In the interests of brevity I am only including one case. The entire list is available for anyone who wants to see it.[15]

Case 25: October 24, 1967. Location – A3072 between Okehampton and Holsworthy, Devon. Two on duty uniformed police officers, PC Clifford Waycott and PC Roger Willey had spotted a pulsating flying cross whilst driving between the above locations. It was seen at low altitude moving above the treetops of the surrounding countryside. Intrigued they began to chase the UFO; however they were never able to significantly gain on it. At times the object slowed to 50 mph and covered a distance of 14 miles. Whenever they did gain a little ground on the object it would simply accelerate away from them. Eventually they reduced their speed fearing an accident themselves. The closest distance they reached to the UFO was 400 yards. At one point they stopped at a farm to wake up the owner so they could gain some corroboration that they were not mistaken in their sighting.

At a later press conference PC Waycott said, "The light wasn't piercing but it was very bright. It was star-spangled – just like looking through wet glass and although we reached 90 mph it accelerated away from us." Before the object disappeared from view they saw a second UFO that was also cross-shaped, very bright and made no noise. Both officers were impressed by the relevant speeds of the objects as they quickly departed, especially the first one. Enquiries at nearby RAF Chivenor proved negative. Within 48 hours numerous other witnesses began to report sightings of similar objects. A 'fiery cross' was witnessed above the skies of Glossop, Derbyshire by six police officers.[16]

The next few pages relate to one of the areas of greatest concern on the part of our neighbors from other planets and galaxies. It is one that we will have to address before we can expect the kind of help essential for the preservation of our planet as a beautiful homeland of unlimited promise.

The Children are Playing with Matches

A recurring theme in most of the literature I have read, as well as in private interviews, is that the frequency of visits from outer space increased markedly about the time the U.S. set off its first test atomic bomb. Not only did the number of visits multiply rapidly, much of the celestial surveillance centered on military installations – especially top secret bases directly connected to the nuclear proliferation. The Roswell crash, or crashes, as there were allegedly two incidents, fit this pattern as they were so near where the U.S. had tested its early nuclear weapons and the Army Air Force had stationed its first squadron of nuclear bombers.

While I was in Hawaii in June 2006, Mike Bird, a Canadian delegate, recommended a nearby restaurant for dinner. Sandra and I took his advice, and asked him to join us. When we arrived Mike recognized one of the presenters, Capt. Robert Salas, and his wife Marilyn, so we persuaded them to join the party. Not only were they delightful dinner companions, the story that the Captain told bordered on science fiction, but it was real – only too real – because he was there. The following is a very brief summary based on that conversation, his presentation, his book *Faded Giant*, and the evidence he provided Dr. Greer as part of the Disclosure Project.

The incident occurred on the morning of March 16, 1967. Capt. Salas and his commander, Fred Mywald, were on duty at Oscar Flight, a part of the 490th strategic missile squad. It was still dark and they were sixty feet underground at the ICBM launch control facility. Early that morning Salas received a call from the topside security guard who said that he and some of his colleagues had been watching some strange lights flying around the site launch control facility. The guard said it was quite unusual, because they were just flying around. "You mean a UFO," Salas asked? The guard didn't know what they were; they were not airplanes but there were lights and they were just flying around. They weren't helicopters, either, but they were making some strange maneuvers that he couldn't explain. Salas says that he just shook his head and said: "Call me if anything more important happens."

Some time later the guard called again and this time he appeared to be very frightened. Salas could tell by his voice that he was "very shook up." "Sir," the guard said: "There's a glowing red object hovering right outside the front gate – I'm looking at it right now. I've got all the men out here with their weapons drawn." The Capt. didn't know what to make of it and was somewhat uncertain as to what order he should give in the face of unprecedented circumstances. Salas thinks he said something like: "Make sure that the perimeter fence is secure." At that point the guard said he had to go because one of his men had been injured climbing the fence.

Salas went over to his commander who was taking a nap during a rest period and started relating the information he had received and, as he spoke, the missiles – Minuteman One missiles with nuclear-tipped warheads – started shutting down, one by one, as a result of guidance system failures. At the time, Salas recalls, he felt that they were losing them all but later in reviewing the incident with Fred Mywald, his commander, they concluded that only seven or eight had been rendered inoperable.

The Air Force did an extensive investigation of the entire incident and was not able to come up with a probable cause of the shutdowns. Each missile was independently controlled and the system was very reliable. Failures were rare and seldom, if ever, had there been more than one shutdown at a time. Weather was not a factor, and power surges were ruled out. A Boeing engineer who did some laboratory tests thought that some kind of electromagnetic force or field might have caused the signal to go. Needless to say, as with all other matters related to the Extraterrestrial presence, the whole incident was kept secret without any public awareness.[17]

**

In the previous chapter I mentioned that I had met Nick Pope, the officer in charge of the UFO desk at the U.K. Ministry of Defence, when visiting London, and that he had given me two files that looked especially interesting. One related to the Rendlesham Forest incident just outside the US Air Force's twin NATO bases at Bentwaters and Woodbridge, Suffolk, in 1980. Unlike most sightings this one had been widely reported due to a memorandum sent to the U.K. Ministry of Defence by Lieutenant Colonel Charles I. Halt, who was Deputy Base Commander RAF Woodbridge at the time. Pope thought that Halt might be willing to talk to me. So that fall I wrote to the Colonel, who lived in Virginia, and asked if he would see me when I was in Washington for the National Prayer Breakfast in early February 2007. He replied that he didn't usually respond to correspondence on that subject, but he knew and trusted Nick Pope, so he would be happy to see me.

On February 2, 2007, I hired a car to take me to the gated city that the Colonel runs, and we had lunch at their country club. His story follows. Normally I would just include the highlights but I am putting in much of the transcript because it includes so many of the significant points including the inevitable incredulity, the attempt by officialdom to discount what happened and other aspects of the UFO saga that I consider both worthwhile and important to share with the wider community. Unless otherwise noted, the words are his.

Okay, as I said earlier I really got involved to put it (the UFO matter) to rest because what had happened in the first instance was such a 'thing' the security people became obsessed with the fact there was something they didn't know and directed all their attention to looking for this 'whatever' versus their normal routine…

So what happened the first night, from interviewing the young men that were involved in it, three of the four were very responsible people, the other one wasn't irresponsible, but just an average person. Two of the people involved were very, very responsible, I've known them for some time having served time with them when they worked with me in the command in various exercises and I had seen them under stress when they reacted very well, very intelligently.

Bentwaters and Woodbridge were known as the twin base complex, two bases geographically separated by forest in East Suffolk … just east of the Ipswich area … right along the coast … a couple of miles inland.

It was December 1980 and Christmas evening. The police routinely patrol the back gate where you can transverse between the two bases and take a shortcut … but we locked it at night because we didn't have the personnel to man the … two bases … so if you had to do something at night you drove all the way around which was seven miles versus a mile or two, so part of the check list for that particular patrol man was to go out and check the integrity of the gate because people occasionally would find the combination for the lock … and the maintenance people like to sneak back and forth because they could save themselves fifteen minutes, four, five miles of driving, so it was normal. If they could figure a way to do it they would do it.

Somewhere after midnight the police patrol went to check the back gate and he saw something glowing in the forest. He thought it was a downed aircraft. So he called for the other patrolman in the other car, who came up and they both looked. They called their desk sergeant, the dispatcher, and told him what they saw and they called central security control.

The security police have two divisions, law enforcement and security. The law enforcement section are usually policemen, while the security people are primarily trained to guard assets, although they do get enough training that they can move back and forth a bit if they are short-handed. Generally they prefer to keep law enforcement doing law enforcement. There are legal issues if someone gets involved with people and things, that one has to be trained on how to respond properly. With respect to security people they tend to be a little harder and a little more aggressive. They are authorized, under some circumstances, to use deadly force.

They called central security control and asked if they had any information and asked for a supervisor, the senior law enforcement NCO on duty. He came up and called the desk sergeant, their dispatcher and said it looks like a downed aircraft, please call the tower quickly and see if they have any reports about it. So they called the tower and were told that nothing was active, nothing in the area was flying, there was no night flying. The tower at Woodbridge was inactive but they had a person in the tower in case of emergency. He saw nothing. The tower reported nothing. They called Heathrow for reports of anything and they called Eastern radar which was responsible for that sector. Eastern radar reported that they didn't see anything. Later one operator admitted seeing some blips. A couple more policemen come up to the gate and security, and the supervisor said you will have to leave your guns with me. We didn't go off the installation carrying guns. They [the British] were very strict about that.

Three of them went out to where they saw this object in the forest, glowing red light, and what not. They left one patrolman halfway to relay the radios because the radios were wacky now ... and two of them proceeded on foot and approached what they said was an object ... it was triangular, eight or nine feet on the side, on a pedestal, three legs, and it had multi-colored lights on it.

The one security policeman, probably the most responsible one, actually went up and touched the object and saw its markings which he later described in science fiction terms, as hieroglyphics. He made sketches but I don't have them with me now. But he's made sketches of what he saw, can't exactly say it's triangular ... but strange markings, nothing like we have. And they (the policemen) had a lot of problems with the radios ... interference even though the terrain is nearly flat.

So they didn't know what to do. They went back after several hours to take some pictures. The security people normally carry cameras because it wasn't uncommon to have intrusions of curiosity seekers, who would climb over the fence and try to get a close look at the airplanes – not to do damage or anything. So he took pictures of the object; he turned the film in to the base photo lab and they subsequently disappeared, very conveniently disappeared.

P.H.: Lots of things disappear ...

Especially when certain agencies get involved ... things disappear ... this information comes out. They come back to the base ... they are in shock ... nobody gave them any real good guidance. So they called their flight chief who is a lieutenant, a former marine, in other words it wasn't some nineteen-year-old kid, this was a twenty-five or thirty-year-old guy who had been on a tour duty in the marine corps, then was commissioned in the air force. He told them – you know – to put it aside and the desk sergeant said what do I put in the police blotter ... that's a chronological record that they make up every night ... everything is documented. And he told them just put in something ...

So the next morning I went to the desk sergeant's office early, as I would occasionally go early to pick up a blotter and see what was happening. It was my job to be the eyes and ears for the base commander. At that time I was the deputy base commander. And the desk sergeant started laughing. I said, 'What's so funny?' and he said, 'Well so and so and so and so were out in the woods chasing UFOs all night and the lieutenant said don't put anything in the blotter.' I said, 'You have to put something in there, what did they see?'

Anyhow the lieutenant said don't put anything in the blotter and I said you can't do that, specifically what happened? He said, 'I don't know, I wasn't there. They saw lights in the forest and they went out' ... they didn't tell him the whole story ... they didn't tell me the whole story at that time because they were afraid to say anything. If they admitted to all this they would probably lose their security clearance – they would probably be drummed out of the service. Because there have been some instances where people were pretty harshly treated after they reported UFOs.

I said to the desk sergeant, 'Well if they saw lights put it in there, whatever, if it can easily be substantiated, you can put that in the blotter.' He put it in there and I picked them up and took them to my office and my boss came in, looked at me, raised an eyebrow and said, 'What's this?' and I said 'I really don't know, but I'm a bit suspicious. The people involved are responsible but I had trouble believing this and I'm sure there's some explanation.' I went to a staff meeting where the senior officers gather every morning to discuss whatever the status and the activities and whatnot … the plans for the day and everybody kind of had a chuckle over it. Nobody really believed there was any substance to this.

P.H.: A good joke of some kind.

Not a lot more was said about it but a rumor went around through the security police squadron and they were all very concerned. The police knew the parties involved were responsible people and they would not make up something like that. Nobody knew what to do. So this went on for a day or so. I interviewed the three people and they gave me statements but they were very bland and didn't say anything … except they saw some lights and so on. There was an object … they didn't tell me they approached it, they didn't tell me they took pictures so I could follow up with the photo lab. Everything was sort of closed down and nobody was really willing to talk much.

Two nights later we were heading to the combat support group Christmas dinner, two days after Christmas. We were at the Woody Bar. Now the Woody Bar is where they filmed *Twelve O'Clock High* … you may not be familiar with that … it was a very famous World War II TV series shot in a Quonset hut that was made into a bar and restaurant, but it wasn't a bar that night. We had rented the restaurant part for the year-end dinner where we gave awards and recognized people for various and sundry things that had happened during the year. The presentations were made at this dinner and the families brought dishes and desserts, whatever.

We were just getting ready for dessert when the on-duty police flight lieutenant came in, white as a ghost. He looked as if he'd seen a ghost, and was in shock almost. 'It's back,' he said. 'What's back?' 'The UFOs.'

We took him to the cloakroom because it was the only place we could talk privately – the whole place was full of people. We looked at each other and said tell us, what do you mean, and he said, 'Well we've been back out in the woods' ... 'What were you doing in the woods? You're not supposed to be leaving the base.' 'We saw some lights out there again so we went out to investigate,' he replied. 'We took two light-alls; (motor generators with big fluorescent lights on top ... used to work on aircraft late at night and for security) they wouldn't run ... we couldn't get them to work right, three of them wouldn't work right.' 'At first they complained that somebody didn't fill them with fuel but that wasn't the problem ... there was something interfering with them ... and then we saw this glow in the woods,' he said, 'so we came back to get help.'

So I said to my boss we've got to put this to rest. 'I've got to make all the presentations in a few minutes,' he replied, 'Why don't you go?' So just in case, to help put it to rest, I said to the disaster preparedness officer, 'Who is your standby person tonight?' They always have somebody on standby. She told me, and I knew that he was a professional photographer, too. 'Well call him and tell him to meet me at your office, pick up a Geiger counter, calibrate it and bring his camera along so we can take some pictures to show that there was nothing there and I can show that there was no radiation.' Then I went by the office and picked up my cassette recorder because I didn't want to use pencil and paper.

We all met at the disaster preparedness office. I went home and changed clothes and the police picked me up in a jeep ... we traipsed over to the site ... Woodbridge... and went out there and there were probably twenty or thirty security police milling around and lots of vehicles with night vision scope. I could see ... a glow much brighter than the rest ... if you've ever looked at one ... yellowish-green tint but there was a bright spot in there and they said that's where it was.

I'm still very suspicious of all this, okay. Five of us went into the forest ... and I told the rest of them stay back, we didn't need a whole lot of people clomping around in the farmer's woods and causing a lot of commotion with the possibility for poor publicity. So they took me out to this area where there were three indentations of equal distance apart, about so deep and about so big around. We took the Geiger counter and were getting radiation readings that were higher where the indentations were and much higher in the center formed by the triangle ... and the trees in the area, it was pine forest … it looked like something had come down as there were a lot of branches on the ground.

The reading on the inside of the trees toward the triangle formed by the indentations was higher than it was on the outside. Now these were not fantastic readings or enough to cause you any bodily harm but they were much higher – five to ten times higher – than background radiation. So I took some soil samples and placed them in a film canister, one of those 35mm film canisters, I filled it up with soil samples as we were taking readings and making some notes on my tape recorder when somebody said look over there.

This is a very controversial area because off to the side the lighthouse was beaming; I'm intimately familiar with it as I've been there many times. About thirty degrees from the lighthouse was this blinking object like an eye, it looked like an eye with a black center. We stood there watching it for a while and when we tried to move a little closer it started moving towards us. It moved up into the forest and moved through the trees horizontally, thought not smoothly. It was zigzagging around the trees and whatnot, and it did that for a minute or two, maybe less than a minute, it seemed like a long, long time, then it came towards us again and then it receded. We went through the forest and tried to approach it to see if we could get close to it. It was very frightening. What is it? We didn't know.

It receded out in the farmer's field – the farmer's house was on the other side of the field – and his house looked like it was on fire. We could see the reflections of the object in the farmer's windows, like a flickering fire. I was very concerned for the people that were in the house if anybody was there. I'm sure there was. And while we were watching it (the object) silently exploded into five light objects … exploded … silently … I forgot to tell you it was dripping like molten metal. If you've ever seen a steel crucible pouring, that's what it was like, dripping off the sides of it … dripping … this can't be … ball lightning or something … ball lightning doesn't stay stationary … I don't think particles drip off it … so I said let's go out in the field and see if we can find any evidence where whatever that was had dripped off … maybe it was hot. So we are out in the field and the only thing we found were cow pies. We didn't find any evidence of anything.

So we crossed the farmer's field, crossed his road and over the ploughed field across the street there were objects in the sky. They were doing what I can best describe as a grid search. They were doing sharp angles, then turn and come back. At first they were like half circles, then they turned elliptic, and they had multiple colored lights on – three to the north and one or two to the south. We watched this for probably fifteen, twenty, maybe thirty minutes just standing in awe and what we saw suddenly started moving at high speed toward us, probably, I guess, 5,000 feet high, but it was moving at a very high speed, came overhead and stopped, and hovered silently – we never heard a noise – and sent a beam down. The best way I can describe this is a laser beam because it didn't fan out like light radiates, it came down straight just like a laser beam. It landed right over there ... at a white spot about that big.

Is it a signal? Is it a warning? Is it trying to hurt us? Or is it just trying to take a look at us. No idea. And it stayed on for maybe ten seconds, just like that, off. And the object moved over. Then I saw another object shining a beam – something comparable – into a weapons storage area. And there are people now that deny that anything happened over there at that time, but one or two people that were there say they remember seeing it ... including the tower operator ... a security tower observation located inside the storage area. This was the alternate control center.

The ultimate control center was down in the blockhouse but there was an alternate control panel in case they lost the main center. He could turn the lights on, you name it he could do it. And he did see something too. We were out until about 2 o'clock in the morning; it was cold, wet, we were getting tired and we came back in.

I didn't have a good explanation. Oh my god, why did I ever get involved in this? What am I going to do now? How am I going to explain ... a lot of people to explain this to? The next morning I talked to my boss; he didn't seem to be too concerned. He laughed about it; and the wing commander came in (we shared a common office, a common hallway) and he's heard about it.

I told him about the tape and he said give me the tape, so I gave him the whole tape, recorder and all. The following Wednesday there was a meeting with General Baizley. General Baizley looked around the staff and said what do we do? Everybody ... don't ask me ... I don't know ... finally, he said, 'Well it happened off the base I guess it's a British problem.' And he did say to the wing commander, 'Is he a responsible person?' He said 'Yes.' 'Do you believe him?' and he said 'Yes.' That's what he told me when he came back. He gave me the tape back and I said what do I do?

He said, get together with squadron leader Morland, who was the liaison officer with the RAF, and who was on vacation at the time.

So there is a gap between when the incident happened and when I wrote that memo that you may have seen. That's because I had to wait for the squadron leader and ask him, What do you want? And he said I don't know either. He made a phone call and said, give me a summary. So I wrote a very, very cleaned up abbreviated version of what happened (the one Nick Pope gave me in London). And I kept waiting and waiting and waiting and I would go back and ask every few days is anybody going to come around, is anyone interested in this, anything going to happen. He kept telling me I don't know. I've no idea. They won't tell me either.

So I finally just put it aside to be honest with you and thought no more about it. We had no copy in the office because this was before word processors; we used carbon paper. We were just transitioning into the word processors and our secretary hadn't accepted the fact that we were getting them yet. So I took a carbon copy and put it in my file. Then, apparently, Don Morland sent a copy over to his boss at Third Air Force.

I thought no more about it. We joked about it for a while. People called me the UFO guy, whatnot. There were a couple more sightings and instances … nothing really that I could substantiate … although I was told about them. I did respond once to one … whatever it was … So I kind of put it all aside. Well two years, three years later somebody at Third Air Force gave a copy of that memo to somebody who gave a copy to somebody and then it ended up in the hands of … Larry Fawcett, who is a writer … a Connecticut police officer … he was writing a book. So he came in under the Freedom of Information Act and demanded the base to give him all pertinent documents … he apparently already had a copy but he wanted to verify … I didn't know that at the time because my boss then wrote back and said we have forgotten about this. We didn't say we didn't know anything about it, we said we had no documents. We didn't, officially.

So I went back then with (Jim) Penniston who was one of those involved with the original incident the first night and we went looking for the old police blotters, the security blotters. Guess what? They were both missing. Missing. We went into the archives and both were missing. Very interesting isn't it?

P.H.: Yes it is. How convenient.

That would have been helpful to substantiate ... to check some times and dates and see what was put in ... I couldn't remember all of the details that we put in the blotter ... I remember but I don't remember exactly how we worded it. So I kind of gave up on it and then my tape recording ... I had made a copy for Ted Conrad, who at the time was my boss, and he left it in the desk drawer when he went back to the States. His successor found it and thought it was hilarious and took it to a cocktail party and played it to a whole lot of British civilians and let them make copies, unbeknownst to me. Well then it hit the fan so to speak. The next thing I knew there was a guy calling me from the *News of the World.* You may not be familiar with them but they're like the *National Inquirer.* My life got very complicated for a while because people just came from everywhere, I mean from Japan, Germany, the local radio, TV stations, and it just became a nightmare.

That's in essence a summary of what happened. I do still have one of the plasters ... I didn't tell you ... that one of the airmen involved originally went up the next day and took plaster of Paris and made a cast of all three indentations. A man by the name of Jim Penniston – one of the people that was involved the first night, the one that actually touched the object. When he put them with his household goods to ship home that box disappeared. It's interesting to see how these things happen. Now that could have just normally happened. American households were coming back from overseas ... boxed in cardboard ... and then they go into big shipping crates ... they are nailed and caulked shut, weatherproofed hopefully, not always but ...

So someone would have to open a box and find the right cardboard box and have the inventory to know where to look. Or somebody could have set it aside and not put it into a box ... that's certainly a possibility ... but so many things happened that were strange.

The navy, that had responsibility for all secret activities with the police in England, did come to the base. I know that. But the local commander at the office of the special investigation (OSI), the air force equivalent of the CIA, who was a personal friend of mine denied all knowledge or any interest in the subject. Now why wouldn't he have some interest in the subject?

P.H.: That is a very interesting question.

I didn't press him because I didn't want to put him in a spot. I realized he couldn't talk to me ... they did a lot that they didn't tell anybody on the base about.[18]

**

I found this verbatim report from a tough, no-nonsense U.S. air force colonel totally compelling. It was also very revealing in the sense that it underlined the Visitors pre-occupation with the American nuclear capability. I have read that the ETs have carefully surveyed every U.S. military base worldwide where nuclear weapons are either installed or stored. And for a very good reason. Their use could create a nuclear winter that would end human habitation.

Contact with some Celebrities

His Serene Highness Prince Hans-Adam of Liechtenstein

The first Monday after Sandra and I returned from our honeymoon I received an e-mail from a complete stranger, following up on a telephone conversation first-thing that morning. He wishes to remain anonymous so I will just call him George. "Further to our telephone discussion of this morning, I am confirming details via this e-mail. H.S.H. The Prince indicated to me his interest in discussing with you certain aspects of how to formulate global policy in response to ET involvement in human affairs, past, present and in the future, after learning about your recent presentation at the U. of Toronto Exopolitics Symposium. He will be in Memphis, TN attending to business matters, arriving in the late afternoon of Monday November 14. He is free all day Tuesday, Nov. 15, with the exception of a few hours of meetings which can be rearranged that day to suit your schedule.... I would be happy to book a flight for you if you wish."[19]

I was flattered and immensely interested by the invitation but, regrettably, our availability didn't match. I don't know how my schedule becomes so complex but often it does and a couple of alternate dates were equally untenable. So I had to settle for a telephone call, which was pretty general in nature, and at the end of which the Prince issued an invitation to stay at the castle on my next visit to his principality. To date, I have been unable to accept his kind hospitality despite the magnetic attraction.

A substitute was the opportunity to read a manuscript that the Prince had written for publication but which had been turned down as being too esoteric and theoretical. It is probably another case of the Prince, like other pioneers in the subject, being too far ahead of his time. It may be a while, however, before the majority of us are sufficiently informed about the subject for it to become cocktail or dinnertime conversation. I hope that day will come. Meanwhile, "George" has become a mentor who advises me how to avoid the many land mines and improvised explosive devices that await people who speak too openly on the subjects of this chapter.

Shirley MacLaine

At suppertime on Thursday May 11, 2006, the phone rang. Our inclination was not to answer because the majority of calls during the dinner hour are telemarketers and it taxes our sense of restraint to get rid of them without appearing obviously rude. Sandra decided that she would take the risk in case it was her daughter Wanda who was calling. So she said hello, and told me that it was a lady asking for me.

"Hello Professor Hellyer," she said, "this is Shirley MacLaine." After explaining that I was not a professor, but that I was Paul Hellyer, she asked about dinner Saturday or Sunday. I said that Saturday was out because I was taking the family to the Stratford Festival that day to see "Hello Dolly," but I would take her number and get back to her about Sunday, when Sandra planned to be in Montréal visiting her mother on Mother's Day. Sandra gave me her blessing to accept – provided I reported in full – so I made a reservation for two and called Ms. MacLaine to finalize the arrangement.[20]

I was not totally surprised to receive the call because Shirley – it was first names from the outset – had tried to track me down through the Canadian Action Party head office in Vancouver, which is probably where she got my phone number. The attraction, I knew, was my well publicized interest in UFOs, a subject that was both old hat and of deep concern to her. When Sandra revealed the news to the family at dinner, after the Saturday matinee, conversation with Grandpa gained a new and brighter currency.

When I met Shirley at the Park Hyatt Sunday night she decided that it would be preferable not to go out – it was not a nice evening – so the concierge canceled the reservation I had made and we dined in the hotel restaurant that was well and favorably known to me. We got along well from the start. Shirley proved to be quite charming, and very down-to-earth, which was reassuring for an actress of such wide renown.

For about three hours we carried on a wide-ranging discussion, mostly about UFOs and her life-long interest in the stars and the possibility of life on other planets that began when, as a child, she was given a telescope for Christmas. She would spend hours gazing at the heavens and wondering. Then on Saturday night, July 19, 1952 (she remembered the date because she recorded it in her diary) just after she had graduated from high school, a pilot reported seeing UFOs over Washington and two Air Force jets took off in hot pursuit. A week later more UFOs buzzed the White House knocking the Korean War and the presidential campaign off the front page. Shirley recalled that a few days later Air Force Intelligence Chief Major General John Samford, speaking for President Truman, told his television audience that the crafts were not from the Soviet Union, though he couldn't say where they were from.

These events confirmed for Shirley that there is "life out there" and that she should seek all the information possible on the subject. So through the decades she has built up a truly impressive roster of witnesses and informers from across the political and diplomatic spectrum. It was a very candid exchange that was as fascinating as it was informative.

She must have enjoyed the encounter as much as I did because on Tuesday, Sandra phoned my office to tell me that Shirley MacLaine had called and invited us both to have dinner with her Thursday evening at 6 o'clock. I said sure, why not. When the time came Shirley was wearing a shawl and prepared to go out so we went around the corner to Roberts Steak House. The place was packed and we didn't have a reservation but they quickly "found" a suitable table.

This time she really let her hair down and talked about personal and family matters, which was good because Sandra believes that UFOs are real but doesn't enjoy spending a lot of time talking about them. We also talked about Faith. I told her that my God was the God of Abraham, Isaac, Jacob and Ishmael, and that Jesus was my role model. She wanted to know if I would go to the cross and I admitted that I would probably "chicken out." It was a wonderfully revealing evening, but she wanted us to keep mum about the details. I am respecting that undertaking.[21]

Before we parted she invited the two of us to visit her ranch in New Mexico, with its twelve dogs, four horses, numerous cats and assorted other animals. She is going "off the grid" in favor of wind and solar power in conformity with her concern about the future of the planet. It sounds like a wonderful spot that would be nice to visit, but for now, at least, that is in the future. Meanwhile we have maintained the relationship based on common interests.

Edgar D. Mitchell, Apollo 14 Astronaut

There is something quite exciting about getting a call from a friend saying that Apollo astronaut Edgar Mitchell will be speaking in Toronto soon and has indicated an interest in meeting you if that can be conveniently worked into your two schedules. Sandra, good scout that she is, said: "Why don't we invite him to dinner," so that is what we did. He was to arrive in Toronto the evening before his speech on July 8 and would come directly to our place from the airport.

The plan was simple and straightforward, but sometimes the unexpected can intervene. As his flight approached Lester Pearson International Airport the pilot reported a cracked windshield. So, instead of landing, he turned the plane around and went back to Pittsburg to get a new one installed. So we were "in the dark," so to speak, until the plane returned to Toronto and Mike Bird, who had been the go-between, finally delivered Mitchell and his traveling companion, Susan, an hour and a half later than expected. Mike and his friend Susan – later to be his wife – made up the balance of the sextet.

There was much joy and relief when everyone was well and truly settled in. I poured drinks and put the salmon in the oven only to find that, due to its size, the fish took twice as long to cook as I had estimated. But no one complained, and the delay provided a head start with the fascinating and quite unusual conversation that ranged from Earth to the far reaches of the Cosmos and back again. Ed expressed the unique view that the universe may be flat, and we see it as a hologram – a proposition that few of his colleagues agree with. I started dinner with grace, which led to a discussion of the nature of God. Ed described some of the transcendent experiences he and others had encountered. When Sandra asked if he didn't think that God had something to do with this, he said it depended on how you define God. He does not believe in a grandfather God with long gray whiskers sitting in the heavens. Rather, he defines deity in general – the universe as God's body, with a collective mind.

Ed denied having seen UFOs on his trip to the moon, an answer that I had to respect. But at one point when he mentioned the alleged crash at Roswell I interjected: "Why do you use the word 'alleged?'" A tell-tale smile a mile wide came across his face. Shortly after that he asked me how many species (of Visitors) I thought there were. I replied, "Somewhere between two and twelve." "That's what I think, too," Ed said in response.

An important area of agreement came when we discussed possible reasons for the extended cover-up. The two most obvious were religion and economics, and the power base associated with each. In Ed's words:

"You can make a good argument for that, it's hard to decide which; but it's certainly entrenched power in any of these areas. It's putting self-interest ahead of the common interest and that is exactly the mission we have (to overturn). I try to work at it every damn day."

The one question Ed dislikes most is: "What does it feel like to set foot on the moon?" When one is in a critical survival mode, as he was, you don't have time to think about "feel." Fortunately, Ed was willing to stay with us long enough for a great journey of discovery with an amazing man who is going all out in an effort to help save our beautiful planet. It was a privilege to have him with us and we follow his endeavors with much interest.[22]

Edgar is the founding chair of the Institute of Noetic Sciences (IONS), a non-profit membership organization exploring the frontiers of human consciousness. It is hard to imagine a more fascinating and significant area of exploration. In his case, too, we have kept in touch in mutual support.

Update 2007

I read numerous books on various aspects of the "broader reality" that we humans must adjust to and each one helped my understanding in one way or another, although I must admit that the boundaries of my "broader reality" kept getting stretched like a scroll being opened in both directions from the center. So even though I had moved from about grade one to the grade four or five level in two years, I decided that before beginning to write about the subject I would go to another symposium and just listen to the experts in order to ensure that there were no dramatically new developments that I was unaware of.

I signed up for the 5th Annual UFO Crash Conference at Las Vegas, Nevada, held in November 2007. The conclave was sponsored by Ryan Wood, and his father Dr. Robert Wood. Ryan had sent me a copy of his book *Majic Eyes Only* that told the stories of 78 UFO crashes over a period of about a century beginning in 1897. Wood admitted that the evidence in some cases was stronger than for others, but if even half of them were adequately authenticated, and that would be on the conservative side, there had been a large number of crashes. At the conference he told me that since the book had been published he had learned of fifteen more cases and I had one additional new one from the Canadian experience.

Equally important as the information about government crash retrievals, and their extensive cover-up, was the revelation of allegedly authentic information concerning the Top Secret/Majic Eyes Only, or MJ-12 as they are more popularly known, the small group originally established by President Truman to monitor and exercise control over the whole spectrum of the Extraterrestrial presence, and the exploitation of their technology. The document purports to show the extraordinary lengths that were to be taken to keep the public in the dark

The conference also gave me the opportunity to renew acquaintance with two additional pioneers, Stephen Bassett, executive director of Paradigm Research Group, sponsor of the X-Conferences, and Richard Dolan, author of *UFOs and the National Security State*. Both of these men had presented in Toronto in September 2005, where we had appeared at a joint press conference at the end of the program. I also had the good fortune to break bread with Danny Sheehan, the Keynote speaker, who had defended the Berrigan brothers as well as the late Dr. John Mack, the Harvard psychiatrist, and author of *Passport to the Cosmos*, who became one of the world's top experts in the field of human-extraterrestrial contact.

Another rare opportunity occurred when I had lunch with Linda Moulton Howe, author of *Glimpses of Other Realities*, Emmy Award winning TV producer, and acknowledged to be one of the world's most thorough and successful investigators. Her presentation at the conference was limited to a single recent case, but that didn't disguise the fact that her contacts in government, the military, and among abductees are probably without parallel.

While planning the trip to Las Vegas I had managed to work in another important experience at the same time. Except for a very brief exchange in Toronto the day I went public, I had never spoken at length to an abductee and I decided it was important for me to do that, and make up my own mind concerning their authenticity, before sticking my neck out on the subject. My Guardian Angel cooperated, and I managed to arrange two significant meetings by simply extending my time in Vegas by one day.

Travis Walton

A U.S. Navy veteran, Ed Cochrane, who had phoned me about UFOs on several occasions, told me about his friend, Travis Walton, who had been the subject of a movie, Paramount's *Fire in the Sky*. His friend knew about my interest in matters extraterrestrial, and would be willing to meet and talk to me. I filed the offer in the back of my memory bank until I reached the stage in this book that I was giving serious thought to what I would say about UFOs and related matters. Ed gave me Travis' phone number and when I contacted him he told me that he lived in Snowflake, Arizona, not too far from Vegas by plane. So he and his wife Dana agreed to come and meet me there on the weekend.

We were able to spend quite a bit of time together, and I interviewed him at length about his story that may be the best documented case of alien abduction ever recorded. The story, in brief, is that on the evening of November 5, 1975, Travis and his six co-workers were returning home after a day's work in the Apache-Sitgreaves National Forest not too far from where they all lived. As they drove along they saw an unusually bright light shining through the forest gloom, and decided to follow it. Eventually they got close enough to observe this incredible object in the sky.

Travis, his curiosity piqued, recklessly left the safety of the old truck they were riding in to take a closer look. He was soon knocked to the ground by a blast of mysterious energy that left him motionless. When they realized what had happened the other near-hysterical men took off in fright. Eventually they decided that they were morally obliged to go back and see if there was any trace of Travis but, when they reached the clearing where the episode had occurred, there was no sign of him.

They had to report their stories to the authorities who were understandably incredulous. They then were interrogated at length and when there was no sign that alcohol might be the source of the mystery, a hint of foul play became inevitable. The interrogations and lie detector tests spanned five and a half days until the space ship dropped Travis off not too far from the scene of his disappearance. His next problem was to walk to a pay phone and face the unenviable task of convincing his brother-in-law that his return was real, and not just another hoax, so he would agree to come and get him.

There was general rejoicing that Travis was back alive but there was not universal acceptance of his incredible story. He told me that his friends and acquaintances were divided about fifty-fifty between believers and skeptics. The effect on his psyche was severe and it took years for him to fully recover and hold his head up high. Speaking personally, I am totally convinced of his truthfulness and anyone who is interested in the drama and the trauma of this stranger than fiction story should read Travis' book *Fire in the Sky*, and skip the movie of the same name that contains a nightmare scene that must be part of the "jazzing up" that Travis admitted had been done to make it more saleable. It may have filled seats in the theater, but if the Visitors had legal rights on Earth they could launch a big class action suit against Paramount Studios for the monstrous misrepresentation of what the Visitors are really like.

Jim Sparks

The other abductee that I met and interviewed at length was Jim Sparks, who has the distinction of being one of the best-informed "experiencers," as Dr. John Mack liked to call them, anywhere. I was fascinated by his early encounters with his abductors – he has been abducted dozens of times – but I was even more interested in what he had learned from the Visitors in the later years, after he had accepted the fact that he had some kind of role to play and that he might just as well relax and enjoy it. So he eventually became comfortable in their presence. Jim has the added distinction of having been conscious throughout most of his encounters, whereas the majority of abductees only recall significant details under some form of hypnosis.

The ETs have a message for us that should make headlines in every newspaper and magazine in every language in the world – "*We are hell bent on the destruction of our planet as a hospitable place to live or visit."* The ETs may have an agenda or agendas of their own – there are more than one species so there is no more assurance that their agendas are identical than there would be find the U.S., Russia, China and India in absolute agreement. But what the Visitors have in common is the concern that we are in the process of making our planet uninhabitable and that is not in their interests or ours.

On one occasion they showed Sparks and other abductees a video of sparkling streams and lakes teaming with fish, beautiful forests, blue skies and snow-capped mountains. Then the scene slowly changed and the same streams and lakes had dead bloated fish floating on the surface, the skies were darkened with smog, the forests were dying or being cut down at such a pace that they no longer had the capacity to renew the atmosphere. It was a chilling scenario but no different than the one we see in our newspapers daily as we slowly but surely adjust to the reality that we are rapidly destroying the Earth's ecosystems.

Another of the ETs' preoccupations, as I have already mentioned, is our military's love affair with nuclear weapons. They rightly anticipate that if we don't reduce our stockpiles dramatically, and soon, that some megalomaniac will opt to bring about a nuclear Armageddon that will reduce the planet to a barren wasteland. This just confirmed my earlier suspicion, based on the incidence of sightings, that there is a direct connection between their concerns and our intransigence.

Their greatest revelation to Sparks, however, is that they have met with humans and collaborated in sharing technology. The deal, however, included specific timing for the release of this information to the public. This treaty, like many others, has been observed in the breech. The excuse for continued secrecy is that the public couldn't handle the truth. That is the same old nonsense that we get from the ruling elite. Admittedly, there would have to be major adjustments to accommodate the new and broader reality. But there are, in fact, exciting opportunities including the possibility of saving this marvelous planet for the benefit of generations to come.

One interview Jim had with a group of Visitors was so powerful in its message to us Earthlings that I asked permission to reproduce it verbatim here, a wish to which Jim cheerfully agreed. The excerpt from his book *The Keepers* follows.

**

It was night, but I wasn't frightened for some reason. In fact, I was so calm and relaxed that I was enjoying the ride. Twenty feet from the ground, I started to rock slowly back and forth several times like a pendulum, almost as if I were being guided to a target and this was the final adjustment. The transport method was the same, but the technology was notably much more gentle. When I was a few feet from the ground, I saw the profiles of about a dozen large creatures standing in a semi-circle, and then I blacked out.

"WE WOULD HAVE GIVEN IT TO YOU, BUT WE KNEW IT WOULDN'T HAVE MEANT ANYTHING UNLESS YOU EARNED IT. IT WAS THE ONLY WAY YOU COULD POSSIBLY UNDERSTAND WHAT YOU HAVE BEEN A PART OF AND WHAT YOU HAVE TO DO."

The message came to me loud and clear as I began to regain consciousness and opened my eyes. I later understood that by "IT" the Voice meant knowledge.

I found myself standing in that abandoned carnival yard, clear-headed and fully conscious. There were those creatures again, and I could see that holograms of human faces were cast over their faces, to disguise their true appearance and make me feel less apprehensive.

I noticed that each alien seemed to be concentrating and communicating or transmitting its thoughts to the creature to my left. They seemed to be of like mind, as though combining their consciousness into one telepathic Voice. They continued:

"THERE ARE SOME THINGS YOU NEED TO UNDERSTAND.

"YES, IT'S TRUE THAT WE HAVE BEEN IN CONTACT WITH YOUR GOVERNMENT AND HEADS OF POWER.

"IT IS ALSO TRUE THAT AGREEMENTS HAVE BEEN MADE AND KEPT SECRET FROM YOUR PEOPLE. IT IS ALSO TRUE THAT IN THE PAST SOME OF YOUR PEOPLE HAVE LOST THEIR LIVES OR HAVE BEEN BADLY HURT TO PROTECT THIS SECRET.

"OUR HANDS HAD NO PART IN THIS.

"WE CONTACTED YOUR LEADERS BECAUSE YOUR PLANET IS IN GRAVE TROUBLE. YOUR LEADERS SAID THE VAST MAJORITY OF YOUR POPULATION WASN'T READY

FOR ANYTHING LIKE US YET, SO WE MADE TIME AGREE-
MENTS WITH YOUR LEADERS AS TO WHEN YOUR PEOPLE
WOULD BE MADE AWARE OF OUR PRESENCE. THIS PART
OF THE AGREEMENT HAS NOT AT ALL BEEN KEPT.

"IT WAS ALSO AGREED THAT IN THE MEANTIME
STEPS WOULD BE TAKEN TO CORRECT THE ENVIRON-
MENTAL CONDITION OF YOUR PLANET WITH OUR AD-
VICE AND TECHOLOGY. WE SAY 'ADVICE' BECAUSE WE
RESPECT THE FACT THAT THIS IS YOUR PLANET, NOT
OURS. THEY ALSO BROKE THIS AGREEMENT."

I felt an awful wave of emotion from them – the feeling of abandonment. To feel any emotion from them at all was amazing, but this was
quite overwhelming.

"You aren't giving up on us, are you?" I asked.

There was a long silent pause and I received the transmitted feeling
of tremendous loss.

"Well, are you?" I asked.

"NO."

I felt an immediate sense of relief – straight from my own emotions!

"YOUR AIR, YOUR WATER, ARE CONTAMINATED.

"YOUR FORESTS, JUNGLES, TREES AND PLANT LIFE
ARE DYING.

"THERE ARE SEVERAL BREAKS IN YOUR FOOD
CHAIN.

"YOU HAVE AN OVERWHELMING AMOUNT OF NU-
CLEAR AND BIOLOGICAL WEAPONS, WHICH INCLUDE
NUCLEAR AND BIOLOGICAL CONTAMINATION.

"YOUR PLANET IS OVERPOPULATED.

"WARNING: IT IS ALMOST THE POINT OF BEING TOO
LATE, UNLESS YOUR PEOPLE ACT.

"THERE ARE BETTER WAYS OF DERIVING ENERGY
AND FOOD NEEDS WITHOUT CAUSING YOUR PLANET
ANY DAMAGE.

"THOSE IN POWER ARE AWARE OF THIS AND HAVE
THE CAPABILITY OF PUTTING THESE METHODS INTO
WORLDWIDE USE."

I let this digest for a moment. I definitely had the feeling that these creatures were speaking as one.

Then I asked, "Why aren't we doing that now?"

Silence. I was willing to wait. I had come a long way to be treated like this by them, to have this kind of meeting. Apparently I had earned their respect and trust. The best part was that I was getting direct, truthful answers to my questions. I decided that I would milk this rare situation to its fullest, asking as many questions as I could get away with, even personal questions.

I repeated my question, and they answered.

"THOSE IN POWER VIEW IT AS A MILITARY AND SECURITY THREAT."

That upset me. "You mean to tell me the people in power have the ability to save and better this planet, and they aren't doing it?"

"AMNESTY."

"What do you mean?"

"COMPLETE AMNESTY TO THOSE IN POWER, GOVERNMENTS AND LEADERS WHO HAVE BEEN SUPPRESSING THE TRUTH. THEY CAN'T BE HELD LIABLE FOR ANY PAST WRONG DEEDS. IT IS THE ONLY WAY THESE LEADERS CAN COME FORWARD WITH THE TRUTH. IT IS NECESSARY THAT YOU DO THIS IN ORDER TO WORK TOGETHER AND SURVIVE."

Of course, they were suggesting forgiveness. My anger at all this faded as I thought about it. It made sense. Heads roll whenever cover-ups are exposed. And this was a cover-up of galactic proportions – no pun intended.

If anyone had a good reason to hate their government for covering up this information, it was me, and others like me. Most abductees still consider themselves victims who constantly suffer ridicule. When your government's policy is to say, "You're just plain crazy," it only deepens the pain.

I let my intelligence rule over my emotions and calmed down.

"How do I fit in all this? What can I possibly do?"

"WHAT YOU ARE DOING ALREADY. WE WILL SHARE MUCH MORE KNOWLEDGE WITH YOU IN THE FUTURE.

ALTHOUGH YOU UNDERSTAND A LOT, WE WILL SHOW YOU MUCH MORE.

"CONTINUE TO WORK WITH PEOPLE THAT COME TO YOU. WE ARE AWARE OF THE SMALL GROUPS THAT ARE FORMING AROUND THE WORLD AND WE HAVE ADVICE. YOU WILL RECEIVE MORE KNOWLEDGE IN THE NEAR FUTURE."

These were not the exact same aliens who had worked with me all those years – but there was a link between them, and the pain and learning I went through all led up to this.

I asked my questions and they continued to give me some personal advice. They also said:

"CONTINUE TO WORK WITH PEOPLE WHO COME TO YOU. THESE GROUPS FORMING AROUND THE WORLD ARE PEOPLE WHO ARE PREPARED TO LEARN. CONSIDER THEM THE CORE. THEN YOU WILL HAVE THOSE WHO WILL SEEK YOU OUT, WHO ARE STILL IN FEAR. ONCE THEY ARE OVER THE FEAR, THEN THEY WILL BE READY FOR THE CORE GROUP.

"MOST IMPORTANT IS THE CONDITION OF YOUR PLANET. THE FIRST STEP IN SOLVING THIS SERIOUS PROBLEM IS AMNESTY."[23]

One Fact, and Several Observations

One fact is beyond intelligent dispute. UFOs, or space ships, originating from planets other than our own are as real as the airplanes flying overhead! They have been visiting Earth for decades and, in all probability, for centuries or millennia. The following are some observations based on evidence and literature believed to be substantially reliable.

(a) The size of the vehicles range from the very small Foo Foos, that were probably unmanned but intelligently controlled reconnaissance machines, to very large "mother ships" wider than a mile across.[24] The mother ships may carry smaller craft capable of operating independently, at least for short periods. The most frequently observed space ships have been estimated to be in the order of twenty-five feet to one hundred and fifty feet in diameter.

(b) The Visitors comprise more than one species from more than one source. These include Zeta Reticuli, the Pleiades, Orion, Anromeda and Altair star systems.[25] The short greys, as they are called, have been the most often reported, and they are the ones recovered from various crashes including Roswell. There are others including Tall Grays, Nordic Blonds, Semitics and Reptilians, each with their own distinct characteristics.[26]

(c) They appear to be benign because they certainly possessed the technology to immobilize our power sources, and command and control facilities. General Nathan Twining an Air Force Regulation 200-2 issued when he was Chief of Staff in August 1954, wrote under the heading of Air Defense. "To date the flying objects reported have imposed no threat to the security of the United States and its Possessions." Despite that assurance untold sums have been spent developing the aliens own technology in an effort to control them militarily.

Of the many books I have read Timothy Good, the U.K. author of *Need to Know* is the only one who makes a point of reporting incidents of unacceptable harassment and the destruction of some of our aircraft.

What is less clear are the causes. We do not know for sure how many accidents have been caused by close proximity to the very strong electro-magnetic fields surrounding the visitors ships. These are said to disturb the molecular composition of certain metals and cause them to disintegrate.

Similarly we don't know if some or all of the alleged attacks were in retaliation for our constant efforts from the earliest days to shoot them down without any evidence that they were unfriendly. So the nature of the threat, if indeed there is one, will remain a mystery until there is full disclosure and military witnesses are subject to thorough cross-examination.

(d) The Visitors' technology is much more advanced than our own. For example, they have craft that can travel faster than the speed of light, that we have long assumed to be impossible. Earthlings have reverse-engineered some of their technology retrieved from crash sites that may include advanced lasers, integrated circuitry, fiber optics networks, accelerated particle-beam devices, and even the Kevlar materials in bulletproof vests.[27] It is widely believed that the United States has developed anti-gravity space vehicles that are indistinguishable from those of the star visitors but which may not yet have the same highly developed propulsion systems.

(e) Some of the visiting space ships have demonstrated their ability to beam both humans and cattle from the earth to their ships on a shaft of bluish-gray light. Some species, including the greys, have the capacity to walk through doors and walls that we know and describe as solid objects.[28]

(f) It is difficult to determine the agendas of the different species. Some, the greys specifically, extract human sperm and ova for the purpose of replenishing their own reproductive capability after allegedly genetically engineering themselves to the point where live births are difficult or impossible. This is a principal purpose of the mass abductions. What is not clear is whether they have been given permission to do this in exchange for technology, or whether it is done without permission because they have the technological ability to do it on their own initiative.

(g) The question of cattle mutilations is also in the gray area. One school of thought suggests that the incredibly precise incisions, far superior to what our medical profession use in current practice, is related solely to the harvesting of genetic material. Another school argues that the cattle mutilations are primarily a wide-scale experiment to determine the amount of residual radioactive contamination that exists as a result of the earlier testing and use of nuclear weapons.

(h) There is a spiritual overtone to much of the Extraterrestrial activity. Reports from many sources indicate that at least some species of Star Visitors are much more spiritual than Earthlings, and more reverential toward the Creator, the Source, the One, Allah, the Great Spirit – God by whatever name He is known.

The late Dr. John Mack, an American secular Jewish psychiatrist, who became a world leader in interviewing abductees – or "experiencers" as he preferred to call them – came to this conclusion in his startling book *Passport to the Cosmos*. "Although the aliens are not themselves gods – their behavior is sometimes anything but godlike – abductees consistently report that the beings seem closer to the Godhead than we are, acting as messengers, guardian spirits, or angels, intermediaries between us and the Divine Source."[29]

CHAPTER 4

THE (POLITICAL) GOSPEL OF JOHN

"All truth goes through three stages: First, it is ridiculed,
Then it is violently opposed, And finally it is accepted as self-evident."

Arthur Schopenhauer

A wise man once said: "Don't just tell me what he said. Tell me why he said it, so that I will better understand the meaning." This wisdom came to mind when I learned about the political climate that existed at the time the Gospel of John was written. I had always wondered, as others undoubtedly have, why it was so different from the synoptics – Matthew, Mark and Luke – and especially why it appeared to be so much more anti-Semitic. Why did it say "for fear of the Jews," instead of "for fear of the crowd," or whatever phrase would have been appropriate to a situation where Jews were supposedly writing about their fellow Jews?

Why did John say: "At this time the Jews began to grumble about him because he said, 'I am the bread that came down from heaven.' "[1] Why didn't he say "At this time the crowd began to grumble," etc.? Similarly, "Then the Jews began to argue sharply among themselves, 'How can this man give us his flesh to eat?' "[2] Wasn't John just talking about "the people?" Or later: "Jesus said, 'My kingdom is not of this world. If it were, my servants would fight to prevent my arrest by the Jews. But now my kingdom is from another place.' "[3] Why didn't the relative sentence just end "to prevent my arrest?"

This substitution of the word "Jews," in a pejorative way, when it should have been the crowd, worshippers, Pharisees or something else is systemic in the Gospel of John. The noun Jews and the adjective Jewish are used more than twenty times in a highly negative context. This could not possibly be the "true" testimony of the Galilean fisherman John, son of Zebedee, as claimed at the end of the book.

Whenever I would ask a religious leader why John was so different the answer, almost invariably, was that it had been written later than the synoptics and represented a more advanced theology. True, there was a question of timing. The majority of scholars believe that Mark was written first in about 70 CE, Matthew and Luke in the late 80s and John somewhere in the vicinity of the late 90s.[4]

All four were written by unknown authors and circulated anonymously until sometime later when they were attributed to important figures in the early church.[5] Surely, however, ten or twenty years should not have made such a profound difference in how the story was told. It is true that memory fades and the details of any record based on an oral tradition would inevitably become increasingly fuzzy as the years went by; it is also true that the perspective of the gospel writers must have been deeply influenced by the traumatic reverberations of the post-revolution era; but that still doesn't explain the sea change that occurred in just a few short years from the synoptics, and their nod in the direction of historicity, and John's preoccupation with theology. What had happened that would trigger such a change?

In the early days after Jesus' death the "people of the way," as his followers were called, were just one of several Jewish sects; Jesus' disciples, who were Galileans, moved to Jerusalem "since the prophecies declared that the temple would be the pivot of the new world order."[6] Members of the Jesus movement worshipped together every day in the temple but met later for communal meals while continuing to live as devout, orthodox Jews.[7] In addition to that orthodoxy, they had Jesus' teaching to uphold.

"It seems that Jesus had recommended that his followers practice voluntary poverty and special care for the poor; that loyalty to the group was to be valued more than family ties; and that evil should be met with non-violence and love. Christians should pay their taxes, respect the Roman authorities, and must not even contemplate armed struggle."[8]

"Jesus' followers continued to revere the Torah and keep the Sabbath, and the observance of the dietary laws was a matter of extreme importance to them. Like the great Pharisee Hillel, Jesus' older contemporary, they taught a version of the Golden Rule, which they believed to be the bedrock of the Jewish faith. 'So always treat others the way you would like them to treat you; that is the message of the Law and the Prophets.' "[9]

Following the fall of Jerusalem in 70 CE, the whole landscape became increasingly hostile to the followers of Jesus, some of whom were even accused of reveling in the destruction of the Temple, a most unlikely charge. People of the way became increasingly unwelcome in the synagogues where they proclaimed that Jesus was the Christ, the anointed one of God.

Stephen, described in the Acts of the Apostles as "a man full of God's grace and power,"[10] was challenged by members of the Synagogue of the Freedmen who, when they couldn't equal him in debate, trumped up charges of blasphemy. At the end of Stephen's defence before the high priest and the brethren, the crowd were so infuriated that he was dragged out of the city and stoned to death.[11]

With the death of Stephen, and the systematic harassment by Saul of Tarsus, the followers of Jesus were forced to disperse. The movement began to send missionaries to the Galilean district where Jesus had taught, and also the surrounding territories like Damascus, Phoenicia and ports around the Mediterranean including Cyprus and Antioch in the Jewish Diaspora.

Their message was primarily directed to their Jewish brethren but some spoke also to the Greeks, especially in Antioch. When news of this reached the church in Jerusalem they sent Barnabas to discern the legitimacy of the Antioch experience. He was so impressed with what was happening that he went to Tarsus to look for Saul, whom he had befriended and supported in Jerusalem following the former persecutor's dramatic conversion on the road to Damascus.

Saul, who became the apostle Paul, followed Barnabas to Antioch where they worked together for a whole year and taught great numbers of people.[12] It was here, in Antioch, that the disciples were first called

Christians. That was the beginning of Paul's incredible life journey that laid the foundation for Christianity as we know it today.

The majority of the disciples believed that gentiles who accepted Jesus should become Jews. Paul became the most notable exception. He soon became convinced that it was not necessary for gentile converts to be circumcised and adopt the Torah. This did not sit well with some of the Christians in Jerusalem, but a visit from Paul convinced them when they heard how the holy spirit was working through the pagan converts. In response to Paul and Barnabas the apostles and elders sent a letter to the Gentile believers in Antioch, Syria and Cilicia that read in part as follows:

"It seemed good to the Holy Spirit and to us not to burden you with anything beyond the following requirements: You are to abstain from food sacrificed to idols, from blood, from the meat of strangled animals and from sexual immorality. You will do well to avoid these things."[13]

Not all were convinced, however, and some were thorns in Paul's flesh to the point he became deeply resentful. It was to be just the first of the doctrinal disagreements that would plague the life of the church.

Judaism, Too, was in a State of Transformation

The fall of Jerusalem had a profound and in many ways traumatic effect on the practice of Judaism. The Jewish Rabbis regrouped outside the ruined city and met in conclave at Jamnia, a city four kilometers from the Mediterranean and ten kilometers south of Jaffa, in order to reconstruct Judaism in a situation where Temple worship could no longer be the linchpin of their faith. The result was an extended debate, sometimes civil, but often not, between Rabbis of very different opinions as they sought to resolve the numerous conflicts and divisions that had multiplied since the Temple had been destroyed.

At a tense, confrontational assembly in an upper room guarded to prevent entry by dissenters, eighteen decisions were resolved unanimously. The eighteen rules concerned the bread of the pagans, their cheese, their oil, their women, their sperm, urine, rules on gonorrhea and laws on morals. Beside these rules, ten others were taught which made the *terouma* (the priestly tithe on the produce of the land) unfit for eating.[14]

"As far as the (Jewish) Bible is concerned, they decided to determine the canon, in other words they decided which books would 'dirty your hands.' The Tosephta *Yadaim* gives all the details concerning pure and impure books. The Song of Songs was saved by R. Akiba who imposed an allegorical reading of it. The book of Ezekiel was accepted after much discussion. It was at this time that Ben Sirach was excluded from the canon."[15] Thus Judaism was effectively redefined for the post-Temple era.

It is doubtful that these developments had much influence on the writer of John. But there was one development that did. It was the insertion of the "benediction of the *Minim*" into the prayer called *Shemone Esre*. The text of this benediction as it appears in the Geniza of Cairo is as follows.

"May apostates have no hope and the kingdom of impertinence be uprooted in our day. May the *Nozrim* and *Minim* disappear in the twinkling of an eye. May they be removed from the book of the living and not be inscribed among the just. Bless you, Lord, you who cast down the proud."[16]

Three categories of people were affected by this benediction. First, Jews who collaborated with the Romans, second, the Roman Empire itself and, finally, Jews who followed Jesus. The latter were designated under the title *Nozrim* and *Minim*.[17] The practical result was that *The People of the Way*, Jews who followed Jesus, were driven out of the Synagogue. They had been excommunicated.

In the opinion of Father Fréderic Manns, author of *John and Jamnia*, the Jamnia purges were carried out in order to save Judaism. The Law now became the center of religion. Its interpretation had to be made according to the principles of the Hillel school. Enemies from within and without had been removed. Judaism could now survive.[18]

The prospects for the followers of Jesus, however, had just become much more uncertain. Prior to excommunication they had been a Jewish sect, and entitled to the protection afforded Jews under Roman law that exempted them from having to worship the Emperor. Without that "special status," the followers of Jesus became criminals in the eyes of the Roman officials and subject to prosecution by the local magistrates.

The writer of John was obviously not amused, to use a profound understatement, and began to use the Jewish Scriptures to debate the Rabbis and religious leaders in a futile effort to win them over, in addition to giving courage to the Johannine community, where there had been defections based on the understandable desire to avoid becoming fugitives under Roman Law.

The Johannine community decided to fight back through the Gospel of John. Even a cursory reading of its attitude toward the Jews shows that it was not written in Jesus' love. On the contrary, it appears to have been written in a mood of anger unprecedented in the early Church. So, in the opening paragraphs of his book, the writer of John made a deliberate attempt to elevate Jesus to the status of God in an effort to convince the Johannine community – as well as the Jewish Rabbis – that unless they accepted the divinity of Jesus they were beyond salvation and, consequently, eternal life.

The writer of what became the Gospel of John was not the only one to express this point of view and may not have been the first to do so. But he went far beyond earlier Christian statements about the divinity of Jesus and had the most profound influence on the theological evolution of orthodox Christianity. The seeds were sewn for a giant schism between "People of the Way" and more orthodox Jews. Reacting to Jamnia's "for us or against us" ultimatum, the Johannine community developed its own "children of light and children of darkness" distinction and that, regrettably, has been the way it has been interpreted by too many for far too long.

The Struggle for Supremacy in Doctrine

By the middle of the second century nearly all the books of the New Testament had been completed, but there were many others that didn't make the cut when eventually the canon of the New Testament was chosen. These included the lost gospels of the Ebionites, Nazarenes and Hebrews, that catered to Jewish-Christian congregations.[19]

The differences between groups were quite extreme. "The Ebionites were Jews who insisted that being Jewish was fundamental to a right standing before God. The Marcionites were Gentiles who insisted that Jewish practice was fundamentally detrimental for a right standing before God ... The former saw Jesus as completely human and not divine. The latter saw Jesus as completely divine and not human."[20]

"The new religion had a very large problem with pagan and Roman converts who were deeply suspicious of anything 'recent.' The strategy that Christians pursued to overcome this obstacle to conversion was to say that even though Jesus did live just decades or a century or so ago, the religion based on him is much, much older, for it is the fulfillment of all that God had been predicting in the oldest surviving books of civilization, starting with Moses and the prophets."[21]

The argument was not enough to prevent the Roman Emperor Nero from persecuting the Christians, though largely for his own self-interested purposes, in the 60s of the first century. After that, according to Martin Goodman in *Rome and Jerusalem*, there was a long period of relative quiet for about 250 years.[22] As Italian tour guides like to point out the catacombs were burial places, not hiding places. The Christians did meet there for prayer and memorial services, but everyone in Rome knew where the catacombs were, and Christians weren't being hunted there.

The truce had ended by about a decade before the conversion of Constantine. By then Christians were regarded as dangerous fanatics who should be eliminated. "The emperor Diocletian began a war of annihilation against the Christians. This time of terror and anxiety left its mark. [Justin] Martyr, who was ready to follow Jesus to his death became the Christian hero par excellence."[23]

The brutal persecution that believers suffered did not prevent them from their own seemingly perpetual infighting as to the meaning of the gospels. Irenaeus, often identified as a bishop of Lyon, was among the first to champion the Gospel of John and declare that it, together with Matthew, Mark, and Luke constituted the whole gospel. "Only these four gospels, Irenaeus believed, were written by eyewitnesses to events through which God had sent salvation to humankind. This four gospel canon was to become a powerful weapon in Irenaeus's campaign to unify and consolidate the Christian movement during his lifetime, and it has remained a basis of orthodox teaching ever since."[24]

When, much later, Irenaeus arrived in Rome, he found groups and factions that challenged his own understanding of the gospel. "Some members of the new prophecy claimed that the Spirit's presence among them fulfilled what Jesus had promised in John's gospel: 'I will send you the advocate (paraclete) the spirit of truth ... (who) will guide you into all truth.' "[25]

"Angered by such arguments, Gaius, a Christian leader in Rome, charged that the Gospel of John, along with that other controversial book of 'spiritual prophecy,' the Revelation, was written not by 'John, the disciple of the Lord,' but by his worst enemy, Cerinthus – the man whom Polycarp said John had personally denounced as a heretic."[26]

Not long afterward, however, Tertullian, already famous as a champion of orthodoxy, himself joined the new prophecy and defended its members as genuinely spirit-filled Christians. Although to this day Tertullian stands among the "fathers of the church," at the end of his life he turned against what, at this point, he now began to call "the church of a bunch of bishops."[27]

The Doctrine of the Trinity

I have long entertained doubts about the doctrine of the Trinity. It somehow didn't make sense to me – too abstract and convoluted. As the years passed the idea has seemed less and less credible to me so I searched the synoptic gospels for evidence and read a couple of books written by Christian theologians who appeared to be attempting to reconcile the irreconcilable. First, the evidence, which I took from the Gospel of Mark that most scholars agree was the first of the gospels to be written.

I begin with chapter one where John was baptizing Jesus in the Jordan River. And immediately coming from the water, He saw the heavens parting and the Spirit descending upon Him like a dove. Then a voice came from heaven, "You are My Son, whom I love; with you I am well pleased."[28]

Later in the same chapter, when Jesus was teaching in the synagogue at Capernaum, a man possessed with an evil spirit cried out: "What do you want with us, Jesus of Nazareth? Have you come to destroy us? I know who you are – the Holy One of God."[29]

In chapter eight, when Jesus and his disciples were visiting the villages around Caesarea Philippi, he asked them: "Who do people say I am?" They replied, "Some say John the Baptist; others say Elijah; and still others, one of the prophets."

"But what about you?" he asked. "Who do you say I am?"

Peter answered, "You are the Christ."[30] ("The Christ" (Greek) and "the Messiah" (Hebrew) both mean "the Anointed One.")

In the following chapter Jesus took Peter, James and John to a high mountain where he was transfigured in the company of Elijah and Moses. The disciples were frightened out of their wits and didn't know what to say. A cloud appeared and enveloped them, and a voice came from the cloud: "This is my Son, whom I love. Listen to him!"[31]

The next reference taken from chapter ten, I find even more compelling. "As Jesus started on his way, a man ran up to him and fell on his knees before him. 'Good teacher,' he asked, 'what must I do to inherit eternal life?'

" 'Why do you call me good?' Jesus answered. 'No one is good – except God alone.' "[32]

Surely Jesus would not have said that if he had been God incarnate!

Later, in speaking of the end of the age which he seemed to think was not far off, Jesus said: "No one knows about that day or hour, not even the angels in heaven, nor the Son, but only the Father."[33] It is inconceivable to me that Jesus would say that if he had been God in a human body.

And on the night of his arrest, when his soul was "overwhelmed to the point of death," he petitioned God and prayed that if possible the hour might pass from him. "Abba, Father," he said, "everything is possible for you. Take this cup from me. Yet not what I will, but what you will."[34] Clearly, this was a direct appeal to a "higher power."

The clincher came as he hung near death on the cross, when Jesus said: "My God, my God, why have you forsaken me?"[35] To me it is quite inconceivable that Jesus would have uttered these words had he been God incarnate.

It is very telling that the Gospel of John omits these words from the passion story, and for good reason. Including them would have undermined the whole case that had been so meticulously constructed.

In the books that I have read on the doctrine of the Trinity I found that invariably the evidence presented was not really supportive of the doctrine. Then, however, the authors had to reconcile the unhelpful evidence with the Gospel of John that alternates between referring to Jesus as the Son of God, on the one hand, and the Word, that was God, becoming flesh – on the other. This requires a kind of literary gymnastics that would put any Olympian to shame.

Inevitably, as I would read on, a sermon that I had heard in my youth at Villa Nova Baptist Church would return to mind. The young minister, a protégé of my parents, was preaching on the evils of alcohol. He was well aware that most of the audience was quite familiar with the Bible, especially the New Testament, so he felt it necessary to try to reconcile the Baptist prohibition with the well-known fact that Jesus enjoyed a glass of wine with dinner.

So near the end of the sermon he stopped and said something like this. "Now, let's see what conclusion it is that we want to reach." He then went on to make the case that the wine Jesus had enjoyed was a natural product, whereas beer and liquor were artificial products, and this made them unacceptable. The inconsistency became painful, however, when he neglected to add that if "natural" wine was okay for Jesus, it should be equally all right for his Baptist congregation to follow the Master's example if they were so inclined.

I have heard more than four thousand sermons in the course of my life, to date, ranging from the superb, in a few cases, through various degrees of acceptability, to the very bad, and utterly boring at the other end of the scale. Few, however, have been as memorable as the one mentioned above that attempted to reconcile the irreconcilable. Unhappily, I get the same impression when I read the attempts to make a claim for Jesus that he would find shocking, and that he would never have considered making on his own behalf.

It is not surprising, then, that people have been debating this issue since the days of Jesus' earthly ministry. In the early fourth century, the emperor Constantine convened a group of several hundred in Nicea to try to resolve the issue once and for all.

Former U.S. Congressman Mark Siljander in his marvelously insightful book *A Deadly Misunderstanding: A Congressman's Quest to Bridge the Muslim-Christian Divide*[36] describes the narrow divide between factions as follows.

"At one point the raging debate boiled down to a disagreement between two words – actually, to be more precise, between *two letters* in a word. One group wanted to describe Jesus as *homoiousious*, 'of a *similar* substance' to God, while another insisted that he be described as *homoousious*, 'of the *same* substance' as God. Constantine came down on the side of the homoousians, and thus today we have the Nicene Creed, which declares that Jesus is 'begotten, not made, being *of one substance* with the Father.'

"But imperial edict or not, it was an issue that just wouldn't die. A second council followed in 381, a third in 431, a fourth in 451 – and in the year 681, half a century *after* the death of Muhammad, the seventh

Ecumenical Council was *still* dealing with the debate around the divine versus human nature of Jesus."[37]

The Only Begotten Son?

The author of John also makes the claim, consistent with his thesis, that Jesus was "The only begotten of the Father."[38] But that isn't what the Bible says.

In Genesis, chapter six, we read the following. "Now it came to pass, when men began to multiply on the face of the earth, and daughters were born to them, that the sons of God saw the daughters of men, that they were beautiful; and they took wives for themselves of all whom they chose."[39]

Similarly, in Job we read. "Now there was a day when the sons of God came to present themselves before the Lord, and Satan also came among them."[40]

So the literalists can't have it both ways.

And what was Satan doing there amongst the sons? Is it conceivable that he, too, was a son who had rebelled against the father in a manner similar to that of Absalom, who rebelled against his father King David, and tried to seize his throne only to lose the war and his life in the attempt?

Perhaps the problem is one of nomenclature. In Psalm 2:7 after God had chosen David and he had been anointed as King of Israel, David was able to proclaim: "I will declare the decree: The Lord has said to Me, You *are* my Son, Today I have begotten You."[41] Other translations, including the New International Version state: "Today I have become your Father."

Christians used the same imagery when talking about Jesus after the resurrection. One could speculate that there could have been some confusion in nomenclature between the word that the Romans used for their god "deus" and the one applied to their emperors "divus" (divine) – a distinction we may not have explored when reciting the creeds.

What is not speculation is that the Gospel of John and other claims that Jesus was God set off a chain reaction that led to many disastrous consequences. First, and foremost, it separated those of us who follow Jesus from our Jewish and Muslim brothers and sisters. Consequently, instead of working together to establish the Kingdom of God on earth, we have been working at cross purposes, and fighting each other both verbally and militarily, the pogroms, the crusades, the Inquisition and currently the war on terror. This has all been directly contrary to the good news that Jesus preached. He said: "Blessed are the peacemakers"[42] but there has been precious little of that in the two millennia since he died – and the void remains.

And, as a devout and dedicated Jew who would never have thought in terms of starting a new religion, Jesus would be appalled to see what has happened to his people as a result of the schism that erupted between his followers and more orthodox Jews. He must weep as he sees the atrocities committed in his name.

The Jews Got a Bum Rap

It is interesting to speculate what the last two millennia would have been like if the Gospel of John had not made the canon, if it had been excluded, or the Gospel of Thomas had been substituted in its place. Certainly the Jews would not have been referred to in the pejorative in Christian circles, as has been the case. I have seen far too much of it first hand in the course of my political career and the source has been, for the most part, the Christian church. So it breaks my heart to say that John's contribution to anti-Semitism has been incalculable.

At the same time it would be unfair to hold this one author exclusively responsible. There were other Christian communities that were angry at the action of the Rabbis that turned them from law-abiding citizens into criminals and fugitives. But if they had been true to Jesus' admonition to love their neighbors and turn the other cheek, they would not have reacted in the spiteful way that many did. It was not just and right to hold the Jewish people collectively responsible for the actions of a few elite money-changers who conspired to get rid of Jesus for their own protection, and a handful of Rabbis desperately trying to salvage an ancient religion from the ashes of military defeat.

The crowd who called for Jesus' crucifixion was no different than your average "rent-a-crowd" that any rabble-rousing politician can whip into a passion with a little provocative rhetoric, of which the chief priests and elders would have been capable. Matthew records that when Pilate washed his hands of the whole affair the people answered "Let his blood be on us and on our children!"[43] If I were a betting man I would say that the odds were ten to one that the sentence was added to the story by Matthew's community in direct retaliation for the excommunication. It sounds very much like something that the "dirty tricks" department of a political party might conjure up.

Not in their wildest dreams, however, could the early Christians imagine the horrific consequences of such inflammatory words. The Inquisition, for example, was almost beyond description. Sandra and I saw Verdi's opera "Don Carlos" in early 2008. It was a great performance at Toronto's new Four Seasons Centre for the Performing Arts. But we sat in our chairs and winced as we saw the evil Inquisitor at work.

Even the horror of the Inquisition, however, pales when compared to the holocaust of the 1940s. Seldom if ever has the world seen such stark, unvarnished evil. Jews were rounded up like animals and shipped in railway cattle cars to almost-certain death in the gas chambers. That this could happen in a country that, on the surface at least, held the name of Jesus in reverence, is really beyond belief. Is it possible that the Passion Play at Oberammergau might have contributed in some way to an attitude of intolerance? The people there must have thought so because someone who saw the play some years ago reported that the program contained an essay of significant length accepting blame for anti-Semitism and declaring that they had changed the script to be less inflammatory. And to what extent were the Allied leaders aware, and remained silent? A bum deal is far too gentle to express the depth of the injustice.

The Muslims, Too

I am ashamed to admit that I was in my eighties before I knew that Allah was my God. I asked a Christian clergyman about it one day and he said something to the effect that the two were similar but not quite the same. When I finally got around to reading the Qur'an, however, I found that they were in fact one and the same. Allah is the God of Abraham, Isaac, Jacob and Ishmael, as well as those of us who are of the Judeo-Christian tradition. You would never know this, however, from the history of the second millennium and the many battles between opposing armies ostensibly worshipping the same God.

The Muslims have a slogan which translates as "There is no god but God." The Arabic word for god is *allah*; Hebrew is *elohim*; Greek is *theos* … We are prejudicial when we say people are doing things in the name of Allah. They're doing it in the name of God, just like George W. Bush was.

Both Jews and Christians underestimate the accomplishment of the Prophet Mohammed. He was able to persuade the children of Ishmael to worship Allah (God) fervently and consistently, something the Jewish prophets had been unable to accomplish, and most of the rest of us only give lip service to. In looking to the future it is important to understand the different and opposite perspectives of the cross that history has spawned.

I was raised in a tradition that enjoyed singing, "Onward Christian soldiers, marching as to war, with the cross of Jesus going on before." Sometimes you could almost imagine the soldiers marching, arms swinging, as they prepared for battle. So for us, the cross is a symbol of sacrifice and victory.

The Muslim perception is just the opposite. Rooted deeply in the Crusades, the cross is a symbol of invasion, war, rape, pillage and conquest. The fact that the Crusades were sponsored and supported by the leaders of a centralized Christian Church, allegedly based on the teachings of the prophet Jesus who is widely and favorably quoted in the Qur'an, only underscored their distress.

It should come as no surprise, then, that some of our Muslim friends are willing and anxious to work with us to build a better world in the "Spirit of Jesus," provided the distinction is made between "the Jesus of Christianity," and "the Jesus for the world."

**

All followers of Jesus of Nazareth should be deeply disappointed that his message of love and compassion became so distorted within a few centuries of his death. It lost all resemblance to its roots. Christianity substituted rules for compassion in the same way that Judaism had, and that Jesus objected to. The wheel had turned full circle to the point where the most profound elements of Jesus' teaching had been lost.

The Doctrine of Exclusivity

"I am the way and the truth and the life. No one comes to the Father except through me."[44] This sentence has probably caused more strife and turmoil than any other sentence in history. The group of scholars known as the Jesus scholars believe that the statement was the creation of the Johannine community, and that Jesus never said it. I agree, because it sounds so unlike the Jesus I know.

But let's assume, just for the sake of argument, that he did say it. What he did not say was that only card-carrying Roman Catholics and "born again" Southern Baptists need apply.

Will Mahatma Gandhi, who set an example to the world as to how to bring about change without the use of violence, spend eternity in Hell? No way!

Will the Dalai Lama who has taught love and compassion between peoples of all faiths be subject to the eternal fire? Positively not!

Will Stephen Lewis, former United Nations Ambassador for AIDS, who did such a magnificent job of alerting the world to the human tragedy that had developed in Africa be destined to Hell? Hell no!

Will the English woman I read about who married an Iraqi and converted to Islam in order to work amongst the poor in Baghdad be eternally damned? Definitely not! Jesus will say "welcome friend" because she, along with the others, will qualify in accord with his own definition, which reads:

"Then the King will say to those on his right, 'Come, you who are blessed by my Father; take your inheritance, the kingdom prepared for you since the creation of the world. For I was hungry and you gave me something to eat, I was thirsty and you gave me something to drink, I was a stranger and you invited me in, I needed clothes and you clothed me, I was sick and you looked after me, I was in prison and you came to visit me.'

"Then the righteous will answer him, 'Lord when did we see you hungry and feed you, or thirsty and give you something to drink? When did we see you a stranger and invite you in, or needed clothes and clothe you? When did we see you sick or in prison and go to visit you?'

"The King will reply, 'I tell you the truth, whatever you did for one of the least of these brothers of mine, you did for me.'

"Then he will say to those on his left, 'Depart from me, you who are cursed, into the eternal fire prepared for the devil and his angels. For I was hungry and you gave me nothing to eat, I was thirsty and you gave me nothing to drink, I was a stranger and you did not invite me in, I needed clothes and you did not clothe me, I was sick and in prison and you did not look after me.'

"They also will answer. 'Lord, when did we see you hungry or thirsty or a stranger or needing clothes or sick or in prison, and did not help you?'

"He will reply, 'I tell you the truth, whatever you did not do for one of the least of these, you did not do for me.'

"Then they will go away to eternal punishment, but the righteous to eternal life."[45]

If one reads that passage literally there may be quite a few complacent born again Christians who will find that their passports have expired.

A Few Reasons Why the Jews May have had Difficulty Accepting Jesus as the Messiah

Needless to say this is a subject to which I have given considerable thought over the years. My views are not based on weighing the conflicting claims of scholars who insist that Jesus was the fulfillment of the prophecies found in the Jewish scriptures and those who say that the relevant passages had other meanings leading to a very different result. That is a debate that I am singularly unqualified to enter. My case is based on other more general consideration.

Jesus' claim to be the Messiah became an uphill battle from the day he was born. He was of humble birth, and the majority of Jews I have known – and I have worked with scores of them in both business and politics for most of my life – displayed no particular attraction to people of humble birth. On the contrary! So the fact that none of the fine scholars I have read found any credible evidence that Jesus had been born in either the Bethlehem Ritz or the Nazareth Hilton would be strike one against him from the start.

Jesus' nondescript beginning did not soon lead to any visible ladder of success. His occupation and residence were both marks against him. Tradesmen, despite the essential nature of the services they provide, have never been amongst the favored in social circles. So the name of a carpenter's apprentice would not likely have been listed with the village socialites. And the fact that Joseph's shop was in Nazareth was another negative. The Jerusalem elite would have considered it as being on "the wrong side of the tracks," to use the modern vernacular. As Nathanael said to Philip of

Bethsaida in response to the claim that they had found the one of whom Moses and the prophets had written, "Can anything good come out of Nazareth?"[46]

Jesus' choice of disciples didn't strengthen his claim one little bit. They were mostly local chaps, many of them fishermen. The majority would have been illiterate. How could they possibly stack up with a list comprised of the most learned scribes and teachers of his generation? It almost looked as if Jesus was giving his finger to the establishment and their rigid ways and, in a way, he probably was. He was introducing the revolutionary idea that God had to be worshipped with the mind, as well as the Book.

His teaching, including his choice of miracles and when and where to perform them, turned out to be strike two. In particular, when he chose to heal the sick on the Sabbath, in blatant violation of the Mosaic Law as the orthodox Rabbis interpreted it, they were outraged, and would happily have punished him physically as well as verbally. The idea of treating some ill person as they would want to be treated if they were that sick person, was apparently not a factor. The law, as they interpreted it, trumped compassion!

When Jesus went to Jerusalem and he and his gang – today they would probably be called protesters – went into the Temple and over-turned the tables of the moneychangers, he struck out. No one, no matter how popular with the crowd, can mess around with an elite group of bankers positioned to exploit the powerlessness of the poor, and expect to get away with it. The greed factor will trump the law and the prophets. So Jesus' fate was sealed.

The bottom line was that God sent the messiah that the Jews needed rather than the one they wanted. Jesus' advice to render unto Caesar the things that are Caesar's and unto God the things that are God's did not sit well with the authorities. They wanted a warrior king who would lead them into battle and end the Roman occupation. Little did they dream where this warlike stance would lead.

At the time of the Platonic philosopher Philo's death, "there were pogroms against the Jewish community in Alexandria. Throughout the Roman Empire there was widespread fear of Jewish insurgency, and in 66 CE a group of Jewish zealots orchestrated a rebellion in Palestine that, incredibly, managed to hold the Roman armies at bay for four years.

Fearing that the rebellion would spread among the Jewish communities of the diaspora, the authorities were determined to crush it ruthlessly."[47] The emperor Vespasian was assigned the task.

"When Vespasian arrived at the gates of Jerusalem, he said to the inhabitants: 'Fools, why do you want to destroy this city and burn the Temple? What do I ask of you? Only that you hand me over a bow and an arrow and I will go away.' They answered him. 'Just as we went out against your predecessors and defeated them, we will go out against you and defeat you.' When Rabbi Johanan ben Zakkay heard that, he went and found the people of Jerusalem and said to them: 'My sons, why do you want to destroy this city, and burn the Temple? What does he ask of you? Only a bow and an arrow and he will go away.' They answered him: 'As we went out against his two predecessors and defeated them, so we will go out against him and will defeat him.' "[10]

When R. Johanan realized that his pleas for reason were falling on deaf ears he asked two of his disciples to put him in a coffin and carry him out of the city in the guise of a corpse. When he came before Vespasian he was given the opportunity to ask what he wanted. "He answered: 'I don't want anything except Jamnia where I can go and teach my disciples, establish prayers and observe the commandments prescribed by the Law.' He said to him: 'Go and do what you want.' "[49] This was the genesis of the row between the rabbis at Jamnia and the Johannine community that lead to such tragic consequences for the antagonists.

The moral of the story, as I read it, is that the whole course of history would have been different and infinitely preferable if the Children of Israel had recognized that Jesus had been sent to remind them of the Law and the prophets. And what is that in a nutshell?

"Hear, O Israel, the Lord our God, the Lord is one.

"And you shall love the Lord your God with all your heart, with all your soul, with all your mind, and with all your strength. This is the first commandment.

" And the second, like it, is this. You shall love your neighbor as yourself.

"There is no other commandment greater than these."[50]

Jesus went on to add that we should also love our enemies,[51] which is not an easy thing to do. But our enemies, too, are our neighbors, and should be treated as such. Jesus was referring to *agape* love, meaning to get to know our enemies, try to understand where they are coming from, and then treat them with the same deference and compassion with which we would want to be treated.

None of this may be new, except the addition of loving God with our minds, which makes a lot of sense, but it is the gap between the ideas and the fulfillment that was the problem in Jesus' day, and hence was the foundation of his mission.

If the Israelites needed Jesus' message at the time he was here on earth, they need it even more today. Peace in the Middle East seems to be as elusive today as it has ever been, yet it remains the cornerstone of peace on Earth. Unless Jew and Gentile, Muslim and Christian can demonstrate the collective goodwill to sort out this immensely complex puzzle we will never see the kind of world that is our true God-given legacy.

Ironically, as I was writing this chapter, I picked up a copy of *The New York Times International*, Sunday, July 6, 2008, when my wife and I were returning from a wedding in Ottawa. You can imagine my surprise when I saw a front page headline entitled "Ancient Tablet Ignites Debate On Messiah and Resurrection."[52]

An ancient artifact that was probably found near the Dead Sea in Jordan, has been described as "a Dead Sea" scroll on stone. The tablet from the late years BCE has already sparked a major debate on the meaning of a message that has been dubbed "Gabriel's Revelation." It is a document of some length that is open to various interpretations but the core message is this. "In three days you shall live, I, Gabriel, command you."[53] That suggests that the idea of a resurrection was not unique in Jesus' time.

The tablet will provide exciting opportunities for Biblical scholars that will include study of the scroll and moral issues of that era. It is these issues that are the compelling priority of our time.

CHAPTER 5

WRITING HISTORY YEARS AFTER THE EVENTS OCCURRED

"Memories are hunting horns whose sound dies on the wind."

Guillaume Appollinaire

As one who has twice written some history several decades after the events occurred, I can state categorically that there is absolutely no way that the very extensive passages attributed to Jesus in the Gospel of John could be authentic without benefit of a tape recorder or a court stenographer capable of transcribing perfect shorthand. Reconstruction of homilies and dialogue from the oral tradition with the kind of detailed certainty demonstrated by the Johannine community is quite impossible.

To give you an example, my father died in 1971, thirty-eight years before I wrote this, and there are only four things he said that I can recall clearly enough to swear in a court of law that they are direct quotes:

1. "Stand up straight boy." Repetition of that short sentence engraved it on my mind.

2. "Are you going to Sunday school this afternoon?" This one, too, was repeated so many times that I would swear to its accuracy.

3. "You run in Toronto, you crazy?" This was his spontaneous response when I phoned to tell him that I intended to contest a Toronto riding as a Liberal candidate in the 1949 federal election. I could never forget those words that were conditioned by his belief that I didn't have a hope in Hades running as a Liberal in what was, at that time, an almost exclusively Conservative city.

4. "Play ball!" Dad was a softball (now fastball) fanatic and long time president of the local league who often reminded complacent teams that the time had come – or passed – to start the game by cupping his hands and yelling "play ball" at the top of his lungs.

Of course I could write a whole chapter or two on what Dad thought and did and how he practiced during the week what he taught on Sunday. But none of it would be precise enough that it could be red-inked as direct quotes.

The fallibility of memory was underlined for me recently when I had lunch with two senior colleagues from the Trudeau government era to see what they could recall about events related to a big kafuffle in cabinet over my chairmanship of a Task Force on Housing and Urban Development. I had been asked to alter the record and remove all references to my chairmanship, a suggestion that I considered comparable to altering the books and consequently obliged to reject. To my mild surprise, neither of them could remember anything of significance even though they were eyewitnesses forty-one years earlier. That was clear evidence of both the fallibility and selectivity of memory. I remembered because it was very important to me and led to my resignation from the Trudeau government. I have no doubt that events in their political careers that were difficult or traumatic for them would be equally vague in my memory bank.

Some of my friends have registered their skepticism about the gospels because even the synoptics, though they have much in common, recorded different events and sometimes remembered the same event differently – like three or four eyewitness accounts of an accident. This has never bothered me, and especially since I have learned from my own experience that it is par for the course when writing history.

It isn't the detail that you should rely on; it is what I call "the essential facts."

The Essential Facts

A classic case from my own experience is totally illustrative. My friend Keith Davey became National Director of the Liberal Party of Canada in 1961. The following are three versions of how it came about; first his, then that of my one-time cabinet colleague Walter Gordon, and finally mine. Take your pick as to the one you consider most likely to be the correct version.

1. Keith Davey:
"We met at length in Walter Gordon's Wellington Street office to discuss who should succeed Jim Scott, but no one seemed to fit the bill.

"After the meeting I was driving Royce Frith home when he exclaimed, 'I've got it! I've got it!' His idea was that I should become the national director of the Liberal party. It was the last thing in the world that I wanted, when my political ambition was to be a provincial Liberal candidate in Toronto Eglinton. Yet to my own amazement I heard myself telling Frith that I was interested.

" Frith called Walter Gordon who asked that I meet with him the next day. Walter was explicit. The job was mine if I would agree to take it. I made a positive decision on the spot and only later learned that there had been a number of other names in contention from other sources in Ottawa. But it was Walter Gordon who had the ear of Mike Pearson."[1]

2. Walter Gordon:
Jim Scott, who had been appointed National Organizer about a month before the rally was held, fell into bad health about this time and was forced to resign. I had become increasingly impressed with the enthusiasm and drive of Keith Davey, President of the Toronto and Yorks Liberal Association, and recommended that he should be appointed National Organizer to succeed Scott. This was done in May 1961. Davey was what the party needed.[2]

3. Paul Hellyer:

Walter Lockhart Gordon was, at the time, Mike Pearson's closest friend and advisor. When the question of a successor to Scott arose, Walter proposed that his brother-in-law Charles (Bud) Drury, a wartime brigadier general and Montréal businessman, get the nod. All of the privy councillors who were members of the Leader's Advisory Council – Paul Martin, Lionel Chevrier, Jack Pickersgill and I – instinctively felt that this would be too great a concentration of power in Walter's hands, in addition to the inevitable charge of nepotism. So we began to consider other names and finally settled on Keith Davey.

Walter remained opposed until the eleventh hour. When the Advisory Council broke for coffee the morning that the decision was to be made, Walter took me aside and said: "Will you swear in blood that this man can do the job?" To which I replied that I thought he was well-qualified for the position. The Council and the Leader agreed and Keith got the job. Within a few days, he and Walter were as thick as thieves.

So which version would you be most likely to accept as the correct one? Two of the accounts were written by eyewitnesses, and the third by the man directly affected.

It doesn't really matter which one of us got it right, although you can probably guess my preference. The essential fact is that Keith got the job, and served with distinction.

Another example that I am very familiar with is various accounts of the Pearson years. If you were to choose two or three books from that era such as *Memoirs of a Bird in a Gilded Cage*, written by a colleague from the Pearson cabinet, Judy LaMarsh, former minister of health, *Damn the Torpedoes*, my account of the unification of the Canadian Armed Forces, and Walter Gordon's *A Political Memoir*, all basically about the same period when Mike Pearson was prime minister, you would certainly wonder if they all related to the same administration.

Once again, it wouldn't really matter because they all contained the same essential points. L.B. (Mike) Pearson became Leader of the Liberal Party of Canada soon after winning the Nobel Peace Prize. He contested the 1958 general election against Prime Minister John Diefenbaker and lost badly. The same two antagonists met again in 1962 and the result was much closer but Diefenbaker had the most seats, so he clung to power. In a 1963 rematch, Pearson had more seats, though not a majority, and he was able to form a government of which Judy, Walter and I were all members.

The PM called another election in 1965 in order to win a majority, but failed to do so, although he had sufficient support to carry on. Despite the two minority governments a number of significant initiatives were undertaken including medicare and the introduction of a new flag for Canada, which became part of his legacy.

**

The similarities with the gospels are striking and significant. Scholars spend years comparing the differences in the composition of the stories – often in order to say that they can't be authentic because they are not identical. Based on my experience, however, substantial differences are inevitable, especially when they were written with different audiences in mind. Eyewitnesses to accidents often give wildly different versions of what happened, though, in most cases, trying to be objective.

None of the four gospels – including John, though it is highly suspect for other reasons – disagree on the essential facts. Jesus was born in Palestine during the Roman occupation. He lived in the small town of Nazareth in the district of Galilee. At a mature age he became a very popular itinerant teacher, who also performed many miraculous works. These included healing the sick on the Sabbath, in violation of the Mosaic Law. He and his supporters overthrew the tables of the moneychangers and, in the three synoptics, at least, the enraged leaders soon had him arrested, tried, and executed by Pilate, the Roman governor. Because this happened on Friday, before the Sabbath, he was given a hasty burial. On the morning of the third day the tomb was empty and he was subsequently seen by several of his followers.

There was a time when there was little debate concerning these essential points. In recent years, however, scholars have increasingly challenged the historicity of the gospels, and a more highly educated populace has entertained an increasing level of doubt in respect of any phenomenon that cannot be readily proven. Today even the most basic tenet of Christianity, the story of the resurrection, is widely questioned.

This is relatively new in my experience. For decades I can recall skepticism concerning the virgin birth, and many of the miracles including Jesus' ability to walk on water. But the resurrection was always sacrosanct until quite recently. This seems to be a reflection of what has been taught in some of the more liberal Christian seminaries including one attended by students for the ministry in the church to which I belong. It was such a major departure from orthodoxy that it took several decades to become the conventional "wisdom" with the more avant-garde liberal clergy.

I have absolutely no objection to writers who make no pretense of being believers to be as skeptical and critical as they wish, as long as they don't expect me to agree. Michael Arnheim's book *Is Christianity True?*[3] is probably the most meticulous hatchet job of any of the critical books I have seen. When Beatrice Orchard, a research assistant, read it she observed: "He produces some interesting critical points, but does not prove them."[4] That is fair ball. He takes the references from the Old Testament that Christians use to support our claim that Jesus was the Messiah forecast in the Jewish scriptures, gives them a completely different interpretation that appears more contemporary to the time in which they were written, and claims this disproves our case.

In effect, he does what Christians have done, but in reverse. I wouldn't dream of getting involved in this kind of debate. I have often wondered if some of our claims were not a bit far-fetched, but like all of the fine print that I have been discussing, it doesn't matter. It is not fundamental. Arnheim does make one statement, however, that is open to serious challenge. He writes of the Shroud of Turin as a fraud, and quotes the Bishop of Troyes as confirming the fact. Since his book was written, however, a series of tests have established the shroud as an authentic relic of the early Common Era.

The Shroud, that is alleged to be Jesus' burial cloth, never has been and never will be a factor in my faith, yet its history and possible origin fascinate me. So much so that I wrote a whole chapter on the subject but decided to omit it at the last minute due to the length of this book. I will content myself with three references for anyone who would like to do their own research.

The first is a book by the late Dr. John Heller, entitled *Report on the Shroud of Turin*[5] It records one of the most meticulous scientific examinations I have ever read. Both Dr. Heller and his partner Dr. Alan Adler were convinced of the authenticity of the cloth.

Then, despite the objection of the scientists that a single test might not be conclusive, the shroud was submitted to carbon-14 dating that determined its origin as between 1260-1390. The public relations damage was done with screaming headlines indicating that the cloth was a fake. This is the image that stuck with many of the people I talk to. Unconvinced, the scientists struck back.

A book entitled *The Mystery of the Shroud of Turin* reports experiments that claimed to prove that the linen had been affected by the intense heat (960 degrees Celsius) generated by a fire in 1532 – impacting the carbon dating leading to the conclusion "that the actual calendar age of the Shroud of Turin would be closer to the first or second century CE."[6]

Finally a Public Broadcasting System documentary aired in 2004, "Shroud of Christ?" stated on its video jacket that "In the summer of 2002, a team of textile restorers was invited to Turin to undertake an unprecedented renovation of the shroud, which called for the removal of the shroud's backing cloth and all its medieval patches. The results were staggering – brand-new forensic evidence that the shroud is indeed 2,000 years old, dating from the time of Christ."[7]

In the course of the broadcast the world-famous textile historian Mechthild Flury-Lemberg said the stitching on the shroud was unique in her experience with one exception – a cloth from Masada, King Herod's ancient fortress, that also would have dated from the first century.[8]

This still leaves the question unanswered as to what caused the image. Scientists who studied the Shroud directly are pretty well agreed that the image was formed by an accelerated dehydration, oxidation and degradation (rapid aging) of the Shroud's topmost cellulose fibrils from an energy source (heat or light) causing a scorch-like effect. This rapid removal of water caused discoloration creating a straw-yellow, sepia one-tone color. But it doesn't explain where the heat or light came from.

In the 1960s British philosopher Geoffrey Ashe suggested that Jesus underwent an unparalleled transformation in the tomb. As he wrote: "It is at least intelligible that the physical change of the body at the Resurrection may have released a brief and violent burst of radiation, perhaps scientifically identifiable, perhaps not, which 'scorched' the cloth. In this case the Shroud image is a quasi-photograph of Christ returning to life, produced by a kind of radiance or incandescence analogous to heat in its effects."[9]

At this point I will venture to relate my own hypothesis, influenced by the "broader reality" discussed in an earlier chapter. I believe that when God resurrected Jesus from the dead that he converted the mass of Jesus' body into light energy as an interim step before his reappearance to his friends and disciples. A number of our Star Visitors from other planets are able to dematerialize and rematerialize seemingly at will. And while we don't know how this is done the day will come when we will. In the meantime we will learn about the extent of heat loss and radiation generated in the process.

I realize that despite the agreed authenticity of the Shroud that there will be those who say that these realities do not prove that the image on the cloth is that of Jesus of Nazareth. That is correct in the absence of DNA or some other test that would provide proof positive.

To those who are not convinced by the image and the existing evidence, I suggest that you make your own short list of Semites crucified by the Romans about two thousand years ago, whose image bears signs of a wreath of thorns, a pierced side, and legs that were unbroken, in contrast to the near universal custom at the time, and whose followers thought was important enough, to them at least, to flout Jewish law concerning the handling of burial shrouds and then to preserve the relic at great risk and cost for two millennia. Consider your short list carefully, and make up your own mind.

Still, the debunkers never give up. In October 2009 Italian debunkers, who had received financial help from a group of atheists and agnostics, announced that they had succeeded in reproducing the Shroud using materials that were available in the 14th century. This proved, they claimed, that the Shroud of Turin was manmade and, consequently, a medieval fake.[10]

They proved nothing of the sort. All that their extraordinary effort accomplished was to show that they could produce an image similar to the one on the Shroud. For the Shroud of Turin to be man made would have required some poor soul to be crucified, and shed blood and blood serum from wounds in the head, sides, hands and ankle.

It would also have been necessary for the fakers to be familiar with the unique stitching from the early years CE, to find a pair of ancient coins to place in the eyes of the corpse, to lay it on linens containing traces of cotton fiber that occurs naturally in the Middle East and to contaminate the cloth with pollen exclusive to that area.

In August 1999, two scientists, Dr. Avinoam Danin of Hebrew University in Jerusalem, and Dr. Alan Whanger, a retired Duke University medical professor, published the results of studies they had made on pollen found on the Shroud of Turin. Their findings, presented to the 16th International Botanical Congress in St. Louis, Missouri, indicated that the Shroud is much older than had been indicated by the carbon-14 dating in 1988.

The pollen was from flowers that only occur in the Jerusalem-Hebron area, and flower sometime between March and May, the time when Jesus was crucified. The flowers on the Shroud only bloom an hour a day, so they were picked sometime between 3 and 4 p.m. – about the time Jesus died and was taken for burial.[11]

Anyone who has taken the time to read the evidence of many scientists who painstakingly spent more time and effort examining the Shroud of Turin more thoroughly than any other artifact in history would guffaw at the pretensions of the debunkers and their cheap publicity.

Arnheim is entitled to believe what he likes. I draw the line, however, when churchmen take up the cause of the unbelievers. Two examples are illustrative. The first is the writing of John Shelby Spong, Bishop of Newark. Over the years he has written many fine books opening up the dialogue on the interface of fact and fiction in the Christian tradition. He has tackled increasingly sensitive issues including the bookends of the virgin birth and, finally, the resurrection.

In *Born of a Woman: A Bishop Rethinks the Birth of Jesus*,[12] Spong was simply elaborating and redefining what was fast becoming the new conventional wisdom, namely that virgin births had occurred several times in earlier mythological history, and the Jesus story had been borrowed from these precedents.

More fundamental is Spong's treatment of the resurrection, first in *Born of a Woman*, and later in *Resurrection: Myth or Reality?*[13] a revised version of earlier works on the same subject. The Bishop rightly points out that, "The birth of Christianity was an Easter event, not a Christmas event."[14] He goes on to explain that if one accepts Q as the first written part of the Gospel tradition, "It seems clear that the exaltation of the Jewish Jesus was the original meaning of Easter rather than the later explanation that came to be called resurrection."[15]

That, in my opinion, is the cop-out. Why would anyone think that the two were contradictory? Why would anyone exalt a dead Jewish criminal? Is it possible to stretch the imagination far enough to believe that Jesus' eleven cowardly followers, hiding away from the authorities, were "exalting" their crucified leader? It is inconceivable that these men would have been willing to go out and risk martyrdom in the name of their dead teacher unless they had been witness to some soul-stirring event so startling and profound that their cowardice had been transformed into the realm of extraordinary sacrificial courage.

A Canadian writer, Tom Harpur, has traveled even further down the slippery slope of disbelief. An Anglican priest, and former Religion Editor for the big circulation newspaper the *Toronto Star*, began on the same route of searching for the historical Jesus as opposed to the Jesus of the church bearing his name. I remember reading one of his books titled *For Christ's Sake*, disclaiming the doctrine of the virgin birth but clinging tenaciously to the authenticity of the resurrection as the bedrock foundation of his belief.[16]

Times have changed. His *The Pagan Christ: Recovering the Lost Light*, published in 2004, not only denied the resurrection, it claimed that there was no historical Jesus on which a religion could be based.[17] This is a tragedy because the first part of the book is an interesting history lesson in early religious practices that predate Christianity, and the extent to which the Church has borrowed from their beliefs and practices. If he had stopped there I would have considered it a good read, and worthwhile.

Most unfortunately, however, he goes on and on in an attempt to prove that the historical Jesus didn't exist, that he was just a figure the evangelists had borrowed from mythology. It was by far the most convoluted and weakest case I have read in the whole library of religious commentary. The best evidence concerning Harpur's conclusion is the fact that not one of the learned commentators I have read has even hinted at the non-existence of the historical Jesus, despite their profound differences concerning who and what he may have been.

In *Truth and Fiction in The Da Vinci Code*,[18] Bart D. Ehrman, one of the most knowledgeable scholars that I have been privileged to read, while acknowledging that there is very little historical evidence of Jesus' life and times apart from the Gospels – including both those that made it into the canon, and those that did not because they were suppressed – quotes the Jewish historian Josephus, author of a twenty-volume history of the Jews from Adam and Eve up to and including his own time, who mentioned Jesus twice. Ehrman elaborates as follows.

"In one reference he discusses a man named James, who was the 'brother of Jesus, who is called the messiah.' That's all he says about him in this reference. In the other reference, however, he gives fuller information: that Jesus was known to be a doer of 'spectacular deeds,' that he had followers among both Greeks and Jews, that he was delivered over to Pontius Pilate by the 'leaders' of the Jewish people, that he was crucified, and that his followers continued down to Josephus's own day."[19] This is the same Jesus that Tom Harpur claims did not exist!

The problem created by Spong and Harpur is that they are both good writers with a large following of readers who are inclined to believe them. Their words are like viruses infecting one churchman after another in what has become an epidemic of disbelief. Nowhere is this more evident than in the United Church of Canada, of which I am a member. Male and female clergymen, one after another, create their own take on the Easter story and while usually proclaiming that something unusual happened, they subtly undermine the possibility that the something included the resurrection.

Worse, at least one minister I know, refers to all of the gospels as "stories" that the writers made up from whole cloth in order to justify their beliefs and actions. To my mind this is much too far-fetched to be given any credence whatsoever. It implies that Jesus' followers rallied to the cause of their dead leader for no better reason than a few happy memories of chats on a Galilean hillside. Sadly, the effect of such attitudes is subversive and deeply hurtful to believers who look to their leaders for spiritual substance and inspiration.

The United Church of Canada, like other mainline churches, has been declining in power and potency in recent decades and there has been much debate as to the reason why. In my opinion, to use one of Jesus' analogies, it is because too many branches have been severed from the vine. When the plug is pulled from the source of the power, the machine just begins to wind down.

Some Personal Beliefs

It is probably easier to criticize the beliefs of others than to state one's own point of view. Still, I think it is only just to raise the flag that you willingly salute even if, in doing so, you present another target for those who choose to disagree.

To begin, I believe that God is alive and well. How do I know he exists? I talk to Him every day, and ask for His guidance in all I do and say. In return, He blesses me greatly in more ways than I can count, including giving me a guardian angel to watch over and protect me when I do dumb things that I do with regularity.

In concert with my Jewish and Muslim brothers and sisters, I believe that God is One, and not three, as I have already explained. In the course of my life I have had only one vision and one revelation. The vision, occurring in the night, was clear and unequivocal. "The Lord thy God is One." I believe that, and proclaim it.

I also know that Satan is alive and well. How do I know? I talk to him almost every day, too. He regularly gives me advice that I usually recognize as being wrong, even though it can be skillfully subtle. So I have to repeat over and over again, "Get thee behind me Satan," or sometimes "just buzz off, and leave me alone." I know from experience that the minute I let my guard down Satan will take advantage of the opening. In addition, every morning when I pick up my newspapers I read about the rapes, murders, riots and frauds committed by people who have fallen under his influence.

Since writing this I found confirmation of my beliefs in God and Satan that Linda Moulton Howe one of America's most respected ufologists, obtained from her informed sources.

"I asked Sherman, (a pseudonym for her government informants) 'Is there a Devil out there somewhere?'

"There is an evil force. Even the Ebens (visitors from other planets) talk about it. There is a Supreme Being and then there is the Evil One, The Evil Entity. The Ebens are as scared of that Evil Entity as we are of the Devil. The Devil or Satan. It's the same."

"Where is the Devil?"

"I don't know. But what worries me is that if the Ebens are scared of him, I'm damned scared of him because the Ebens can control everything! They have been around this universe and done everything. And if they believe in the same Supreme being that we call God, and they say there is an Evil One – then there really is a Devil.[20]

Elaine Pagels, in *The Origin of Satan* writes a fascinating story of "the accuser's" place in religious literature over the centuries.[21] One point became very clear to me from reading the book. Religious people have given

Satan credit for virtually all the erroneous views and practices of others. They are much less inclined to admit that he played a part in their own misconceptions and actions. For a humorous exception I am reminded of the one time television star Flip Wilson who, when he was given to mischief of one sort or another, would invariably say: "The devil made me do it."

It is my belief that the human consciousness comprises a combination long and short wave radio transmitter and receiver. The long wave is the one we use to take in information of all kinds, the sights, sounds, smells, written and verbal communications of our immediate environment. The short wave section is the one we use when communicating with the spirit world, both God and Satan, or their graduate student instructors when they are too busy to give us their instant attention. Constant communication with the former, including saying thanks for His many blessings, leads on to a path of spiritual growth and wellbeing. Switching channels fills our minds with wrong information that leads to decisions that are ultimately hurtful to us, other humans, and the planet of which we are stewards.

In the introduction to the book I proclaimed that Jesus of Nazareth has been and remains my role model. His story of peace and goodwill impresses me as being the only solution to the seemingly intractable problems of the world. God's kingdom will not come until we, as Earthlings, start loving our neighbors as ourselves, and treating them accordingly. So, loving God and our fellow mortals in order that His will be done on Earth as it is in Heaven, remains the essence of the Gospel (good news) that Jesus taught. The problem is that what he said has been ignored for far too long, even by those of us who count ourselves among his followers.

On the question of core beliefs about Jesus, the virgin birth was never a deal breaker for me. I didn't necessarily disbelieve it, but at the same time I didn't feel it necessary to proclaim it because to me it was not fundamental. Only the resurrection was fundamental because without it, as St. Paul deeply believed, the whole story was a lie. The birth story, however, has always been central to the practice and enjoyment of my religion. Christmas is a wonderful celebration and it doesn't matter if the date chosen by the church was that of the sun god Mithras, coinciding with the winter solstice; for those of us in the northern hemisphere, at least, the timing is perfect as the long winter nights begin to shorten and the distant hope of spring is reborn.

For many years as I listened to the Christmas story the part played by the Star of Bethlehem has always intrigued me. It has also engaged the interest of astrologers and astronomers for centuries. Some have concluded that it was Haley's comet, but that choice was never very convincing. Others have turned to the extremely rare conjunction of three planets Jupiter, Saturn and Mars which astronomer Johannes Kepler calculated occurred every 805 years which placed the relevant one in 6 BCE the year usually assigned (because of changes in the calendar) to Jesus' birth.[22] But none of these speculations came close to satisfying the niggling doubt as to how a star could be so localized that it could lead strangers first to a small town, and then to the exact place where the baby could be found.

The dilemma was recognized by the late highly-respected Catholic scholar Raymond Brown. For him as reported in a *Time* magazine story titled "Secrets of the Nativity," the star was a puzzle, a celestial body engaged in a maneuver a little like a car attempting a three-point turn. "A star that rose in the east, appeared over Jerusalem, turned south to Bethlehem, and then came to rest over a house," he ruminated, "would have constituted a celestial phenomenon unparalleled in astronomical history. Yet it did not receive notice in the records of the time."[23]

It was only after I became conscious of and convinced of interstellar travel going back millennia, that I found a plausible answer. The "star" must have been one of God's spaceships assigned to that special mission. It would have been capable of every characteristic and maneuver described.

Another interesting observation related to the extraterrestrial presence and technology, is the probability that Jesus did not have a human father. The evidence is based on the characteristics he shared with what we know about our Star Visitors. The first and very significant similarity was his ability to read peoples' minds and tell them what they were thinking, as he is reported to have done so many times. Our "Star Visitors" do exactly that.[24]

The same can be said about the similarity in healing power. The visitors' medical prowess is much advanced from ours. Then there is the question of levitation. The visitors can levitate with ease and that solves the riddle of walking on the water. But it was the post-resurrection characteristics that are most strikingly similar. The visitors can walk through walls just as Jesus did to join his disciples after he rose from the dead. The Star people can also materialize and dematerialize as Jesus did when he appeared in the disciples' midst and then, later, to vanish from their sight.[25]

The extraterrestrials can easily change their configuration at will, an ability that could account for the difficulty some of Jesus' followers had in recognizing him until he revealed himself to them. There is really no need to elaborate further because it is easy to read the similarities for yourself, and see where that takes you. One final point. Bishop Spong, in commenting on the ascension story, as recorded in the Acts of the Apostles, says that Jesus wouldn't have gone to Heaven, he would have gone into orbit. I don't know if he was trying to be funny or not but he was obviously speaking from what I now call the narrow reality – the view that if you haven't seen it with your own eyes, or it can't be proved in a laboratory, that it can't be true. The "broader reality" is that Jesus would have been "beamed up" to one of God's spaceships waiting for him just above the clouds through which he disappeared.

The narrow reality is a point of view that I hope will soon be a relic of the past. I have always assumed that anything within the realm of human imagination is possible, even though we are not yet aware of the knowledge and technology necessary to achieve it. The "broader reality" as I like to call it, opens up possibilities that we can barely dream of. So when people ask me if I believe all of Jesus' miracles, I say that I don't disbelieve them just because I wasn't an eyewitness. I have an open mind.

The "broader reality" may provide the clue to some of the Old Testament miracles, as well. For example, I had always wondered what happened to Elijah's body when it disappeared somewhere on the east bank of the Jordan River. He was probably beamed up and flown away. The same thing might have happened to Moses.

But the "miracle" that now makes total sense to me was Elijah's victory over the four hundred and fifty prophets of Baal when, after much praying to their god, nothing happened to their sacrifice. Then it was Elijah's turn. He had an altar prepared, the bull cut in pieces and laid on the wood, all of which was then drenched with water, enough to fill a trench around it. Elijah called on the Lord to prove to the wayward children of Israel that He was indeed their God.

"Then the fire of the Lord fell and consumed the burnt sacrifice, and the wood and the stones and the dust, and it licked up the water that was in the trench," and the people fell on their faces and said, "The Lord, He is God!"[26] I never disbelieved but always wondered how this was possible. I now know that one well-aimed zap of a laser from one of God's spaceships would produce exactly the result described in I Kings.

So the Bible, which I have just re-read from cover to cover for the third time, is still the most marvelous book on the shelf. Much of it is fascinating reading, and often reading a passage for a second, third or fourth time reveals new insights. But anyone who has read Karen Armstrong's *The Bible: The Biography* or Bart Ehrman's *Misquoting Jesus*[27] would want to read it with discernment. God didn't write a word of it and although the Holy Spirit, that I equate with the Spirit of God, which predated Christianity, undoubtedly inspired many of the writers, that was not universally true.

I can't imagine the Holy Spirit counseling John, whoever he was, to write an anti-Semitic essay that, read literally, condemns fellow Jews to eternal damnation. On a similar note, I can't imagine the Spirit of God counseling the Jewish Rabbis to write a *minim* that would invoke God's eternal punishment on all outsiders including all Romans, Greeks and Jews who were followers of Jesus. In neither case could they have imagined the tragic consequences first to the Christians, and then to the Jews.

In summation, there is one key point where Bishop Spong and I agree. "Fundamentalist Christians distort the Bible by taking it literally. Liberal Christians distort the Bible by not taking it seriously."[28]

CHAPTER 6

A RELIGIOUS AGENDA

"For I know the plans I have for you," declares the LORD, "plans to prosper you and not harm you, plans to give you hope and a future. Then you will call upon me and come and pray to me, and I will listen to you. You will seek me and find me when you seek me with all your heart."

Jeremiah 29:11-13

Many years ago when I was Canadian Minister of National Defence, my boss Prime Minister Lester B. Pearson showed me a letter he had just received from Canada's ambassador to the Soviet Union, Robert A.D. Ford. In the letter the ambassador blamed religion as a principal cause of strife and conflict in the world. I considered myself a "religious" person and I must admit that I took some offense at the accusation.

As the years passed I came to realize that Ambassador Ford had a more mature worldview than I did, and that he was right in his belief that organized religion was a major contributing factor to the constant unrest and conflict that plagued world society. I recalled, of course, some of the major wars and atrocities that history recorded as being of religious origin. But the ones that I was most familiar with were in the past tense. Soon

I realized, however, that it has never stopped. It is as much a part of the late twentieth and early twenty-first centuries as it was of earlier times. People are still fighting and dying in support of their religious beliefs – all over the world.

Originally I had included several pages of old and recent examples of religious conflicts between Buddhists and Hindus, Communists and Buddhists, Hindus against Muslims, Hindus against Sikhs, Sikhs against Hindus and other examples to illustrate that there is a long and appalling history of conflict between one religion and another. A commentator pointed out to me, however, that in some of the examples I had cited there were factors other than religious such as tribalism and territorialism, where land and resources were also contributing factors. So I have reduced the number of stories to a mere handful that are sufficient to underline the continuing nature of these complicated conflicts and the absolute necessity of finding means of resolving them without resort to the use of force.

Christians Against Muslims

The conflict here is very old and dates back to the Crusades, in which Christians thought they had the right to kill in the name of the Christ. Tensions have ebbed and flowed over the centuries but more recently there have been some dust-ups in Africa and Americans have been waging wars in two predominantly Muslim countries in the name of fighting terrorism.

At a World Religions after September 11 Congress, "Cindy Wesley, a religious studies professor from the southern United States told the conference U.S. President George W. Bush has found allies in the religious right, particularly the leaders of the Southern Baptist Conference. 'The Southern Baptist Convention began formulating a "just war" argument within days of 9/11,' she said, and has continued to back the war on theological grounds ever since.

" 'The Baptists, who were historically among the most vocal of the need for the separation of church and state are now among the most nationalistic,' said Wesley, a professor at Lambuth University in Jackson, Tennessee."[1]

It was most surprising for someone raised in the Christian tradition to learn that the Southern Baptists were supporting a war – indeed a war based on geopolitics and oil – when their leader, Jesus, eschewed violence

118

of any kind, and would be hurt beyond belief to see such a war being justified in his name.

At the same conference, Nobel Peace Prize laureate Shirin Ebadi said "Political leaders, both Christian and Muslim, who exploit the religious beliefs of their people to justify war and violence are the greatest threat facing the world today. To justify war, leaders take advantage of the religious sentiments of their people."

"Ebadi also faulted the United States for using democracy and human rights concerns as a pretext for war in Afghanistan and Iraq, saying 'Democracy cannot be spread through a cluster of bombs.'

"At a news conference after her speech, she said the world has become less safe since the invasion of Afghanistan, noting terrorist attacks around the world have increased in the last five years. Human rights had nothing to do with the U.S.-led invasion to unseat Iraqi dictator Saddam Hussein, she said, noting the U.S. tolerates many dictators. 'The difference between Saddam and other dictators is that he sat on a lot of oil and the others do not.'"[2]

Christians Against Christians

"Monks wield sledgehammers in ungodly battle. Rebels holding Greek monastery go toe-to-toe with rival Orthodox brethren backed by patriarch; seven injured in clash."

Thessaloniki, Greece – "Rival groups of monks wielding crowbars and sledgehammers clashed yesterday over control of a thousand-year-old monastery in a community regarded as the cradle of Greek Orthodox Christianity, police said.

"Seven monks were injured and transported by boat to receive treatment but released after several hours, police said. No one was arrested, but three monks were banned from re-entering the Orthodox sanctuary of Mount Athos, on a self-governing peninsula in northern Greece."[3]

**

From the time of the reformation Roman Catholics and Protestants have fought for the supremacy of their several branches of what is allegedly the same faith rooted in the life of Jesus of Nazareth. Much blood has been spilled – all of it, appallingly! There has been much progress in

119

bringing the two sides to the bargaining table of cooperation, but much remains to be done.

One of the great achievements of recent years has been to stop Irish Catholics and Protestants from killing each other. "The Irish 'Troubles' that began in the late Sixties cost more than 3,000 lives in a formerly quiet and orderly society."[4] The Provisional IRA terrorists have laid down their arms and put on their political hats as representatives of Sinn Fein, the political wing of the Irish nationalists. Although it may be too soon to say that the power sharing arrangement between the two groups following the 1998 Good Friday Agreement has settled the conflict once and for all, what has happened to date is nothing less than a miracle.

Christians Against Jews

The persecution of Jews by Christians has a very long history going back to the early days of the Church. At that time some of it may have been inspired by the persecution of the followers of Jesus by the more orthodox Jews who succeeded in having them excommunicated from Judaism. As I have suggested elsewhere, Christians were deeply influenced by the extreme language of some of the Gospels and especially by the Gospel of John. This is no excuse, however, for the behavior of Christians who refer to their leader as "The Prince of Peace."

The ultimate horror, of course, was the Holocaust of the 1940s when the German government systematically exterminated more than six million Jews. While it was the Germans who were primarily responsible, there were Poles, French and other collaborators. And as I pointed out earlier, the reluctance of Britain, the United States and Canada to accept Jewish refugees is a serious blot on our calendars.

A sad reminder that anti-Semitism in Europe is not dead was reported from Paris in April 2006. A pretty schoolgirl known as Yalda enticed a handsome young Jewish telephone salesman to have a nightcap at her place. It was to be his last date. "The testimony of this 17-year old femme fatale who happily offered herself as 'bait' in the kidnapping of Ilan Halimi, whose tortured body was found on wasteland, has shocked a country which is haunted by a painful history of anti-Semitism.

"The gang she worked for was known as 'les Barbares', the Barbarians, and included blacks, Arabs and whites from Portugal and France."[5]

Jews Against Muslim and Christian Palestinians

It seems like a never-ending cycle of violence. On a Saturday in June 2006, Israeli commandos carried out their first arrest inside Gaza since Israel's withdrawal the previous summer. The following day Palestinian militants tunneled into Israel and emerged to kill two Israeli soldiers and capture a 19-year old Israeli corporal; three Palestinians were killed. On Monday Israeli Prime Minister Ehud Olmert ordered troops and armor to mass on the Gaza border. Wednesday "Israeli warplanes fired missiles at three bridges in Gaza effectively severing the strip into three sections and isolating the refugee camps along the Rafah border with Egypt, where Israeli intelligence sources suspect the kidnapped corporal, Gilad Shalit, had been held since his abduction early Sunday morning. Israeli army officials said the mission was aimed at preventing the militants from moving the soldier.

"Additional missile strikes incapacitated Gaza's primary power plant, cutting electricity to most of the coastal territory. Simultaneously, an Israeli armored column later began rolling into southern Gaza, creating the impression that a major invasion of the coastal territory was underway."[6] Will the conflict between the Jews and the Arabs never end? More on this subject in the final chapter.

Muslims Against Christians

"In November 2005, a court in Saudi Arabia sentenced a high school chemistry teacher to 40 months in prison and a public flogging of 750 lashes after he had shared his opinion 'on various topics including Christianity' and 'encouraged his students to engage in critical thinking in resolving apparent differences of meaning between the Koran and the words and deeds of the Prophet Mohammed.' He was banned from his trial, his lawyer not recognized. No reply from the Saudi government for requests for information.

"And so it goes: In Pakistan, a 26-year-old Christian died after torture while in police custody. 'It was alleged,' writes the rapporteur, 'that 40 Christians who sought an investigation of the police involved in the case were brutally arrested.' A young Christian drank water from a tap outside an Islamic seminary. According to his deathbed statement, he was tortured for five days by a teacher and students when he refused to convert to Islam."[7]

Muslims Against Jews
Malaysia PM fans flames after remarks cause storm.

Putrajaya, Malaysia – "The gulf between the Islamic world and the West was starkly visible yesterday as a firestorm of condemnation from Europe, America, Australia and Israel scorched Malaysia's prime minister for remarks seen as blatantly anti-Semitic – while officials from major Muslim nations rallied to his defence.

"An unapologetic Prime Minister Mahathir Mohamad fanned the flames, refusing to retreat from remarks he made Thursday, instead accusing his critics of a double standard. 'People call Muslims terrorists, they even say … Muhammad, the prophet, was a terrorist,' Mahathir said.

" 'People make such statements, and they seem to get away with it. But if you say anything at all against the Jews, you are accused of being anti-Semitic,' Mahathir told a news conference after the close of a summit of the Organization of the Islamic Conference, the largest group of Muslim nations. The day before, in a speech calling on Muslims to embrace science and technology, and put behind them divisions over religious dogma that have left them weakened on the world stage, he told delegates of the 57-member organization that 'today the Jews rule this world by proxy. They get others to fight and die for them.' "[8]

**

"A terrifying shooting rampage by a lone male gunman at the headquarters of a Jewish organization in downtown Seattle has left one person dead and five people in hospital with gunshot wounds. Several of the wounded were reported to be in critical condition.

"The gunman entered the Jewish Federation of Greater Seattle building… and began shooting at employees working inside the city's trendy Belltown area. Amy Wasser-Simpson, community services vice-president for the federation, told The Seattle Times the gunman announced to staffers before opening fire: 'I'm a Muslim-American. I'm angry at Israel.'

"David Gomez of the Federal Bureau of Investigation said at the scene that the suspect 'may have been acting out antagonism toward this particular organization (the Jewish Federation).' "[9]

Muslims Against Muslims

When I consulted my files in advance of writing this section I discovered dozens of newspaper clippings reporting the deadly consequences of internecine warfare between competing branches of the Muslim faith in Iraq, Pakistan and Afghanistan. In the interest of brevity I will just quote three 2009 headlines all relating to Iraq.

A January 5 report in *The New York Times* was titled "Bomber at Iraqi Shrine Kills 40, Including 16 Iranian Pilgrims."[10] A May 7 headline in the same newspaper read "Concealed By Potatoes, Bomb Kills 10 In Baghdad."[11] Later, on August 20, the banner heading in the *Wall Street Journal* said "Deadly Blasts Test Iraq's Grip: Explosions in Baghdad Kill 95, Challenging Security Amid U.S. Pullback From Cities."[12]

**

This small and very random sampling of man's seemingly perpetual inhumanity to man is like a random soil sampling that shows that in almost every case they are fertile ground for the seeds of hate and conflict. All too often those seeds of hate are planted and watered by the political and religious poobahs who exploit the masses for purposes of their own power and advantage. Often they reflect a striking resemblance to the manipulation of the crowd when Jesus was arrested and crucified. The power elite recognized a threat to their special privileges and used their power of persuasion over the crowd to stamp it out. It seems that little, if anything, has changed in the intervening millennia.

If we want to save our planet and ourselves, all that must change, and now. Hate must be overcome by love, and conflict must be replaced by cooperation. Men and women everywhere must work together as Team World to build the Kingdom of God on Earth. It sounds like a tall order but it is possible by the universal application of the Golden Rule. Interestingly all major faith communities subscribe to this ideal in one form or another but all too often ignore it in everyday life. The time has come for all of us to match the words and music in a new universal harmony.

To achieve a harmonious result, however, the majority of moderates of all faiths will have to become activists to overcome the walls of intolerance erected by the fundamentalists.

Fundamentalism is a Curse

Fundamentalists are people who know what they know and who are not willing to let the facts stand in the way of their beliefs. There are rare cases of someone being converted to the "open mind" society but they are very rare indeed. It doesn't matter whether they are Christian fundamentalists, Jewish fundamentalists, Muslim fundamentalists, Hindu fundamentalists or economic fundamentalists, they are a breed apart. Reasoning with them is like talking into a microphone that is turned off.

Most of my Christian friends of all denominations are wonderful, open-minded people who reason together and, when the time allotted for talk ends, direct their efforts toward extending the kingdom on earth in the fields of health, education and general well-being. A few of my friends are fundamentalists who insist that the world was made in six twenty-four hour days, and that Eve was created by surgically removing a rib from Adam's chest. They wouldn't think of reading on to Genesis 5:1-2, where it says "In the day that God created man, He made him in the likeness of God. He created them male and female, and blessed them and called them Mankind in the day they were created."[13] That would only confuse the issue.

Fundamentalists would be harmless if they kept their views to themselves, and lived in peace with people of other minds. But when they insist that their views be taught to young minds, and presented as Gospel truths, or when they use the Bible to persecute homosexuals, or kill doctors who perform abortions, or wage wars under false pretenses when the real agenda is to control other people's possessions, they become a major menace to peace and good order. I personally was shocked to read that the Southern Baptists were supporting George Bush's "war of lies."

The Muslim fundamentalists are an equal threat to peace and well-being both to their fellow moderate brothers and sisters and to the rest of us. The idea of spreading a particular faith at the barrel of a gun is a monstrous holdover from the dark ages which should disappear into the history books. That Christians and other faiths are part of that history is no excuse for continuing an inexcusable practice.

The Torah, that has been incorporated into the Christian Bible is clear enough. "Thou shalt not kill."[14] And although that command might have been better translated as "thou shalt not murder," it has always been understood that killing is only permitted when the cause is totally justified, such as a war of self-preservation or to end the evil power of the Nazi regime in Germany in the 1930s. On the other hand it should be read as a total prohibition of preventive wars like the war on Iraq. It should also be a prohibition to dropping bombs on a house or compound in an effort to kill a terrorist in the knowledge that almost inevitably innocent people will also be killed. Yet fundamentalists seem capable of rationalizing such acts.

Similarly, the Qur'an forbids killing unless it is just. Yet suicide bombers invariably kill innocent people in addition to themselves. That, by no stretch of the imagination, can be called just. Yet some Muslim fundamentalists appear to have no qualms about it. To suggest that young boys who are willing to blow themselves up in the course of killing innocents will be rewarded by instant arrival in paradise where they will be waited on by young maidens is grotesque beyond belief. They are destined for a rude shock. Yet the whole practice is condoned by devout worshippers of Allah, the God of Abraham, Isaac, Jacob and Ishmael.

I struggle with the fact that both the United States and Israel have reverted to the pre-Mosaic Law. Even "an eye for an eye, and a tooth for a tooth" used to bother me because it was so far from the teachings of my mentor who said we should turn the other cheek. The "an eye for an eye" is a quotation from Exodus 21:23-27, in which a person who has taken the eye of another in a fight is instructed to give his own eye in compensation. At the root of this principle is the belief that one of the purposes of the law is to provide equitable retaliation for an offended party. An eye for an eye defined and restricted the extent of retaliation. This early belief is reflected in the Code of Hammurabi and in the laws of the Hebrew Bible.

This rule was intended to end the practice of unequal and unfair retaliation practiced by primitive peoples. Unfortunately, both the Americans and the Israelis have either forgotten or deliberately chosen to ignore this important restriction of the Jewish law.

In the dastardly attacks on the World Trade Center in 2001, 2,752 people were killed. In retaliation, the United States, under the pretext of a war on terror, launched two wars against Afghanistan and Iraq where military and civilian casualties will probably exceed fifty times that figure.

The Israeli government has long followed a similar practice. When the Lebanese Hezbollah faction captured two Israelis in a disputed area between the two countries in 2006 and took them hostage, the Israelis launched an all-out war against its beleaguered neighbor. It not only attacked the Hezbollah stronghold in the south, it launched a series of air attacks on the north including the capital city of Beirut which had just been rebuilt following the devastating 15-year civil war, and reduced it to rubble once again.

This policy of massive retaliation will never produce the kind of good relations necessary for peace and understanding between neighbors. On the contrary!

Economic fundamentalists are almost as great a menace to the prospect of a better world as their religious counterparts. Experience shows that neither Keynes nor Friedman got it right. Both considered the economic system to be self-regulating, when it has been proven over and over again that it is not. Keynes at least was willing to use government intervention to even out the extremes of business cycles. Friedman was prepared to leave us at the mercy of a system that hasn't in the past and never will work properly.

It should be self evident that there is no hope for a world of peace and security where cooperation crowds out fear and hysteria unless we, the moderate majority, play a more active role in our own affairs and expose the Neanderthals as the impediment to progress that they really are. Before suggesting a detailed agenda, however, there are a few policies and practices in the faith realm that we should reflect on as they, too, have consequences that may affect the quality and tranquility of our lives.

Policies and Priorities to Reflect On
Evolution and Creationism

One of the most hotly debated subjects between Christian fundamentalists and others, especially scientists, is how man – Homo sapiens – arrived at his or her present state. For the fundamentalists, the answer is clear. God created man, planted him in the Garden of Eden, and that is that. So that is what should be taught in the schools. Agnostics and scientists object. Darwin's theory of evolution has been proven to their satisfaction and, consequently, the school system should teach facts, not fiction.

As is often the case, the facts are not as clear-cut as both sides have been arguing. The general theory of evolution has been proven to the satisfaction of the scientific community. It is going on all around us, even as we debate. At the same time, it is being increasingly recognized that in the case of man there was a break in the chain somewhere along the line. When we embrace the new reality of life elsewhere in the cosmos we come into contact with entities who insist that there was genetic manipulation in our history. So we, in our present form, were created to be different from our animal ancestors. Is it possible that both sides are in possession of the truth?

It is simply amazing to see how many scientists are opening their minds to new possibilities as their total knowledge expands. Sandra and I attended the National Prayer Breakfast in Washington in February 2007 where Dr. Francis S. Collins, Director of the Human Genome Project was the principal speaker. Dr. Collins said that the group of scientists he works with are trying to figure out "God's little instruction book" for the human body in order to find cures for cancer, diabetes and many other life-threatening diseases. A former agnostic, Dr. Collins had become a Christian, and his closing statement to the vast assembly in the Washington Hilton Hotel said it all. "It is not a question of science or religion: They are marvelously complementary."

Population Control

Birth control is another contentious issue. The Vatican is still sticking to the "natural family planning" method which shows just how far removed from reality it has become. The rationale must be a four thousand year old Biblical injunction to be fruitful and multiply. At that time, however, the total population of the world was miniscule and there was room for a lot of multiplication. Succeeding generations took the injunction seriously to the point where there are now far too many people for the Earth to sustain and fewer, rather than more people would be the injunction that would make sense today.

We must, however, find more humane ways of reducing the World population than starving people or letting them die agonizing deaths through want of available medication. But all legitimate means such as education and the provision of prophylactics should be adopted. George Bush's policy of sexual abstinence is a non-starter in the world of reality.

It is almost beyond belief that religious communities continue to refuse to approve the use of condoms, and especially so in areas where HIV is epidemic. This is a murderous decree, causing not only the death of millions of women and children, but the appalling "child-headed households" in villages where the entire parent generation has died. Grandmothers are doing their best but seeing an 86-old grandma trying to take care of eighteen grandchildren is tragic. It is difficult to see how anyone can claim to worship God with their mind and at the same time be so callous toward measures that would relieve human suffering.

Racism

I have never met anyone who was not a racist. I have met dozens who said they were not, but on scratching just a little bit beneath the surface one finds trace elements of a deeply seated universal disease. I am not sure about the mechanism by which this occurs, because I don't think children are born with it. It is only after they have been exposed to their home and social environment that they begin to take on the prejudice of adults.

Most whites I know have a deep seated fear of blacks and call them by epithets that my wife and I would never allow to be used in our home, and that I won't repeat here. Some blacks have been known to refer to us as "whitey," "honkey," "The Man," etc. when they intended to be less than complimentary. A visit to Malaysia years ago convinced me that the Malays harbor a general dislike of the Chinese members of their society due in part, no doubt, to the success of the latter in business enterprises.

Similarly a short stop in Japan was enough to indicate that they have a low regard for blacks. Many Jews find it difficult to say anything good about Arabs, and the reverse is true. Anti-Semitism is a near universal disease perhaps related to the Jews entrepreneurial success as well as the influence of the Christian Gospel stories surrounding the crucifixion of Jesus. Many black African tribes are constantly at odds with each other over the ownership of resources or other issues of power and influence. And on it goes.

Christian Sunday schools teach children a song that includes this line "Red and yellow, black and white, all are precious in His sight, Jesus loves the little children of the world." It's a nice song, but the sentiment is not carried forward into adult life. When it comes to feeding the hungry, or healing the sick "we" come first, and "others" last – if indeed there is anything left after our needs and wants have been met.

I don't really believe that there is a cure for such a deeply entrenched and fundamental problem, at least in this century. But it can be substantially controlled by means of an all-out effort on the part of every one of us. Every time ugly thoughts come to mind we must say to ourselves "What if our places were reversed? Would I want them thinking such evil about me?" We have to remember that we are all God's children and there is no reason to believe that He doesn't want us to practice the Golden Rule in our thoughts as well as in our actions. It's a tough one – I know from working at it. But practice does help, and if we persist in our efforts to really love others as ourselves it does ultimately make a difference.

Women's Rights

One of the most difficult yet most important questions on the religious and social agenda is the place that women should play. Great progress has been made in some Western countries, while there has been considerable foot-dragging in others. In many Eastern and Third World countries women are still regarded as chattels, and considered inferior to their husbands in almost every way. The reason for this, of course, is that all the religious books and rules were written by men – macho men who considered that women had their place, but it was first in the cave, and then in the tent.

Progress has been painfully slow. Even in my own country of Canada women did not have the right to vote in federal elections until 1918. And they were not considered as "persons" under the law and consequently qualified to be appointed to the Senate until 1930.

The first female elected to the House of Commons was Agnes Campbell Macphail on December 6, 1921 and the first to hold a cabinet post was Ellen Fairclough in 1957, long after I had become an MP. The number and clout of female ministers has never come close to equality so there is still a long road to tread.

Some of the Old Testament rules die hard. Women had few rights, whereas if a man wanted to divorce his wife all he had to do was say so. Fortunately Jews have long since abandoned the "death for adultery" rule, but some Muslim societies still observe it. It is an archaic rule that has no place in the 21st century. God endowed all men and women with free choice. Consequently we are free – or are intended to be free – to make our own choices without being subjected to either religious or civil sanctions. If we make wrong choices the day of reckoning will be with the Creator Himself, and not by any one of us pretending to stand in for Him.

This was one of the great moral lessons that Jesus taught. When a woman accused of adultery was brought before him by a group of vigilantes, who had planned to trick him by asking what should be done to her, Jesus suggested that the one of them who was without sin should cast the first stone. One by one the men sheepishly filed away beginning with the eldest. It seems to be an appropriate test for today.

Some Muslim fundamentalists would put a girl to death for unmarried sex while her male partner, who more times than not would be the instigator, is allowed to go without any penalty. Such a double standard is a gross miscarriage of justice. The penalty should apply equally, either to both parties or to neither. Some of the stories of young girls being killed by their relatives are sufficient to melt the hardest of hearts. Also, "what's fair for one should be fair for both" should be applied to female circumcision. If women are to be denied sexual pleasure by what strange logic should a man be allowed the satisfaction of orgasm?

The role of women in churches, synagogues and mosques is another big area where the rules have all been written by men. Often in Christian churches the excuse has been given that because Jesus had twelve disciples and none of them were women, that was to be the standard set for us. A close reading of the Bible indicates clearly that it reflects the mores and social values of the times in which various parts of it were written. If Jesus were picking twelve today, I have little doubt that half of them would be women, and they would add invaluable insights concerning any subject under discussion. Still the churches, and especially the Roman Catholic Church, operate as if women are still second-class citizens.

This trait is not limited to the Catholics, however. I remember attending an Anglican service in London, England, some years ago where I heard the Bishop of London say that if his church ordained women priests he would join the Roman Catholics who, no doubt, would have been happy to have him. I have often wondered if the Bishop lived long enough to have to make good on his threat. Still there is hope, however faint. Not too long ago a good friend to Sandra and me was ordained a

Deacon in the Roman Catholic tradition, and his wife a Deaconess. So that is a beginning. Another close friend wants to be the first ordained priest in the Catholic Church. It would give me great pleasure to live long enough to see her wish granted.

It takes a while to get used to the fact that women can fill just about any job that is not based primarily on physical strength, and do it well. I confess that it took me a while to appreciate what I have just said. Some years ago when I was CEO of an organization called the Canadian Foundation on Compulsive Gambling, subsequently renamed the Responsible Gambling Council, one of our board members, a medical doctor, began to negotiate the availability of four beds for gambling addicts in the hospital with which he was associated. An appointment was made with the CEO of the hospital to discuss the fine print.

When I arrived for the appointment I was more than a little surprised to find that the person in charge of the hospital was a female. Following the introductions, she called the meeting to order, handed out a well-prepared and succinct agenda of the principal points to be considered, and began the discussion. I was soon impressed – favorably. She was friendly, flexible, and willing to listen while at the same time ensuring that we did not wander too far off the relevant item.

I am happy to say that the session ended with a meeting of minds and a decision that we could get on with our experiment with in-house addiction treatment, while the way the subject was addressed and resolved was inspiring. My most lasting impression was the way this woman ran the meeting and the intellectual prowess she brought to the decision-making process. The experience was something of a turning point in my life and I resolved that in future I would assess people strictly on merit and never again on gender.

Abortion

God, by definition is pro-choice. That doesn't mean that He is pro-abortion, but that He leaves decisions like that to the individual's discretion taking into account all of the circumstances involved. That is the way we were created. We were given free choice and will be held individually responsible for the choices we make, either good or bad, as is the case with all moral decisions. It follows that the state has no business trying to second-guess the decisions we make.

I say this on the basis of long years of experience with the state deciding what personal behavior was criminal and what was not. When I was first elected in 1949 adultery was a criminal offense in Canada. At the same time polls indicated that fifty percent of all adult Canadian males were adulterers. If the law had been rigorously enforced half of the adult males would have been in jail and the rest would have been required to work twice as hard to keep them under lock and key. Mercifully, my first boss, Prime Minister Louis S. St. Laurent, had the good sense to repeal that section of the criminal code.

Homosexuality remained on the books as a crime for almost twenty more years, however, and anyone indulging in same-sex activity was a potential felon. It was left to the third prime minister under whom I served, Pierre E. Trudeau, to repeal that section. He became famous for a line that he either invented or borrowed namely. "The state has no place in the bedrooms of the nation."

I became aware of the complexity of the abortion issue during my time in political office. One of my secretaries, near the end of her term of employment, confided that she had helped arrange abortions for a number of MP's employees and others where she felt the circumstances warranted. Some of the cases were really pathetic, and Solomon in all his wisdom would have had difficulty deciding between right and wrong.

My secretary justified her actions by describing the physical risk involved for women having abortions performed by "the back alley butchers" as she called them. She provided me with chapter and verse of several cases of women who had died as a result of inadequate medical assistance including one beautiful young nun. With this background information I, for one, was not disappointed when our Supreme Court struck down the law prohibiting abortions and it became possible to have them in properly-equipped hospitals and clinics. And to the vigilantes who try to kill doctors who perform abortions I would say that killing for such reasons is not only a civil offense, it is a moral offense as well.

Homosexuality: What God has Created Let No Man Disdain

Of all the literal readings of the Bible few, if any, have caused greater injustice, injury, pain and heartache than the references to homosexuality. I would go so far as to say that it is not homosexuality that is the abomination; that word more appropriately applies to the consequences of treating the dictum as a divine proclamation. The Holy Spirit undoubtedly influenced the content of the Bible but a careful reading suggests that too often the Spirit was trumped by the prejudiced views of macho men. You certainly did not hear any condemnation of homosexuality coming from the mouth of Jesus when he was on Earth.

Full acceptance really requires getting to know homosexuals as individuals and this can be a lifelong learning process. One of the young men in the Bible class I taught was gay. He and his partner entered into a lifelong relationship. He has played an active role in a successor Bible class and took his turn as president with full support of the membership.

One of my grandsons is gay and the characteristics were clear from the time he was a young child. It only became official when Joshua turned twenty-one and wrote a delightful little autobiography titled *Give Life a Squeeze: Juicy Observations from my Life's First Quarter*, disclosing his personal journey of acceptance in the hope it might help other young people who struggle with their sexuality. He is wonderfully supported by all the members of the family who love him dearly and unreservedly.

Not all homosexuals are as fortunate. Two case studies from real life are illustrative. The Calgary, Alberta, Prayer Breakfast Group membership was primarily but not exclusively comprised of urban businessmen whose theology and politics were both decidedly conservative. They assumed that their waiter was gay and whispered slurs loudly enough for him to hear.

Outraged by the insult he asked to be heard. He told the group that he was a born again Christian who had a masters degree in theology. His father, the senior pastor at a conservative evangelical church in the United States, had completely disowned him years earlier and refused to see either him or his partner. He reminded the group that Christianity is supposed to be an inclusive religion that celebrates the value and dignity of all people. Nevertheless the group decided to change their meeting place, much to the dismay of the female members and one or two of the more liberal participants.

I was witness to a good news story on the same subject. One Wednesday morning, just before Christmas, one of the more conservative members of the Prayer Breakfast Group that I attend shared that his daughter had just told him that she was gay. His first instinct, he told us, was to ask her to move out and never darken his doorstep again.

To a man, every one of us advised him to go home, put his arms around his daughter and tell her he loved her and wanted her to be home for Christmas. Furthermore her partner would be welcome, too. And this is what he did.

One of the two ministers at the downtown church that Sandra and I attend is gay, as is a significant percentage of the congregation including many of the "pillars" of the church. Not only could we not get along without them, they are all delightful people and a joy to be with both at work and socially.

The litmus test of our sincerity is the Golden Rule. If, by accident of birth, we were "one of them" would we want to be subject to stinging slurs and epithets? Or would we want to be fully accepted as one of God's glorious variety of children and allowed to joyfully share our common heritage?

Rules Versus Compassion

One of Jesus' biggest complaints against the scribes and Pharisees of his day was their adherence to rules at the expense of compassion. Strict enforcement of rules for the Sabbath trumped healing a sick person, or allowing the disciples to find food. And the major point of the story of the good Samaritan was that the priest and the Levite walked by a dying man because if, perchance, he had already succumbed, they would have been considered "unclean" from having touched him. A Samaritan, not bound by the rules, had compassion and attended to the needs of the sick man.

Somehow the three religions that sprang from Abraham's bosom have all become obsessed with rules. Soon after the destruction of the Temple in Jerusalem in 70 CE, Judaism was reborn on the basis of a long list of rules ranging from the sublime to the less than sublime. The Qur'an is the source of a long list of very strict rules still observed by Muslims. Not to be outdone, the Christian Church has, at different times and places, come up with its own list of do's and don'ts. Thou shalt not drink; thou shalt not smoke; thou shalt not wear lipstick or earrings; thou shalt not dance; thou shalt not play on a public stage. And with some, I suspect, "Thou shalt not be born a lesbian or a homosexual if you want to be a member in good standing." The alternative, of course, would be that if you are so born you will forever keep your mouth shut about it.

I am constantly appalled by the priorities of some of the faith communities. The right wing Christian community, in particular, spends far too much time and energy on issues like abortion and homosexuality while ignoring really important problems like the fact that millions of people are dying from starvation and lack of health care. And how can people who call themselves Christians spend such vast sums on weapons and war at the expense of health care and education both at home and around the world? Somehow the love and compassion that were Jesus' forte have been largely abandoned in favor of "security and prosperity," the perks of the well-to-do.

The time has long since come when all faith communities should reexamine their priorities. Do we want to continue fighting wars between tribes, races, people of different faiths and anyone who doesn't agree with us? Or are we willing to work together in harmony to build the Kingdom of God on Earth, including, as a matter of utmost urgency, saving the planet from destruction as a suitable habitat for succeeding generations? Life is a matter of choices. We can be part of the "me first" generation, or we can be visionaries projecting ahead to the kind of peaceful and just world that is surely within our means if we opt to make it a reality.

So on the assumption that many moderate activists from all races, tribes and colors are ready to act in concert for their own benefit and that of all humankind, the balance of this book will include a series of suggestions for action on various fronts that would literally transform the world if implemented.

Building the Kingdom Brick by Brick

"The sign of being human is to be a friend to the weak."

Jean Vanier

Most of this chapter, to date, has been highly negative – reports of riots, insurrection, wars, racism, male chauvinism, hypocrisy, twisted priorities, neglect and the whole panoply of human frailties. There is an old adage, however, that says every cloud has a silver lining, and certainly there are many members of the human species who have done and continue to do their bit to build the Kingdom of God brick by brick. Or in terms of the vernacular, seed by seed, plough by plough, goat by goat, camel by camel, water well by water well, house by house, food bag by food bag and in myriad other ways that make life better and provides new hope for some other member of the human race.

Members of all faiths have played positive roles throughout history. The Christian Church, for example, has established schools, shelters, universities and hospitals. And it is not alone in its contribution to humanity. One bit of history that intrigued me was that even during the Crusades, Christian scholars were traveling to Spain to learn at the feet of Muslim intellectuals. And one of the reasons that the much reviled Hamas and Hezbollah are so popular is because they have been providing aid and welfare to people in desperate need.

There are many cases where one person has made a difference. Habitat for Humanity is one example. The Stephen Lewis Foundation, Free the Children and the Samaritan's Purse are others as are World Vision, United Nations Relief agencies, etc., etc. This list of good things that are happening could go on and on and fill a whole book. But they are still far from adequate in meeting the immediate, medium and long-term needs of a world population in desperate need. So the idea is to get all faith communities to pool both their prayers and their efforts in Team World to expand what is being done by two, four, ten, a hundred and a thousand-fold until the point is finally reached where no one anywhere in the world, male or female, is without basic food, potable water, shelter, and a reasonable level of education to be adjusted upward over the years and decades as each level of achievement has been reached. We, collectively, have the resources and ability to undertake and carry out such a plan and all that is needed is the will.

I would like to make it clear that it is not my role to tell people what to think. You will think what you like, as has always been the case. All faith communities have gone through periods of dissension and disagreement, and there have been many splits and new groups formed, sometimes with more rancor and hostility than appropriate under the circumstances. The most I would wish for in this realm is to stimulate discussion and debate in a way that might possibly bring some positive results.

My concern, therefore, is not so much what you think as what you do. It is the action side of your beliefs that is critical to the future of all humankind. So here are some steps for your consideration.

Step 1

A Conclave of World Faith Communities

A good place to start would be to organize a World Congress of the six major faith groups, Buddhism, Christianity, Hinduism, Islam, Judaism, and Shintoism with other groups by invitation to discuss outstanding issues that have to be addressed, and old animosities that have to be reconciled. Event planners tell me that a minimum of about eighteen months is required to organize a meeting on such a large scale, so the project should be launched at the earliest practical date consistent with good organization and an agreed agenda. It would have to be understood at the outset that this would not be a convention to debate theology or dogma. The object of the exercise would simply be a general desire to end any hostilities that may exist and to work in harmony to solve the real problems of a world in stress. These conclaves might become biennial events to assess progress and renew vows of cooperation. In the off years there might be regional meetings to address more local issues, and it would be good to have local interfaith councils meeting regularly to iron out the inevitable tensions in special need of immediate attention. These would become the real action centers for cooperation in meeting the common needs of local communities.

A Year of Forgiveness and Reconciliation

An important by-product might be the declaration of a "Year of Forgiveness and Reconciliation" during which Muslims would forgive Christians and Christians would forgive Muslims for atrocities committed against the other, Catholics would forgive Protestants, and Protestants forgive Catholics, Greeks would forgive Macedonians, Ukrainians and Poles would forgive each other, Israelites and Palestinians would forgive each other, and Aboriginals worldwide would forgive those who had sinned against them. In effect, everyone would be asked to forgive anyone who had trespassed against them at any time and agree to move forward together for the common good. It would be silly to suggest that forgiveness and reconciliation is easy. But the bottom line is that it is possible where there is a determination to make it the option of choice.

There is no better example of a modern miracle than the peaceful ending of apartheid in South Africa. So I am going to take the liberty of quoting at some length from the speech by Archbishop Desmond Tutu at the University of Toronto, where he was awarded an honorary Doctor of Law degree. He contrasted what had been happening in Russia, in Bosnia, in Kosovo – "all the upheaval, instability and bloodletting, with what had happened in South Africa.

"We have been richly blessed to have had at such a critical time in our history a Nelson Mandela. He was imprisoned for 27 years. Most expected that when he emerged from prison he would be riddled with bitterness, and a lust for revenge and retribution. Instead, the world has been amazed at this one who, instead of spewing calls for revenge, has urged his own people to be ready to forgive and to work for reconciliation. He has preached this gospel of forgiveness and reconciliation a great deal more by example than by precept. He has had lunch at the presidency with Percy Yutar, who was the prosecutor in the Rivonia trial, where Mandela and his colleagues were sentenced to life imprisonment. He invited to lunch the man who had argued for the death sentence to be passed in that trial.

"Wonderfully, Nelson Mandela has not been the only person committed to forgiveness and reconciliation. Less well known people are sometimes erroneously described as the 'ordinary' people – in my theology no one is ordinary, for each of us is created in the image of God and, thus, is God's viceroy. Many of the previously more anonymous, faceless victims of apartheid have shown that they are the real heroes and heroines of our struggle.

"One woman was injured in a hand-grenade attack by one of the liberation movements. She went into the intensive care unit and when she came out of hospital, she was still so badly injured that her children bathed her, clothed her and fed her. She came to tell us her story – that she could not go through a security checkpoint at the airport because she still had shrapnel in her body and all sorts of alarms would have been set off. She described the experience that left her in this condition – she said it 'enriched' her life. She said she would like to meet the perpetrator, she, a white woman, and he, almost certainly a black man, in the spirit of forgiveness."[15] The Bishop gave other examples.

One of the charges that Michael Arnheim leveled against Jesus in *Is Christianity True?* was that he was impractical for suggesting that we love our enemies. But it can and does happen. One of the most dramatic cases I know of involves Kim Phuc the Vietnamese girl whose photograph, as a napalm-covered child victim of the Vietnamese war, won Nick Ut a Pulitzer Prize. I was privileged to hear her tell her story when she spoke to the Ontario Prayer Breakfast in 1999. Everyone was stunned by the visuals.

On June 8, 1972, Kim Phuc, her family and others feared that their village of Trang Bang was about to be bombed. So they fled from the Cao Dai Temple, where they had taken refuge, and began running down the road toward the safety of South Vietnamese held positions. Alas, they were too late. A South Vietnamese Air Force pilot mistook them for enemy soldiers and attacked.

One of the bombs fell on the road immediately behind Kim. The napalm that sticks to and incinerates anything it touches splashed on her back, engulfing her in a cloud of smoke as her clothing combusted and the fiery jelly peeled the skin from her back and left arm. As the nine year old ran naked down the road, arms outstretched and screaming, "Too hot, too hot, help me," Út took the now famous picture!

Immediately after snapping the photograph, Út took Kim and the other injured children to a hospital where it was determined that the third degree burns to half of her body were so severe that it was doubtful she would survive. It was so painful to have her wounds washed and dressed that she lost consciousness whenever she was touched. But fate and an indomitable will decided she would live. After fourteen months and seventeen surgical procedures she was allowed to return home to the custody of her mother. Út continued to visit her until he was evacuated during the fall of Saigon three years later.

The world seemed to forget about the little girl in the photograph until 1984, when a Dutch film crew inquired about her whereabouts. It was then that the Vietnamese government decided she could be a useful propaganda tool. They tracked her down and began to manage her life. She deeply resented the endless interviews and photographs she was subjected to, and longed for relief from being used as an anti-war symbol.

The prime minister of Vietnam, Phạm Văn Đồng, became her friend and patron and she was granted permission to continue her studies in Cuba. While there, her life was to take an unexpected turn. She met a fellow Vietnamese student Bui Huy Toan, and they became good friends. There was talk of marriage but Kim was reluctant because he didn't share her faith. Four years earlier she had converted from her family's Cao Dai religion to Christianity. She had been attracted to the teachings of Jesus. After praying about it, and seeking God's guidance, she agreed to marry Toan and they were allowed, after Kim's plea to the Vietnamese ambassador, to go to Moscow for their honeymoon.

On the return flight, Kim confided to her husband that she intended to seek refuge in Canada when the plane landed in Gander, Newfoundland. She would get off and not get back on. A startled Toan, first reluctant, agreed. Following a nerve-racking and seemingly intermible wait, the plane took off without them and they were granted asylum. Kim recalls that they had nothing – no clothes, no family, no friends, no money, but they had the one thing she wanted most. Freedom! She was happy and knew that God would help her. The couple settled in a small town near Toronto, Ontario, and began a new life.

An important part of their new life would be Kim's ministry of healing, reconciliation and, most powerful of all, forgiveness. She has taken her message to many audiences but the most painful memories came during a visit to Washington to address a vast crowd of Vietnamese war veterans more than two decades after that fateful attack.

Kim remembers being scared. She began to speak: As you know, I am the little girl who was running to escape from the napalm fire. I do not want to talk about the war because I cannot change history. I only want you to remember the tragedy of war in order to do things to stop fighting and killing around the world. I have suffered a lot from both physical and emotional pain. Sometimes I thought I could not live but God saved me and gave me faith and hope. Even if I could talk face to face with the pilot who dropped the bombs I would tell him we cannot change history but we should try to do good things for the present.

Meanwhile, Reverend John Plummer, the former air force officer who had convinced himself (some say erroneously) that he was the one who had ordered the attack on Trang Bang, and who had suffered years of remorse, waited anxiously at the back of the crowd, desperate to meet Kim face to face and beg her forgiveness.

Plummer managed to scribble a note to Kim and request a private meeting. It must have reached Kim's escort because on the way to the police cruiser waiting to take her back to her hotel her host whispered,

"Kim you know that man you've been wanting to find?" "Yes." "He's right behind you."

She turned around and looked into a face of pain. She held her arms out. "Plummer fell into them. "I'm sorry, I'm so sorry …" "It's okay," she replied. "I forgive, I forgive."[16] The victims of war comforted one another, and for John Plummer, his twenty-four year nightmare was over.

**

Another deeply touching case of forgiveness involved an Amish community in Lancaster County, Pennsylvania, following the shooting death of five of their little school girls on October 2, 2006. As they struggled with the slayings they urged forgiveness of the killer. The Toronto *Globe and Mail* reported as follows.

" 'They know their children are going to heaven. They know their children are innocent … and they know that they will join them in death,' said Gertrude Huntington, a Michigan researcher and expert on children in Amish society.

" 'The hurt is very great,' Ms. Huntington said. 'But they don't balance the hurt with hate.'

"The Amish have also been reaching out to the family of the gunman, Charles Roberts, 32, who committed suicide during the attack … an Amish neighbor comforted the Roberts family hours after the shooting and extended forgiveness to them."[17]

**

A third example flowed from the tragic murder of Jason Lang while at his high school in April 1999, a story that sent shockwaves throughout Canada. The boy's parents, Dale and Diane Lang, riveted the attention of the country again just days later by forgiving the perpetrator of the terrible crime.[18]

I had the privilege of hearing Rev. Dale Lang tell the story at the Ontario Prayer Breakfast June 5, 2009. Like many others present I was moved to tears. When he finished I thought "Here is one of Jesus' followers who walks the talk." Sometimes it is incredibly difficult, but it is possible.

Connecting Faith and Works

I read an interesting article in *Maclean's* magazine of June 25, 2007 entitled "It's Take-an-Atheist-to-Church day: Jim the evangelist and Casper the unbeliever hit the road in a magical mystery sacred tour." Seattle evangelical pastor Jim Henderson wondered about the "lost" – the third of adults who do not regularly attend one of the nation's 335,000 churches – from returning to the fold. So he hired an atheist, Matt Casper, a San Diego copywriter and guitarist/singer in a band called Hell Yeah! to be his one-man focus group in a tour of 12 different churches, most of them evangelical mega congregations and one traditional place of worship with its "wood paneling and formal hymns" that made Henderson think it felt "more like an English hunting lodge than a church."

What was learned? "The megachurches all leave Casper cold, because of what he sees as a stress on self-improvement over help-thy neighbor: 'I didn't hear anything that I haven't heard Tony Robbins say better.'" Casper's politics seem obvious, and on their eighth church visit, he does broach what is probably the greatest source of secular hostility in contemporary America. "In far too many cases, saying you're a Christian means you're a Republican, at least to outsiders," he says. "If I were a Christian I'd be furious that those politicians – the Bush administration – dared to associate themselves with Christianity," he said. I know precisely what he meant. I grimace every time the subject is brought to my attention.

This may be an appropriate time to mention a point that was made at Yorkminster Park Baptist Church in Toronto. One Sunday, early in 2007 I think it was, the Rev. Dr. Peter Holmes, pastor of the church, began his sermon by saying "Sometimes I think the Christian Church should reinvent itself." I felt like shouting Halleluiah at the top of my voice. That would not have been appropriate at Yorkminster Park and, besides, I am just kidding because I am far too shy to open my mouth even if I knew that such an outburst would be welcome.

Yorkminster Park is an outreach church that earns it high marks. But all too often, especially in the uptown churches, there is scant concern for the kinds of people that Jesus cared about most. They very seldom refer to the passage in the Letter of James where Jesus' brother asserts that "Faith without works is dead." Indeed it is, because one is a manifestation of the other. Anyone of faith should be rushing around trying to build the

Kingdom of God on Earth, and not be concerned about tax cuts for the rich if this will result in less adequate education and health care for the poor. It is a point that applies to all faith groups, and not just Christians. So that is the reason we all have to work as Team World in building the kind of society that God has given us the skills and resources to do if we act positively, rather than waging wars for highly questionable reasons.

The Jesus for the World

The Lebanese Muslim friends we met when we visited Beirut in 2006 were quite open about their willingness to work with us in building a better world in the Spirit of Jesus. Not, they made clear, the Christian Jesus, whose name had been invoked by the Crusades, the Inquisition, and George Bush's wars on terror, but by the historical Jesus, one of the five Islamic prophets, who preached peace, justice and humility, and who eschewed violence. His message is one that makes sense in a war-torn, insecure and troubled world. So it is one they can endorse without abandoning their own religion and culture.

Samir Kreidie, who coined the phrase "The Jesus for the World" pointed out the many similarities between the Qur'an and the Bible. There are differences, of course, but the point was that in important ways we have common beliefs that are more important than our differences. Here is some of what he said.

"As a child I studied in the Evangelical School of Beirut. I studied the Bible and I was very impressed by the stories of all the prophets, especially by the teachings of Jesus. My father also put me into the tutelage of a sheikh in order to study our religion, which is Islam. I found I was studying the same stories, the same prophets, the same teachings, and the same principles. One day the sheikh told me that all Christians would go to hell and all Muslims who pray would go to heaven. [Sounds familiar.] It meant my good teacher Mrs. Smith, who I loved so much, was going to hell only because she was born a Christian, while Abu Ali, the butcher who was cruel to me and my friends, was going to heaven just because he happened to be a Muslim who prayed. I cried a lot for Mrs. Smith.

"As I was growing up this question was always in my mind. I started observing the world go into conflicts and wars and noted that one of their basic causes was religion. So I searched for the religion of God. I asked: Is he a Muslim, a Christian, a Jew, a Buddhist or what? I thoroughly studied the Qur'an, the Tawrat and the Bible. Again I found I was studying the same stories, the same prophets, the same teachings, and the same principles. I came to a conclusion that God does not have a religion. God is universal. He is for all the world. He is love. He is mercy. He is giving. I concluded that most conflicts and wars result from our ignorance, from not knowing our own religion and the religion of others. Religion as practiced by many today is a misrepresentation of the real spiritual idea and teaching of God. It is coated and surrounded with ignorance, with cultural, political and economic motives. If we removed all these coatings we are going to reach the same God, the same prophets, the same teachings and the same principles.

"Today many Muslims and Christians live together, study together, work together, and some even get married to each other. In spite of this, many of them do not know about the religion of each other. If only they really knew their own religion and the religion of the others, they would discover that they believe in the same prophets, the same teachings, the same principles, the same God. They would also discover that they agree on a much wider range of issues than it seems on the surface. They share the same religious history, philosophy and values although they differ in religious practices. The two sides think they disagree while actually they agree with each other.

"Let me give you an example that happened to me personally. Four months ago I gave a lecture in Lebanon in English. The topic was 'I am a Muslim and a Follower of Jesus.' The day following the lecture the newspapers wrote, 'Kreidie is a Muslim and a believer in Issa (the Arab name of Jesus in the Qur'an).' Many of my Muslim friends called me and congratulated me. They said it is good that I told the Christians that Jesus is not only for them but for the whole world. The second day another newspaper wrote, 'Kreidie is a Muslim and a believer in Yassoua (the Arab name of Jesus in the Gospel).' So all my Muslim friends called me, criticizing me for believing in the Christian Jesus. My friends, Jesus is Jesus. He is the same whether he is called Jesus or Issa or Yassoua or Nasiri or the son of man or the son of God."[19]

In early 2009 my dear friends Kent and Kay Hotaling sent me a new book titled *A Deadly Misunderstanding: A Congressman's Quest to Bridge the Muslim-Christian Divide*, by Mark D. Siljander, with a Foreword by

Ban-Ki-moon, Secretary-General of the United Nations.[20] It is the most exciting and hopeful book I have read in a long while.

Siljander tells his story of someone who, as an Evangelical Christian, walked out of the National Prayer Breakfast in Washington because a reading from the Qur'an was included in the program. Later he was challenged by a life-long leader in the Fellowship and this started him on a road and a journey that he would not have dreamed possible.

A natural linguist he began to read the Qur'an in Arabic, the language in which it was written. He also read the New Testament in Aramaic and learned that nearly all of the misunderstandings between Muslims and Christians are due to the Greek and then English texts that distort the original meanings. Siljander spends most of his time in constructive debate with Muslim and Christian clerics and scholars.

It is a remarkable story that can't be condensed so I strongly recommend that it be read by all pastors and imams alike. The bottom line is that after reasoned discussion there is wide agreement that God (Allah) is Supreme, and that Jesus' message is one around which we can unite in the pursuit of peace on earth and goodwill toward one another.

Jews, too, should be able to cooperate in the Spirit of Jesus of Nazareth. His message was not new, as they keep pointing out. Loving God with all their heart and soul and strength is the first and great commandment and it just happens to be one that is common to Judaism, Islam and Christianity. The Second Commandment is like it "You shall love your neighbor as yourself." This too, was not new as my Jewish friends like to point out. It was included in the third book of Moses: "You shall not take vengeance, nor bear any grudge against the children of your people, but you shall love your neighbor as yourself: I am the Lord."[21] The only difference is that in Leviticus the rule only applied to the twelve Jewish Tribes whereas Jesus (like some Rabbis before him) identified it as one of the two great commandments.

The idea of treating our neighbors as ourselves – The Golden Rule – seems to be a common thread of all religions. The problem has been, and remains, that all too often we don't pay any attention to it and that is where major change is called for. So we have here a platform on which people of all faiths could build together.

Each group will have to develop its own action plan, but for the Christian Church, the one with which I am most familiar, I have a suggestion for action that might also lead to revitalization. Once a month, cut the weekly worship service by twenty minutes or so by reducing the sermon to a five minute pep talk, and then breaking into small groups meeting around pre-arranged stations where a list of specific kingdom-building projects would be available for discussion and assignments for action. Mechanisms would be required for collecting ideas but these could be supplemented by spontaneous contributions. At each session a review of success with earlier assignments would be a useful guide for new participants and repeaters alike.

Kingdom Builders

Every group will have to make up their own list of items relevant to their country and environment. The following is a brief list applicable to my North American experience. It isn't intended to be comprehensive, but merely a starting point.

* Smile more. This first one is for me. I have often taken myself too seriously. People who greet me with a smile brighten my day, and I readily reciprocate. But I will have to work at taking the initiative more often.

* Plant a tree, or several trees. Not only do they add shade and beauty, the future of the planet is at stake.

* Eat about one-third less, on average. This is especially relevant to our American cousins. When I was peddling one of my books in Chicago a few years ago I ordered lamb, potatoes and yellow beans. When the order came I was presented with a whole platter of lamb – enough for a family of four, at least – and the side dishes, too, were food enough for several people. Cutting back would reduce the level of obesity, and make more food available for export which would help moderate food prices at a time when shortages are leading to riots in some countries.

* Be a Big Brother or a Big Sister to some child in need of the advantage of relating to and being cared for by another adult.

* Cut a neighbor's lawn or shovel the snow from their driveway when they are too old or too sick to do it themselves.

* Contact the owners of businesses that only provide recorded options without recourse to a live person in the event none of the options fits your case. Ask them politely to add the option of speaking to a knowledgeable operator. If after being asked nicely they refuse to act, organize a boycott to get their attention.

* Volunteer some period of time to teach school or work in a hospital in some foreign country desperately in need of such services.

* Buy paint and organize a party to paint part or all of a home – rented or owned – by someone who cannot afford to maintain it properly.

* Take up a collection to buy a goat or a camel for some poor family in Africa. Just a few weeks before writing this I read a story in one of the Toronto newspapers where it reported a young African girl had finished high school and was enrolling in a Canadian university all because her parents had been provided with a goat by one of the several Kingdom-Building NGOs that do such good work.

* Drive more cautiously and patiently. Just remember that the idiot that passed on the wrong side to cut in on you might be a reflection of you on some other occasion.

* Avoid conspicuous consumption. Some of the humungous houses being built for the *nouveau riche* are several times bigger than required. Also, two houses and a couple of cars should be more than enough for most of us. If these and a small yacht don't use up our disposable income give some of the surplus to someone who has no house and no car – perhaps doesn't even have enough to eat.

* Organize a work gang to clean up some garbage-strewn park or river valley.

* Organize a work party to plant or tend some flowers around your church, synagogue, temple, mosque or shrine.

* Collect books and clothing to give to people who can use them.

* Babysit for an evening or a weekend to allow some couple desperately in need of a night off or a weekend away from their children to have one.

* Visit someone in hospital – a friend or even someone you don't know, and take a single rose, carnation or flower from your garden to brighten their day.

* Join a prison ministry and visit someone in prison, or help a former prisoner reintegrate into civil life. His or her success in doing so will be the most important factor in whether or not they are tempted to commit another crime.

* Make a special effort to recycle more and waste less. Make a greater effort to save and collect hazardous waste for special treatment to prevent it from being dumped into landfill sites where it will contaminate your or

your neighbors' water supply. Remember the pollution may not be in your backyard but you never know where that polluted water will wind up and it could be in your drinking supply.

Spend some time thinking about items you would have added to this list and make them part of your own.

ONE WORLD – ONE VISION

The night before writing this last page of the chapter I watched a reprise of the Opening Ceremony of the 29th Olympiad (modern era) in Beijing, China. I was absolutely stunned by the imagination and ingenuity that had gone into the preparations for the show and by the precision and beauty of its presentation. It was beyond doubt the most unforgettable spectacle I have ever seen.

The thought crossed my mind as to what kind of a wonderful world we could have if China, the United States, Russia, India, and the rest of us all pooled our creative imagination and ingenuity to build the kind of world environment that one can only dream of. It could be the brave new world that is so often written about, and talked about, but has so far escaped realization because we spend and waste so much of our best talent and available resources preparing to fight and kill each other.

The greatest challenge of our lives is to change course before it is too late and concentrate on that brave new wonderful world for the benefit of all humankind as well as our cousins visiting from other parts of the cosmos.

Paul Hellyer with his boss Prime Minister Lester B. (Mike) Pearson

Defence Minister Hellyer doing a jackstay crossing from the aircraft carrier Bonaventure to the destroyer Restigouche.

Hellyer having a word with Secretary of State Dean Rusk at a NATO meeting in Paris

Paul being introduced to President Jimmy Carter and Mrs. Carter at the National Prayer Breakfast in Washington.

Paul dropping in to say hello to President Gerald Ford at a formal dinner in Toronto.

Hellyer with Prime Minister Pierre E. Trudeau at Rideau Hall in Ottawa.

The Hellyer family at Arundel Lodge on Paul's 80th birthday. (back row) Peter, Ellen, Paul and David; (middle row) Jordan, Emily, Catherine, Kathy, Mary Elizabeth and Michael; (seated) Joshua and Katie

Kay and Kent Hotaling, Sandra and Paul Hellyer exploring the Middle East in April 2006.

Paul with Dr. Michael Salla and Ambassador John W. McDonald at the Extraterrestrial Civilizations and World Peace Conference, Big Island, Hawaii, June 2006.

Photo of UFO (upper right) taken by Jeff Cherry from the Arundel Lodge dock in Muskoka, Ontario, at dusk, June 26, 2008.

CHAPTER 7

MAMMON RULES THE WORLD

"We are grateful to the Washington Post, the New York Times, Time magazine and other great publications, whose directors have attended our meetings and respected their promises of discretion for almost forty years. It would have been impossible for us to develop our plan for the world if we had been subjected to the lights of publicity during those years. But, the world is more sophisticated and prepared to march towards a world government. The supranational sovereignty of an intellectual elite and world bankers is surely preferable to the national auto-determination practiced in past centuries."

David Rockefeller[1]

There you have it! In a one paragraph "thank you" to attendees at the close of a meeting of Bilderbergers at Baden Baden in Germany, David Rockefeller sums up what the New World Order is all about – the substitution of elite rule for democracy. I believe this is an accurate summation of his philosophy because everything he and his close associates have done since World War II has been a building block in the New World Order, also known as One World Government, by a handful of autocrats controlled either directly or indirectly by a few of the world's richest and most powerful elite.

Worse, the implementation to date has been so slick and smooth as to appear like a natural and inevitable evolution when, in fact, it has been neither. It has been a coldly calculated and ruthlessly implemented business plan to concentrate power, control and wealth in the hands of a corporal's guard of rich men and women – mostly men, as you won't see many women enter the secret conclaves of the Bilderbergers annual meetings.

Why should we be concerned? Because Jesus made it very clear that one cannot serve God and mammon, and far too many of us have chosen mammon. The result, of course, is that the rich are getting richer, and the poor are getting poorer, at least relatively and, of late, in many cases absolutely. Millions of people are dying from starvation and ill health because the distribution systems controlled by, and the priorities established by, the rich and powerful are not geared to meet the needs of the world's impoverished. They make a lot more money by launching cold and hot wars.

It is not always easy to identify the players in the global monopoly game by the colors of their uniforms, especially when some of them have more than one color in their desk drawers. But it is widely known that there are three related teams involved, with the possibility of one more to be identified later. The three are the Council on Foreign Relations, the Bilderbergers, and the Trilateral Commission, in order of appearance.

The Council on Foreign Relations

The Council on Foreign Relations (CFR or Council) is the oldest of the three. Although it was active in the 1920s, it only came into a position of great influence with the outbreak of World War II. As early as October 1940, years before Germany surrendered to the Allied armies to vaporize Hitler's vision of Empire, the Council's Economic and Financial Group drafted a memorandum outlining a comprehensive policy, "… to set forth the political, military, territorial and economic requirements of the United States in its potential leadership of the non-German world area including the United Kingdom itself as well as the Western hemisphere and Far East.[2]

The "Grand Area," as the non-German block was called in 1941, was insufficiently grand. The preferred ideal was all-inclusive – one world economy dominated by the United States.[3] It was at this stage that there was a virtual merger of the Council and the U.S. State Department which, in late 1941, created a special committee to consider positive planning, the Advisory Committee on Positive Foreign Policy, on which Council members played important roles, and set the stage for key decisions that would affect the post-war world.

The Council influenced plans for international economic institutions including the International Monetary Fund (IMF) and the International Bank for Reconstruction and Development (World Bank), no doubt with the noblest intentions. It was also deeply involved in the creation of the United Nations where the motive appeared to be more self-serving. At a meeting in May 1942, one of the Council members, Isaiah Bowman, argued that the United States had to exercise the strength to assure "security," and at the same time, "avoid conventional forms of imperialism."[4] The way to do this, he suggested, was to make the exercise of that power international in character through a United Nations body.[5]

The Council made no attempt to disguise the fact that the purpose of the Grand Area and later world hegemony was to support an expanding U.S. economy – to provide it with raw materials, and markets for its products. This was labeled the "national interest." It was equally clear that the "national interest" was the interest of the ruling elite whose members comprised the Council. The real interests of the majority of rank-and-file Americans was never a factor in the equation.

The Bilderbergers

Bilderberg was the brainchild of Dr. Joseph Retinger, a top aide to General Wladyslaw Sikorski, head of the Polish government in exile in London. Even during World War II he suggested regular meetings of the foreign ministers of continental countries and established close relationships with men who were to become post-war leaders.

After the war, Retinger explained his concern for European unification in a meeting at Chatham House, home of the Royal Society on International Affairs, the British equivalent of the Council on Foreign Relations. His recipe for a divided Europe, which had rejected both Hitler's New World and communism, was to move towards a federal union of neighboring European countries, in which the states would "relinquish part of their sovereignty."[6]

The idea was not new, of course, but Retinger gave it currency at a critical time in the post-war development of Europe. He was also a catalyst in establishing closer ties between Europe and America at a time when there was a lot of anti-Americanism on the continent. It was as a result of this process that the group which became known as the Bilderbergers evolved.

The name comes from the group's first meeting place, the Hotel de Bilderberg of Oosterbeek, Holland, in May 1954. The meeting was chaired by Prince Bernhard of Holland who, along with Paul Rykens of Unilever, drew up the original list of participants, two from each country, with representatives of business, banking, politics, academia, etc. with a fair balance of conservative and liberal views that were not too far left – as perceived by the Prince and the steering committee chosen by him. The group was pragmatic enough to ensure that their views would carry weight regardless of who formed a government of the day.

One should not discount the positive influence the group has had on inter-governmental relations and the resolution of international problems. It has contributed to just about every major debate the West has faced. Membership, which is not officially acknowledged, reads like a Who's Who of power and influence. President John F. Kennedy virtually staffed the State Department with Bilderberg alumni, including Secretary of State Dean Rusk and Under-Secretary of State George W. Ball.

In fact it is only the elite members of society who are asked to attend. They are people who, as a result of their position, power or influence, can help propagate the Bilderberg consensus on any subject. While this has sometimes been a good thing, it can also be a bad thing because Bilderbergers tend to equate their personal interests with the public interest. The New World Order, with its seamless market and vanishing borders, would, for most of them, enhance their power and wealth. They are probably incapable of believing that it would be bad for the world's masses.

The Trilateral Commission

The youngest of the three major groups pushing globalization and a New World Order is the Trilateral Commission, which was officially founded in July 1973. Its roots can be traced to Zbigniew Brzezinski, then a professor at Columbia University. He wrote a series of papers acknowledging Japan's increasing power and influence on the world stage, and then organized the Tripartite Studies under the auspices of the Brookings Institution, known in Washington as the think-tank for democratic administrations.

These studies helped convince David Rockefeller that trilateralism could be a useful instrument in building a community of interest between North America, Western Europe and Japan at a time when relations between the three were deteriorating. When he and Brzezinski presented the idea of a trilateral arrangement to the Bilderberg annual meeting in 1972 it received an enthusiastic response – the endorsement Rockefeller needed to follow up and make the dream a reality.

This organization is the most open with regard to aims and objectives. It is elitist and anti-democratic. A 1975 report entitled "The Crisis of Democracy: Report on the Governability of Democracies to the Trilateral Commission," states: "The vulnerability of democratic government in the United States comes not primarily from external threats, though such threats are real, not from internal subversion from the left or right, although both possibilities could exist, but rather from internal dynamics of democracy itself in a highly educated, mobilized and participant society."[7] Wow, the principal danger to democratic government is democracy! That is a concept that you have to dig deep to come up with. What about the danger to democracy of actions taken by governments "elected" by the people, but only after being chosen and installed in positions of leadership by these elite groups?

The political power of the Trilats, a convenient abbreviation that I will use to cover the joint and several influences of the Commission, the Council on Foreign Relations and the Bilderbergers, is ominous! When they became concerned about the protectionist measures of the Nixon administration, they began to look around for someone to replace him. The name of Jimmy Carter appeared on a short list of three and he was the one who ultimately got the nod. It was the Trilat connections in the media who helped an obscure agronomist achieve national prominence and become a leading contender for the Democratic Party nomination for president. The operation succeeded as planned and when Carter became president he named seventeen Trilats to important positions in his administration.[8]

When after four years the Trilats became somewhat disillusioned with Carter, they decided to replace him with another of their own, George Bush.[9] A small problem arose when Bush ran for the Republican nomination. Opponents in five states ran full-page ads saying: "The same people who gave you Jimmy Carter are giving you George Bush." In the face of this setback the Trilats had to settle for a Reagan-Bush ticket and George Bush had to bide his time while Reagan, who had been looked upon with some skepticism, really came through for them with the Canada-U.S. Free Trade Agreement.

Later, after George Bush finally had his turn the Trilats picked another one of their own, Bill Clinton, to be their standard bearer. Clinton attended the Bilderberger meeting in 1991 where the desirability of a North American Free Trade Agreement was mentioned to him.[10] He returned as the "anointed" one and although his personal life made the road to stardom a somewhat rocky one, with the help of his powerful allies he prevailed.

Clinton's pay-off to his benefactors was profound and continuing. Most dramatic was his successful negotiation of the North American Free Trade Agreement (NAFTA) in order to provide the U.S. Round Table on Business (and Canadian business, too, including U.S.-owned business in Canada that were generous contributors to the propaganda campaign) unrestricted access to an unlimited supply of cheap Mexican labor. This process was ably recorded in *The Selling of "Free Trade": NAFTA, Washington and the Subversion of U.S. Democracy*, by John R. MacArthur, publisher of *Harper's* magazine.[11] It is a case history of the manipulation of the Congress which anyone interested in politics should read.

Of even greater long-term significance, Clinton transformed the Democratic Party from one that sometimes listened to and cared about the concerns of traditional allies including trade unionists, environmentalists, the poor and social activists, into just another party only marginally but not too significantly different from the Republican Party. His robust promotion of "Free Trade," including the proposed Free Trade Area of the Americas (FTAA), robbed U.S. nationalists, and other thoughtful Americans concerned about the serious loss of sovereignty, from any effective voice in determining their future. The Clinton rightward shift was an answer to the Trilats prayers. He also denied American voters the kind of ideological choice that they traditionally enjoyed, and so desperately need.

The Free Trade Panacea

I must admit that I am a free trader at heart, and always have been. One of my first speeches in the Canadian House of Commons more than half a century ago was on that subject. At that time I proposed a two percent annual reduction in tariffs that would see them eliminated in fifty years. It was a rate of reduction that would allow a gradual change that could easily be absorbed without any drastic upheaval in living standards in the more industrialized countries.

Perhaps the same goal could have been achieved in twenty-five years without unacceptable disruption; but there was no way we could foresee the "Shock and Awe" approach that the big guns were eventually able to implement with its gut-wrenching consequences for manufacturing industries in the more advanced countries. But then few of us had any notion of what was really going on in the world as I can attest from the reaction to some of my earlier writings on the subject.

A principal aim of One World advocates was to gain access to cheap labor so they could reduce costs without any corresponding reduction in the prices of their products, thereby increasing profit margins significantly. In the process they succeeded in reversing decades of social progress on every front. They could, at a stroke, undo the wage gains unions had won in the post-World War II years through hard-fought negotiations. As a result of moving production to cheap labor countries, they were able to employ child labor, in a manner reminiscent of Dickensian England. The cheap labor, adult or child, would lack the protection of workplace safety standards, and would toil without the negotiated health and welfare benefits enjoyed by the workers being displaced. And, of course, the industrialists could pollute to their hearts' content in places where concern for clean air, water and soil were not yet on the public radar.

The undeniable benefits to the manufacturers could only be realized in a world where their products could not be denied entry into traditional markets simply because they were made under circumstances that would be quite unacceptable in the importing country. This meant changing the whole woof and warp of international law in a way that would remove from politicians the right to legislate in the real interests of their electors because they were rendered powerless under the terms of new international treaties.

The Canada-U.S. Free Trade Agreement (FTA)

*"The Canadians don't understand what they have signed.
In 20 years they will be sucked into the U.S. economy."*

Clayton Yeutter[12]

Yeutter denies having said this, but an eye and ear witness disagrees, and the prophecy proved to be well founded. The Canada-U.S. agreement, of which Yeutter was a senior negotiator, was one of the first of its kind – a template for the New World Order that the people who really run the U.S. envisaged. Like the vast majority of my fellow Canadians, I was naïve enough to believe that the FTA was a trade agreement, because that is what I heard on television and radio and what I read in the newspapers. It was also what the governments were telling us, and the message that big business was hammering home in its full-page ads.

Most Canadians still believe that "free trade" means free trade. But it doesn't! It is much more complicated than that. Anyone who has actually read the FTA or its successor the North American Free Trade Agreement (NAFTA), as I eventually did, will know that these treaties are primarily about investment and corporate rights.

Of course the FTA eliminated tariffs between the two countries over a ten-year period but these were already coming off under the General Agreement on Tariffs and Trade (GATT). So by the time the FTA was signed, the vast majority of items were already duty free; and for those items where tariffs still applied, Canada had an advantage because our tariffs were higher than those in the U.S. – an advantage we gave up without getting anything in return.

From the outset the two countries had very different objectives. These were stated during an initial meeting of Prime Minister Brian Mulroney's Chief of Staff, Derek Burney, and Senior Deputy United States Trade Representative, Michael B. Smith, on July 31, 1985. Canadians wanted just two things: "Exemption from U.S. Dumping and Anti-Subsidy Laws, and a gradual phase in, indeed a back-end loading of tariff eliminations." The U.S. had two demands: "Immediate abolition of the infamous Foreign Investment Review Board (FIRB), and a faster implementation of tariff reductions, given the fact that Canadian tariffs were already higher than U.S. tariffs."[13]

In the end, the Americans achieved both of their demands and Canada struck out on its two bottom line objectives. We did not get an exemption from U.S. anti-dumping and countervailing duty laws which can be applied almost capriciously whenever the American political situation demands, and have been, as anyone in the softwood lumber or several other contentious industries can attest. So Canada did not get the "guaranteed access" to U.S. markets that PM Mulroney had promised. But the Americans did get their "license to buy Canada" which was what the treaty was all about.

In effect, it was the Trilats first "shot across the bow" to show free countries, in a free world, that they were no longer free to run their affairs in the best interests of their citizens but must bow the knee to "King Capital," who would henceforth be able to determine their destinies. In the first fifteen years after the signing of the treaty about 13,000 Canadian companies were sold to foreigners – the majority to our cousins south of the border. And the pace never slackened as the global monopoly game got under way in earnest.

Of course the European members of the "Club" got in on the act which is now worldwide. The aim of the game is, as always, to eliminate competition to the point where market forces are replaced by market power, at the consumers' expense. In effect the elite wanted to achieve in nickel, aluminum, food and other industries what they had already achieved in oil – a result that is all too obvious at the gas pump.

In recent years some of Canada's few remaining global companies like International Nickel Company and Alcan Manufacturing have been bought out and all of our steel manufacturers are now foreign-owned. In addition, an increasing percentage of our oil and gas resource companies have been bought by foreigners. The march toward oligopoly continues.

In the course of the 2008 U.S. presidential race more than one candidate hinted that if elected, they would abrogate NAFTA and seek a better treaty. Instead of being alarmed at the prospect, I was one of the few Canadians who relished the thought that the U.S. might do what spineless Canadian leaders have refused to do – give the six month's notice for abrogation and start at once to negotiate a "Fair Trade" agreement that would embody "free trade" while allowing us to regain some control over the destiny of our own industries and resources.

This idea is anathema to most of our bureaucrats and editorialists who have been thoroughly brainwashed by the ideology of seamless borders. Canadians point to the benefits of free trade without analyzing the bottom line. They have been mesmerized by the numbers. The cross-border volume has sky-rocketed, so these figures are cited as proof positive that the FTA and NAFTA have been big contributors to Canada's prosperity. But figures lie, or at least they don't tell the whole truth.

Canada's biggest gains in exports to the U.S. since the FTA was signed have been in automobiles and energy. In both cases the connection to the FTA, if any, has been minimal. In the case of automobiles, the increase was largely attributable to the Auto Pact with the U.S. which represented Canadian "protectionism" at its best and most successful – an advantage that no longer exists under the New World Order, so we see more of our hugely successful auto industry now disappearing almost daily.

The most dramatic increase in exports, by far, has been electricity, natural gas and crude oil. This has been due to the nearly insatiable demand for energy south of the border and will continue to increase with or without NAFTA. The agricultural sector, too, has done well. Canadian farmers did everything right; they expanded exports three times but their net income remained static. That has been the bottom line. Despite all of the increased activity, average Canadians are little if any better off vis-à-vis average Americans than they were in 1989 when the Free Trade Agreement came into effect. So some people have benefited from the agreements, but for the rest of us it has just been treading water.

Globalization and the New World Order

"The New World without borders will be like a zoo without cages. Only the most powerful of the species will survive."

Paul Hellyer

It is important to point out at the outset that "globalization" is not just one big ball of wax. An analogy that I find useful is to compare it to cholesterol. There is good cholesterol and bad cholesterol. The good cholesterol is life-enhancing, whereas the bad cholesterol can kill you.

Similarly there is good globalization and bad globalization. The good globalization is technologically driven. The Internet, for example, apart from its addictive qualities, or the temptation to wander of in search of pornography or gambling, is a marvelous benefit of technology. It opens up a whole new world of knowledge and information on a scale hitherto undreamed of. And its benefits are widely dispersed, and can save writers weeks or months in checking facts and sources, for example. Satellite phones are another useful marvel.

These widely-enjoyed benefits are in sharp contrast to bad globalization which is agenda driven. The agenda is the coldly calculated business plan of the richest, most powerful people in the world to re-engineer the global economy and governance in a way that will increase their overly generous slice of the economic pie even further.

In theory, the New World Order, as President George W. Bush called it, is a world without economic borders. It is a kind of *laissez-faire* economic Darwinism, where capital is King of the jungle. It has been labeled neo-classical economics, a revised but unrepentant version of the ideas of Milton Friedman and his colleagues from the University of Chicago, and sometimes known as the Washington Consensus, the rules by which the world must be run. Whatever the tag, the transformation that has been under way is so far-reaching as to be almost beyond belief.

If it is allowed to run its course, no country will be able to protect its industries even long enough for them to mature to the point where they could compete in a global market. Neither could any nation state set higher environmental standards than the market would tolerate, nor protect its labor from exploitation without paying a high price in jobs lost to countries where 19th century standards remain in effect.

No country would be able to prevent the sale of an industry to a foreign player wishing to (a) include it in its empire, or (b) shut it down to eliminate the competition, or (c) move it to another country where lower wages and environmental standards would permit higher profits. Under the new rules, foreigners can buy your natural resources and export them without any value added in the country of origin.

Under its benevolent wrapping, globalization is a plan to strip elected representatives at all levels of government of their power to legislate on behalf of ordinary people, and to transfer that power to unelected, unaccountable international bureaucrats implementing rules laid down by the globalizers. It is a plan to end popular democracy as we have known it and substitute a plutocracy of the wealthy elite.

It doesn't require much imagination to understand what the New World Order will be like. For most people it will be a life of total powerlessness. In the case of small and medium powers, like Canada, for example, there will be the added frustration of seeing the level of excellence already achieved slowly ebbing away, and with it their significance as a nation state. As companies are bought by foreigners, and head offices move, the good jobs disappear. The tax base is also eroded because foreign-owned companies pay less tax than domestically-owned companies.

At the same time, one country after another is losing its right to use its own central bank to help finance essential services when the tax revenue from other sources is being eroded. It is not by accident that countries are being encouraged to adopt either the U.S. dollar or the euro as a replacement for their own currency. It is all part of a scheme to rob people of one of their most valuable assets so the rich can second them – a scam to which I will return later.

Brainwashing

You may well wonder how such a grand larceny, on a global scale, could be sold to an unsuspecting public. So too, apparently, did its sponsors.

Greg Palast, author of *The Best Democracy Money Can Buy*, and whistle-blower extraordinaire, has unearthed some fascinating information about secret meetings between European and American captains of industry and finance. He even managed to get minutes of some of their meetings. In an interview with *Acres USA*, Palast had this to say.

"One of the most amazing things in one of these meetings is when they talk about how to sell globalization to the public. They can't figure out how to sell this thing to the public because they can't figure out what the benefits of globalization really are to the average person. They actually sat there and said: 'Why don't we pay some professors a bunch of money, and get them to come up with a study that globalization is good for people?'

"Then the officer for Reuters, the big news service that's in every big paper on the planet, said: 'You come up with the material and we'll help you out, we'll place the stories in the papers.' It really freaked me out to find this propaganda system to sell people on the means of their own economic destruction.' "[14]

I don't know why Palast was so surprised. The neo-cons, who are mostly a bunch of very rich old cons, have been peddling their propaganda for decades. And they have provided a real "bunch of money" to hire dozens of accommodating professors to write myriad papers proving beyond reasonable doubt that black is white.

As far back as 1943, a group of anti-New Deal businessmen established the American Enterprise Institute. It provided intellectual public relations in the 1950s and 1960s working directly with members of Congress, the federal bureaucracy and the media.[15]

The Heritage Foundation is another one of the best-known U.S. think tanks due to the close association it had with Ronald Reagan, and its powerful influence on his policies. Its success inspired the creation of thirty-seven mini-Heritages across the U.S. providing synergy, an illusion of diversity, and the impression that the experts quoted actually represented a broad spectrum of views. Other, smaller U.S. think tanks include the venerable Hoover Institution on War, Revolution and Peace; the Cato Institute and the Manhattan Institute for Policy Research.[16]

The United Kingdom has its own network including the Centre for Policy Studies, the anti-statist Institute of Economic Affairs, and the Adam Smith Institute. Even Canada is not immune from the propaganda factories. We have the very influential Fraser Institute in British Columbia, the C.D. Howe Institute in Toronto, and a number of new regional institutes based on the same model.

These institutions have much in common. They are financed by foundations and large corporations which are anti-populist in philosophy. In general they believe that the least government is the best government; that nation states have outlived their usefulness; that markets are infallible regulators of economic activity; and that the rich have no obligation to share their wealth with the poor on whom they depend for labor and as customers for their goods and services.

This, then, is the philosophy of the captains of industry and finance that Greg Palast said had been meeting secretly to promote their globalization agenda. These same people, who are re-engineering the world for their own benefit, have no compunction about using both governments and international institutions as batboys to carry their bats for them. They use them to promote international treaties that diminish the power of nation states to act on behalf of their citizens; to jaw-bone poor countries into selling their assets at firesale prices; and to help enforce contracts even when those contracts were not negotiated in good faith and were much more favorable to one side than the other. As Joseph E. Stiglitz, former chief economist of the World Bank says: "There is, in fact, a long history of 'unfair' contracts, which Western governments have used their muscle to enforce."[17] The following few pages cite data and relate stories that are not current but, nevertheless, provide important background as to how the crisis of 2008 became inevitable.

The Axis of Evil: The IMF, World Bank, and WTO

If President George W. Bush wanted to find a real axis of evil he had only to look at the International Monetary Fund, the Bank for Reconstruction and Development (World Bank), and the World Trade Organization.

In an earlier book I refer to the first two, the IMF and World Bank, as "The Enforcers" of globalization. They are the bullies that carry the big sticks and beat the bejeebers out of any country that won't accept the Washington Consensus and open its borders to rape and pillage by international banks and multinational corporations. The Enforcers work hand and glove with the U.S. Department of the Treasury (DOT) and Wall Street, for which the DOT acts as agent.

The World Trade Organization is a new addition to the evil axis. It had earned this distinction for actions past, present and planned. It has been enforcing global rules written by or for Wall Street moguls, for the benefit of the industrial heavyweights at the expense of the lightweights and featherweights. It has invariably ruled in favor of commerce at the expense of the environment and, finally, the rules proposed for a General Agreement on Trade in Services (GATS) will remove from legislators in nation states most of their residual power to act on behalf of their electors. So the WTO has to be admitted as a member of the club but, for now, we should concentrate on the frightening record of the other two.

Both were born in 1944 at the Bretton Woods Conference and both had laudable mandates. The IMF lost its *raison d'être* however, when most of the world switched from fixed to floating exchange rates, and it was no longer necessary to provide nations with the temporary cash to prevent a devaluation of their currency. The World Bank meanwhile, borrowed money on world financial markets and lent it to Third World countries to build roads, bridges and dams – especially dams – until those countries were up to their eyeballs in debt.

They were just able to take an occasional breath in order to survive when along came the monetarist economics of Milton Friedman and his colleagues, with its ridiculously high interest rates, and they were swamped. Servicing enormous debt at 5% interest was extremely difficult. To pay 18%, after U.S. Federal Reserve Board Chairman Paul Volcker raised rates to that dizzying height in 1980, was impossible! Absolutely impossible!

It was Volcker's subsequent determination to rescue the investment of his New York banker friends, that had been put in jeopardy by his interest rate policy, that paved the way to the grand larceny of the 1980s, 1990s and beyond. Chairman Volcker realized that several South American countries were technically bankrupt. He also realized that all of the major New York banks were technically insolvent as a consequence. So he insisted that the banks lend the debtor countries more money so they could pay the interest on their existing debt, until he could persuade the IMF to ride to the rescue with taxpayers' money. That way the loans would appear to be performing when, in fact, they were non-performing. Had the public been exposed to the truth, there might have been a financial panic.

The IMF did in fact ride to the rescue of the poor countries but not in order to save them, it was to rescue the foreign investors. At last it had found a new *raison d'être*. It would be the life raft for international capital to see it safely home after being invested irresponsibly in Third World countries.

The IMF performed this role so well that it was recruited by Wall Street and the U.S. Treasury Department to become the sword-carrier for the imposition of the Washington Consensus on financially destitute countries everywhere. Its "success" was so great that it eventually ran out of money. Consequently its sponsors had to persuade the World Bank, too, to augment its traditional role and learn the skills of a sword-bearer on behalf of market fundamentalism.

The Washington Consensus became synonymous with market fundamentalism, and the principal American intellectual export since anti-communism lost its currency. Although widely known as the Washington

Consensus, and sometimes simply as "free trade," this gospel became the basis for an American "Crusade" to "liberate" people everywhere, and save them from poverty and archaic economic notions – the latter obviously considered as cause and effect in the minds of the "liberators." William Finnegan, in an article entitled "The Economics of Power," published in *Harper's* magazine, describes the strategic battle plan.

"It [The Washington Consensus] is promulgated directly through U.S. foreign policy and indirectly through multilateral institutions such as the World Bank, the International Monetary Fund, and the World Trade Organization. Its core tenets are deregulation, privatization, 'openness' (to foreign investment, and to exports [from foreign countries]), unrestricted movement of capital, and lower taxes. Presented with special force to developing countries as a formula, a theory, of how the world should be run, under American supervision. Attacking America is, therefore, attacking the theory, and attacking the theory is attacking America."[18]

The theory has now been in effect in varying degrees for more than thirty years since the central banks of the western world adopted the monetarist, "markets in, governments out" ideas of Milton Friedman and his colleagues in 1974; and in dead earnest for almost thirty years since Friedman's disciple Paul Volcker decided to put monetarist theories to the test. The time has come to apply the old adage, "The test of the pudding is in the eating." The theory has been given ample opportunity to demonstrate its worth. A few examples, of what could be an entire book on the subject, are illustrative.

In exchange for financial assistance from the World Bank and the IMF the government of Tanzania was required to agree to 157 conditions. Trade barriers were cut, government subsidies were restricted and state industries were sold off. In just fifteen years, according to Nancy Alexander of the Washington-based Globalization Challenge Institute, Tanzania's GDP dropped from $309 to $210 per capita, the literacy rate is falling and the rate of abject poverty has jumped to 51 percent of the population.[19]

Bolivia is a country of great natural wealth but where nearly all the benefit goes to foreigners. When it emerged from many years of military rule in the early 1980s the country was in deep trouble due to looting by the generals. Its foreign debt was overwhelming and its annual rate of inflation was 24,000 percent. It was ripe for the radical treatment recommended by the young American economist Jeffrey Sachs, who later became known for designing "shock therapy" plans for countries emerging from communism – which some have credited with the near-destruction of the Russian economy.

For Bolivia the therapy included a drastic devaluation of the currency, abolition of minimum wages, and drastic cutbacks in government expenditures. As a result the country was plunged into a deep recession. Wages fell and unemployment skyrocketed. But prices were stabilized and the Bolivian government's good relations with its foreign creditors, and especially with "The Enforcers" were restored.

World Bank development loans helped keep the country afloat, and it and the IMF took control of large areas of public policy. Like many poor countries, Bolivia was subjected to the rigors of market fundamentalism, a term William Finnegan describes as: "a set of standardized, far-reaching austerity and 'openness' measures that typically include the removal of restrictions on foreign investment, the abolition of public subsidies and labor rights, reduced state spending, deregulation, lower tariffs, tighter credit, the encouragement of export-oriented industries, lower marginal tax rates, currency devaluation, and the sale of major public enterprises. In Bolivia's case, the latter included the national railways, the national airlines, the telephone system, the country's vast tin mines, and a long list of municipal utilities."[20]

Argentina has been a test case for economic fundamentalism, and the New World Order. It did everything right throughout the 1990s – privatization, deregulation, trade liberalization, tax reform – and became Exhibit A for the true believers in *laissez-faire* economics, until shortly before its collapse in 2001. Since then it has become Exhibit A for those who say that monetarism or neo-liberalism – whatever you want to call it – is junk economics.

In early 2002 Greg Palast got inside documents from Argentina outlining the secret plan for that country which had been signed by James Wolfensohn, the President of the World Bank. As part of its integration into the New World Order, Argentina was required by the IMF and the World Bank to sell off its major public assets. Palast talks about some of the implications in an interview with Alex Jones.

"It's not just anyone who gets a piece of the action. The water system of Buenos Aires was sold off for a song to a company called Enron. A pipeline, that runs between Argentina and Chile, was sold to Enron."[21]

Palast continued: "I actually spoke to a senator from Argentina two weeks ago. [February 2002] I got him on camera. He said that after he got a call from George W. Bush in 1988 saying "Give the gas pipeline in Argentina to Enron." He said that what he found really creepy was that Enron was going to pay one-fifth of the world's price for the gas and he said how can you make such an offer? And he was told, not by George W. but by a partner in the deal, "Well if we only pay one-fifth that leaves quite a little bit for you to go in your Swiss bank account." And that's how it's done… They hand it over, generally, to the cronies like Citibank [which] was very big and grabbed half the Argentine banks."[22]

Palast pointed out, by way of background, that the United States is a major financial contributor to both the IMF and the World Bank.

"So the question becomes, what are we getting for the money we put in there? And it looks like we are getting mayhem in several nations. Indonesia is in flames. He was telling me, [Joseph Stiglitz, former chief economist of the World Bank], that he started questioning what was happening. You know, everywhere we go, every country we end up meddling in, we destroy their economy and they end up in flames.

"And he [Stiglitz] was saying that he questioned this, and he got fired for it. He was saying that they even kind of plan in the riots. They know that when they squeeze a country and destroy its economy, you are going to get riots in the streets. And they say, well that's the IMF riot. In other words, because you have a riot you lose. All the capital runs away from your country and that gives the opportunity for the IMF to then add more conditions."[23]

While Palast drives home his points with flamboyant language, economist Stiglitz confirms the substance in his more scholarly style. In *Globalization and its Discontents* he writes: "(As of January 2002, Argentina is going through a crisis. Once again, the IMF bailout policies failed to work; the contradictory fiscal policies that it insisted upon pushed the economy into an ever deeper recession.) The IMF never asked why its models systematically underestimated the depth of recessions – or why its policies are systematically excessively contradictory."[24]

If globalization and "free trade" are creating poverty, misery, corruption and mayhem on an ever-widening scale, they are also producing economic results that are far less satisfactory than those achieved before the new [old] economic fundamentalism was adopted as holy writ.

The compound annual growth rate of U.S. Gross National Product in the bad old days from 1948 to 1973, before the monetarist counter-revolution conquered the hearts and minds of policy makers, was 3.7 percent. From 1974 to 2001 the GDP grew by an average of 2.9 percent – a reduction of 22 percent.[25] For Canada, the growth rate from 1949 to 1973 averaged 4.9 percent compared to 3.03 percent during the 1974-2001 Friedman era – a reduction of 38 percent.[26]

Latin America and Africa have fared much worse. In those dark ages of increasing national government control and ownership (1960-1980), per capita income grew by 73 percent in Latin America and by 34 percent in Africa. By comparison, since 1980, Latin American growth has come to a virtual halt, growing by less than 6 percent over twenty years – and African incomes have declined by 23 percent.[27]

Obviously market fundamentalism, like other fundamentalisms, is impervious to argument or inconvenient facts. So how do they sell it? Invariably professors attempting to make a case will go back to 1959 for their data. It is convenient, but dishonest, to use the successes of the Keynesian interventionist years to justify the failures of a model which, as Joseph Stiglitz says, doesn't make sense outside the classroom. Listen to William Finnegan's concerns.

"But vulgarity and obtuseness should not be mistaken for sincerity. Not only is the case for President Bush's 'opinion' that 'free trade is good for both wealthy and impoverished nations' empirically feeble, there is plenty of evidence that rich countries, starting with the United States, have no intention of playing by the trade rules and strictures they foist on poorer, weaker countries as 'a single sustainable model.' We practice free trade selectively, which is to say not at all, and, when it suits our commercial purposes, we actively prevent poor countries from exploiting their few advantages on world markets."[28]

The extent of the economic terrorism is all pervasive. The IMF and World Bank not only put poor countries in economic straight-jackets, they lock them tight by refusing to let those countries use their own central banks to create money to help finance the cost of health care and education. Ironically, this is probably one of the main if not the main issue on which the U.S. War for Independence was fought.

Although we were taught that the argument was about tea, that was far from the whole story. True, tea was a factor because it was supplied by one of the U.K. monopolies which exploited the colonists in a manner not too different from the way U.S. multinationals are currently exploiting their "colonists." But in his memoirs, Benjamin Franklin tells us that the real issue was London's decision that the colonies could no longer print their own money.

They had been doing this successfully for some years, especially in Pennsylvania where "ship-building prospered and both exports and imports increased markedly."[29] Even Adam Smith, who was not a fan of government-created money, admitted that Pennsylvania's paper currency "is said never to have sunk below the value of the gold and silver which was current in the colony before the first issue of paper money."[30]

Unfortunately the London bankers found out about it and insisted that Westminster pass a law forbidding the practice. Instead of creating their own money, the colonists were forced to borrow from London banks and repay principal and interest in gold that they didn't have. A depression resulted and when the colonists decided on another currency issue war became inevitable.

Substitute Wall Street for London, and the underdeveloped world for the American colonies, and you have a picture of the scene in the world today. Now, as in the time of the American War for Independence, economic terrorism is backed by military force. But today the U.S. has such overwhelming military power that no country, either poor or relatively well-to-do, can challenge it. And if Wall Street's industrial-military complex has its way, no one ever will be able to.

As long as financial power is concentrated on Wall Street, the impoverished people of the world will have to choose between a form of perpetual slavery, or the loss of most or all of their natural assets – or, in far too many cases, both. It is all embodied in the Project for a New American Century which is the cocaine of the economic fundamentalist marauders, but arsenic for the rest of the world.

Little wonder that even the Hungarian-born American financier George Soros is concerned. Speaking of his student days and recalling a book entitled *The Open Society and its Enemies*, by Karl Popper, Soros says: "At that time, open society was threatened by various totalitarian ideologies – fascism, Nazism and communism – which used the power of the state to impose their final solutions. Open society is now also threatened from the opposite direction, from what I call market fundamentalism. I used to call it *laissez-faire* but I prefer market fundamentalism because *laissez-faire* is a French expression and most market fundamentalists don't speak French."[31]

The New Totalitarians (NEOTOTS)

We have long since passed the point where we have to recognize the elite group for what they are. They are a new breed of totalitarian. It is not that their ideas are new, because they are as old as recorded history. It is just that they used to be called kings, queens, emperors or dictators, and they have a long history of concentrating power and wealth in their own hands and dispensing small portions of it to those who do their bidding, while withholding justice from all who oppose them.

The present bunch, who openly and honestly admit that they do not believe in democracy, have perfected the art of camouflaging their intent by appearing to operate within civilized rules. Meanwhile they have used their power to unseat presidents, prime ministers, chief executive officers and heads of important international bodies who fail to operate within the rigorous unofficial rules laid down by the emperors' game plan.

Some of us were naïve enough to believe that the defeat of Nazism in Germany, in 1945, followed quickly by the defeat of the Japanese dictatorship in 1946, and then the ultimate unraveling of the Soviet Union in 1991 and winning the Cold War would usher in a brave new age of justice, compassion and, above all, liberty, where we would be able to live in some dignity without fear and undue interference in our daily lives. Little did we dream that the people who had made enormous sums by financing these wars, and in some cases both sides of the same conflict, were constantly changing the rules to enhance their own financial interests.

The climate of entitlement – rich payoffs for financial engineering either within or without the law – has become endemic to our system. Fifteen years ago the average CEO pay package was equal to forty times the average of his or her employees. Today, it is more than 237 times according to one report,[32] and 433 times according to another.[33] Nothing has happened in the interim what would justify this kind of an increase. It is simply a function of greed gone berserk in the corporate world.

One of the worst examples I have seen involved John Paulson a hedge fund founder – a breed of institution whose merit has never been adequately explained – earned $3.7 billion U.S. in 2007.[34] Can anyone justify this kind of return in a "civilized" society? The man is a member of a stratospheric league that includes Richard Grasso former chief of the New York Stock Exchange who accepted a retirement package of $188 million.[35] I can find no polite words to describe either the transaction or anyone who would be a party to it.

Some of the Elite Cut Corners

Cutting corners is as old as the world itself but some contemporary cases appear to establish new benchmarks for the magnitude of deceit. The collapse of Enron Corp. is now a textbook example. It would be redundant to repeat the story here, except to say that the collapse revealed that the books had been deliberately and methodically falsified. Worse, this was done with the knowledge and cooperation of some of its auditors.

There was even a Canadian connection. According to a 218-page report by a special committee of Enron's Board of Directors, the company took a $210 million (U.S.) loan from the Canadian Imperial Bank of Commerce and booked it as a profit. "This is a devastating report.... It suggests massive problems. This is almost a culture of corruption here," U.S. Congressman Byron Dorgan said on NBC's "Meet the Press." One billion in profit was booked here that didn't exist. That's trouble."[36] The Congressman was dead on. It did indicate trouble – especially for employees and shareholders who lost jobs and savings in the process.

As a footnote to history, Kenneth Lay, president of Enron when it collapsed, was a director of the right-wing American Enterprise Institute. He was also a member of the Trilateral Commission, was selected to receive the Private Sector Council's Leadership Award, received the 1998 Horatio Alger Award, and was named by *Business Week* as one of the top twenty-five managers in the world for 1999. Mr. Lay, who died before he could stand trial, was also a member of the Texas Business Hall of Fame. A friend of President George W. Bush, Mr. Lay's Enron contributed $113,800 to his 2000 campaign fund.

Not to be outdone, WorldCom topped them all in order of magnitude – the largest Chapter 11 bankruptcy ever filed in the United States. In May 2003, MCI, the former WorldCom, agreed to settle accusations of fraud by the Securities and Exchange Commission by paying a $500 million penalty destined for investors.[37] This figure was just a drop in the bucket compared to shareholders' claims that they lost "tens of billions of dollars" from MCI's misleading accounting.[38]

These major scandals arising from greed, extending into fraud, attracted much public attention and provided the cocktail circuit grist for the mill for months. Many executive reputations were ruined, some charges were laid, investors lost their savings and employees lost their jobs and pensions. But in a way these stellar cases were only the tip of a much more ominous iceberg – widespread cheating by many of the most prestigious firms on Wall Street.

The list read like a Who's Who of world finance. Salomon, Merrill, Credit Suisse Group's CSFB, Morgan Stanley, Goldman Sachs, Bear Stearns, J.P. Morgan Chase, Lehman Brothers, U.S. Bancorp. At firm after firm, according to prosecutors, analysts wittingly duped investors to curry favor with corporate clients. Investment houses received secret payments from companies they gave strong recommendations to buy. And for top executives whose companies were clients, stock underwriters offered special access to hot initial public offerings, according to *The New York Times*.[39]

Brian Miller, writing in the Toronto *Globe and Mail*, said: "There's little repentance on Wall Street these days. Even after 10 major securities firms agreed to pay a combined $1.4 billion in penalties and costs to put the scandal behind them – a tiny fraction of their profits during that era – not one has admitted any wrongdoing and probably never will."[40]

Perhaps this is the point where I should stress that not all businesses, and not all business men and women should be tarred with the same brush! There are thousands of honest and reliable enterprises led by moral and upright men and women. They should be honored for their persistence in observing a moral line.

It seems, however, that the bigger the enterprise becomes, and the more successful it is in financial terms, the greater the temptation to cut corners and attempt to hide the evidence. Furthermore, if caught red-handed, there is often little if any remorse and a general attitude of "let the investor beware" prevails – as was the case with the giants of Wall Street when they were accused of malfeasance.

The Banking System Tops Them All

If one returns to a close examination of the Bilderberger Group, even to the extent that information is available, you will quickly conclude that the hard core of control from the outset has been the banking fraternity. Other invitees include the captains of industry, politicians, heads of international financial institutions, academics and journalists through whom they exercise that control. They even exercise tremendous influence on the central banks, which theoretically control their powers to create money, and the Bank for International Settlements (BIS) in Basel, Switzerland, comprised of central bankers who agree on rules for their own governance.

The BIS, lovingly known as the Gnomes of Zurich, is another secretive organization that few of you will be familiar with. They are so secretive, in fact, that not even secretaries of the treasury, ministers of finance, or even presidents or prime ministers are allowed to attend their meetings. Yet the decisions they make have a profound effect on the solvency and stability of the world financial system and some of its ivory tower thinking contributed fundamentally to the instability responsible for the financial plague of 2007-2008 and beyond.

If one of the initial aims of the Bilderberger Group was to regulate the banking system more intelligently in order to mitigate the effects of the business cycle, their efforts have been a total and disastrous failure.

Friedmanism et al

It only takes a cursory look back at the 1929-1933 fiasco to see what went wrong in that era. It was the banking system, and the way money is created. In the course of reading some economic history I was fascinated to learn that the word "Depression" was applied to create the impression that the economic disaster, that began in 1929, was in some way less than a "panic," the word previously associated in the public's mind with severe economic downturns. In retrospect it was just another economic ruse to mitigate the potential backlash from one more overdose of human misery when the banking system failed.

Will Rogers, the great American humorist and folk hero reported general agreement as to who was responsible for the monetary mess. On February 24, 1932, he warned that: "You can't get a room in Washington … Every hotel is jammed to the doors with bankers from all over America to get their 'hand out' from the Reconstruction Finance Corporation. And I have asked the following prominent men in America this question: 'What group have been more responsible for this financial mess, the farmers?.... Labor?.... Manufacturers?.... Tradesmen, or Who? …And every man – Henry Ford, Garner, Newt Baker, Borah, Curtis, and a real financier, Barney Baruch – without a moment's hesitation said, 'Why, the big bankers.' … Yet they have the honor of being the first group to go on the 'dole' in America."[41] [Ditto in 2008.]

It is as immensely sad as it is curious to note that nothing has changed in the intervening seventy-eight years. Once again the big banks started to make overly generous loans and when asset values began to crumble the whole virtual financial house of cards began to collapse and the banks had to call on central banks to print billions of dollars to bail them out and stave off bankruptcy.

The Great Depression of the 1930s brewed an intellectual ferment both in academic and political circles. In the face of a banking system in crisis, in 1933, a number of economists at the University of Chicago produced what later became known as the Chicago Plan. It called for outright public ownership of the Federal Reserve Banks and the establishment of new institutions that accepted only demand deposits subject to a 100 percent reserve requirement in lawful money and/or deposits with the Reserve Banks.

One of the eight signatories of the six-page memorandum authorizing the plan was Professor H.C. Simons. Three years later, in March 1936, he summed up succinctly the essence of his concern. "Given release from a preposterous financial structure, capitalism might endure indefinitely its other afflictions; but, assuming continuance of our financial follies …, it becomes academic to consider how the system might be saved."[42]

President Franklin D. Roosevelt must have considered the enlightened, though radical, views of professors Lloyd Mints and Henry Simons and their colleagues at the University of Chicago – views similar to those of Yale's Irving Fisher. In the end, however, it was the bankers' interests that prevailed. Congress was persuaded to entrench the fractional reserve system under which bankers were allowed to make loans that were not adequately backed by legal tender.

Fast forward to Milton Friedman and his colleagues at the same University of Chicago. Friedman insisted that his mentor was, in fact, that same professor Lloyd Mints and that he subscribed to the Mints theory of 100 percent cash reserves. "As good a reform as ever," Friedman wrote in a footnote reply to a letter from William F. Hixon, then added… "unfortunately with as little prospect of adoption as ever. I keep mentioning it but feel that tilting at windmills is not an effective way to spend my time."[43] If he had been content to let it go at that, the Nobel laureate would have earned a place among the forward-looking thinkers on a fundamentally important issue. But in subsequent writings he recommended freezing the production of government-created money and the adoption of zero percent reserves.

In a 1986 letter to Professor John H. Hotson, in reply to a question on the subject of reserves and government-created money, he wrote: "In my opinion, either extreme is acceptable. I have not given up advocacy of one hundred percent reserves. I would prefer one hundred percent reserves to the alternative I set forth. However, I believe that getting the government out of the business altogether, or zero percent reserves, also makes sense. The virtue of either one is that it eliminates government meddling in the lending and investing activities of the financial markets.

"When I wrote in 1948, we were already halfway toward one hundred percent reserves because so large a fraction of the assets of the banks consisted of either government bonds or high-powered money (cash, legal tender). One hundred percent reserves at that time did not look impossible of achievement. We have moved so far since then that I am very skeptical indeed that there is any political possibility of achieving one hundred percent reserves. That does not mean that it is not desirable."[44]

Wow! One has to wonder about the judgment of a man who goes directly from advocacy of 100% cash reserves to 0% without any consideration of some mid-point that might prove preferable to either extreme. Professor Friedman goes on to say that the sole reason he stressed the zero percent reserves was "because it seemed to me at least to be within the imaginable range of political feasibility."[45] He was correct on that point as two or three countries, including Canada, have already done it. But that doesn't mean it makes sense. One could argue that it is one of the worst ideas to emerge from the halls of learning in the history of economics. [P.S. I wonder what Professor Friedman would think of newspaper reports of government intervention in the fall of 2008?]

It was another of Professor Friedman's theories that first rocked the financial boat in recent decades. He concluded that all inflation was monetary inflation and, consequently, all that was necessary to maintain stable prices was to limit the creation of money to a rate proportional to the increase in real goods and services. In theory, at least, this was little more than good common sense. In practice, however, it proved to be a near catastrophic disaster.

When Paul Volcker, Chairman of the Federal Reserve Board, a disciple of Friedman, invoked "practical monetarism" he had reassuring words for Congress. "More positively stated, the progress we are clearly beginning to see on the inflation front when carried forward will help lay the base for recovery and much better economic performance over a long period of time."[46] While this was balm to the "true believers" it turned out to be a hollow promise. Not only has economic performance been worse since Friedmanism was adopted by central banks in 1974, wildly fluctuating interest rates have played havoc with the stability of the system as well as with the lives and fortunes of millions of citizens.

2008 Déja Vu

The headlines on July 15 and 16, 2008 tell the story. " 'Watershed moment' for American banking: U.S. bank stocks take worst hit in nearly 20 years," reads one headline.[47]

"Black days in July: Washington's top financial stewards reassure Congress they're on top of the spreading banking mess.

"A decade ago, three of the most powerful officials in Washington – Alan Greenspan, Robert Rubin, and Larry Summers – banded together to squelch a global financial crisis, earning lavish praise and the nickname: 'The Committee to Save the World.' Their triumvirate of successors would doubtless settle for a more modest title: 'The Committee to Save Wall Street.'

"Ben Bernanke, Mr. Greenspan's replacement as U.S. Federal Reserve Board chairman, warned Congress yesterday that the sickly U.S. economy is being dogged by falling housing prices, soft job numbers and rising prices for energy and food staples. Yet he left no doubt as to his chief area of concern: a battered financial sector that has lost hundreds of billions of dollars on bad loans, and whose problems are quickly cascading into other areas of the economy.

" 'All banks are being challenged by credit conditions now,' said Mr. Bernanke, who was joined by U.S. Treasury Secretary Henry Paulson and Securities and Exchange Commission chairman Christopher Cox. 'In general, healthy economic growth depends on well-functioning financial markets. Consequently, helping the financial markets to return to more normal functioning will continue to be a top priority.' "[48]

Will Rogers must be rolling over in his grave laughing to see the big banks lined up for the dole yet one more time, though he would be as sad as he was in the 1930s to see the havoc they have created for themselves and others – particularly all the people who have been losing their houses and their jobs. But what did they all expect? When banks lend people more than their houses are worth, and those people are so far in debt that they have to choose between making mortgage payments or eating, the crunch is on. And, of course, there is a ripple effect that creates giant waves that inundate the just and the unjust alike.

I have been waiting for someone in authority to say that it is an untenable banking and money-creation system that is basically at fault. But so far there has not been a peep out of anyone paid to take the long view. After all, there have been twenty-five recessions and depressions in the U.S. during the last hundred and twenty years,[49] including the one that began in 2008, and none of them has been necessary.

For many years when someone would ask me what was wrong with my country I would say it was the economy. Then, on reflection, I began to say the problem was a moral and spiritual breakdown of our society. Our ethical standards had deteriorated. To put it more bluntly, we have made gold our god. Marry that to a banking system that never has and never will work consistently well and it spells T-R-O-U-B-L-E with a capital T.

CHAPTER 8

UNLESS WE REPENT AND CHANGE OUR WAYS,
WE ARE DOOMED

"Every gun that is made, every warship launched, every rocket fired, signifies in a final scene, a theft from those who hunger and are not fed, those who are cold and are not clothed. This world in arms is not spending money alone. It is spending the sweat of its laborers, the genius of its scientists, the hopes of its children."

Dwight D. Eisenhower

The title of this chapter was originally going to be "Unless the U.S. repents, etc," but on reflection, that seemed a bit too exclusive. So it was changed to encompass the wider net of Western civilization. Still, when one country chooses to usurp the jobs of general manager, head coach and quarterback and you see the players running the wrong way down the field you have to ask pointed questions about the quality of the management team. Consequently this chapter is primarily dedicated to the attention of the people of the United States, but applies to an equal or lesser extent to other countries in the Western world as appropriate to the context.

I like Americans – at least most of them. They are warm, hospitable, generous, industrious, and ingenious people who have pushed the frontiers of industry and commerce to new limits. They have also extended the boundaries of scientific discovery in many areas of great potential benefit to mankind.

A nation comprised of people of many races and religions, Americans have been richly blessed. They occupy one of the most beautiful and productive pieces of real estate on earth. They have become immensely wealthy to an extent far beyond their real needs, though the distribution of that wealth leaves much to be desired.

They are, at the same time, a naïve people and easily convinced by the latest "spin" their government aims in their direction through the mass media. I call the media the weapons of mass intellectual destruction. Their power is sufficient to prove that up is down and that evil is good.

Despite their naivety, my problem has not been with the American people; it has been with the governments they elect. The U.S. democratic process has been hijacked by an elite group whose policies and plans are unrepresentative of the U.S. population, and inevitably antithetical to long-term American interests. President Eisenhower described them as the industrial-military complex of which he warned us to beware. Increasingly this group of high rollers has been pushing poor countries and poor people around to satisfy their lust for power and wealth. As I explained in the previous chapter this became an integral aspect of U.S. foreign policy.

With the installation of the G.W. Bush administration the trait escalated to a new order of magnitude. The details were developed in the Project for the New American Century (PNAC). In essence it is the establishment of an American empire by military or other means. Iraq was just the trial run against a weak and demoralized regime which posed absolutely no immediate threat to the United States. The alleged existence of weapons of mass destruction was just the excuse required to provide justification for the attack under international law, though it proved to be an excuse that didn't meet the objective.

The small Pentagon clique, who have been running the United States, didn't care about international law. They wanted to establish a new benchmark, namely, an open season on any country that wasn't run to their satisfaction and which lacked sufficient deterrent capability to fight back. So, in effect, United States foreign policy came to be determined by the Pentagon instead of the State Department in a classic case of the military tail wagging the foreign policy dog. At the same time that the potential to produce weapons of mass destruction became "legitimate" reason to attack any country, the U.S. Defence Department was undertaking the development of weapons too evil for description.

At a press conference when announcing U.S. rejection of the Kyoto Accord, President Bush said: "A friend is someone who tells you the truth." As a true friend it pains me to say that the foreign and defence policies put into place by his administration have been intrinsically evil. And no real friend would have anything good to say about them. Certainly no country that was a real friend would either endorse such policies, or be part of them. They would speak the truth and pray for a regime change in the U.S.

From One Evil Empire to Another

"When all government, domestic and foreign, shall be drawn to Washington as the centre of all power, it will render powerless the checks provided of one government on another, and will become as venal and oppressive as the government from which we separated."

Thomas Jefferson

Although my economic radicalism was the prime motive for entering political life more than half a century ago, fate would determine that my primary effort would be in the field of defence rather than economics. I became deeply involved in the ideology of the Cold War. From the moment when, as the newly appointed Minister of National Defence, I first visited Canadian troops in Germany in May 1963, I resolved to increase Canada's small but significant contribution to the North Atlantic Treaty Organization (NATO) forces in Europe.

It was all part of an effort to build up NATO conventional forces that would be strong enough to resist an initial thrust by the Soviet Union – without the necessity of using nuclear weapons with potential consequences too horrendous to imagine. Somehow the spread of communism, with its secret police, denial of civil liberties and inefficient economic system had to be contained.

It may have been partly luck that the Soviet Union decided not to test the United States by starting a war that might easily and quickly have presented the option of either losing all Europe to the Soviet system, or a nuclear escalation leading to the virtual annihilation of both the U.S.

and the U.S.S.R. It was the French fear that given that option the U.S. would "chicken out" and sacrifice Europe to save its own skin, that led the French to develop their own independent nuclear capacity.

In any event, the deterrent worked and the stalemate continued for decades. In many ways it was good for the world because both communists and capitalists curried the favor of Third World countries and presented their most benign and attractive face.

No one could have been happier than I when the Berlin wall came down on November 9, 1989. The elation on our side of the curtain was near universal, and very significant on the other side as one country after another regained its freedom. Nearly everyone believed that it was the dawn of a new era of peace and prosperity for people everywhere.

There was much talk of a peace dividend. Without any enemies of military significance, the Western countries, and the U.S. in particular, could reduce expenditures for armaments and divert the savings to myriad essential priorities including health care, education, environmental protection including sustainable growth, and the development of new sources of energy to replace fossil fuels. There would also be more money for the arts and the alleviation of poverty and illiteracy on a global basis. The prospects were dazzling in their scope and diversity. It was a unique and God-given opportunity for a new, braver and fairer world.

We blew it! We blew the chance of a lifetime to do good things!

A small group of zealots undermined our golden opportunity to pursue peace, not war. Little did we dream that they had a vastly different "vision" of the New World Order. The group included U.S. Vice-President Dick Cheney, former Defense Secretary Donald Rumsfeld, former Deputy Secretary of Defense Paul Wolfowitz, Douglas Feith who held the number three position at the Pentagon, Lewis "Scooter" Libby, a Wolfowitz protégé, who later served as Cheney's Chief of Staff before his dismissal, John R. Bolton who was assigned to the State Department to keep Secretary of State Colin Powell in check, and Elliott Abrams, appointed to head the Middle East policy at the National Security Council. Apparently all envisioned a world dominated by the U.S. both economically and militarily.[1]

Their plan, now commonly known as the Project for a New American Century, included preventive wars (in clear violation of international law), regime change wherever and whenever the U.S. desires and if they can get away with it without excessive casualties, and the establishment of a kind of economic and cultural hegemony with America acting as "constabulary" – their word – globally.

This was to be accomplished without authority of the United Nations and without the restraint of existing international treaties. It would involve a military buildup unprecedented in "peacetime" history and could trigger an arms race which is precisely the opposite to the peace dividend that the world had rightly looked forward to.

The Machiavellian scheme involved secret police, the curtailment of civil liberties in defiance of the U.S. Constitution, and a moribund economy, operating way below its potential – exactly those features for which the Soviet Union was held in contempt.

One distinction may be that the "vision" was "on the record." Not since *Mein Kampf* in the 1930s had anyone been so open about their intentions. The problem, as it was in the 1930s, is that decent people refuse to believe that such far-fetched belligerence is planned even when they see it in cold print.

To those of us who have been around long enough to put things in historical context there is no disguising the nature of the beast. The Project for a New American Century was a plan to establish an American Empire unprecedented since the fall of the Roman Empire and with consequences more devastating and demoralizing for greater numbers of people than the Evil Empire from which we thought the world had been liberated.

I have decided to include excerpts from the original PNAC for the simple reason that a test sample of U.S. tourists visiting my small resort in Muskoka, Ontario, revealed that not one of them had ever heard of it. Not one. Based on that sample one can only conclude that the vast majority of Americans didn't know what was really going on in their own country and the far-reaching consequences for them both individually and collectively.

Project for a New American Century

The initial draft of the Pentagon document "Defense Planning Guidance" on Post-Cold War Strategy was dated February 18, 1992. Some of the key sections are as follows:

1. Our first objective is to prevent the re-emergence of a new rival, either on the territory of the former Soviet Union, or elsewhere, that poses a threat on the order of that posed formerly by the Soviet Union. This is a dominant consideration underlying the new regional defense strategy and requires that we endeavor to prevent any hostile power from dominating a region whose resources would, under consolidated control, be sufficient to generate global power.

2. The U.S. must show the leadership necessary to establish and protect a new order that holds the promise of convincing potential competitors that they need not aspire to a greater role or pursue a more aggressive posture to protect their legitimate interests. In non-defense areas, we must account sufficiently for the interests of the advanced industrial nations to discourage them from challenging our leadership or seeking to overturn the established political and economic order. We must maintain the mechanisms for deterring competitors from even aspiring to a larger regional or global role.

3. Like the coalition that opposed Iraqi aggression, we should expect future coalitions to be ad hoc assemblies, often not lasting beyond the crisis being confronted, and in many cases carrying only general agreement over the objectives to be accomplished. Nevertheless, the sense that the world order is ultimately backed by the U.S. will be an important stabilizing factor.

4. While the U.S. cannot become the world's policeman by assuming responsibility for righting every wrong, we will retain the preeminent responsibility for addressing selectively those wrongs which threaten not only our interests, but those of our allies or friends, or which could seriously unsettle international relations.

5. We continue to recognize that collectively the conventional forces of the states formerly comprising the Soviet Union retain the most military potential in all of Eurasia; and we do not dismiss the risks to stability in Europe from a nationalist backlash in Russia, or efforts to reincorporate into Russia the newly independent republics of Ukraine, Belarus, and possibly others ... We must, however, be mindful that democratic change in Russia is now irreversible, and that despite its current travails, Russia will remain the strongest military power in Eurasia and the only power in the world with the capacity of destroying the United States.

6. In the Middle East and Southwest Asia, our overall objective is to remain the predominant outside power in the region and preserve U.S. and Western access to the region's oil.[2]

When a leaked copy of the document prepared under the supervision of Paul Wolfowitz, then the Pentagon's Undersecretary for Policy, was disclosed by the *New York Times* in March 1992, the negative reaction from both the White House and foreign capitols was so strong that it had to be redrafted.

The new sanitized version adopted a much more conciliatory note. It stated: "One of the primary tasks we face today in shaping the future is carrying long-standing alliances into the new era, and turning old enmities into new cooperative relationships."[3] The document made a small bow in the direction of a leveling of military investments coupled with greater economic and security cooperation. The bottom line remained unchanged, however. "It is not in our interest or those of the other democracies to return to earlier periods in which multiple military powers balanced one another off in what passed for security structures, while regional, or even global peace hung in the balance."[4]

As someone who has long observed the techniques of creating politically acceptable language, and a sometimes practitioner of that craft, I would say that the principal difference between the first and revised drafts is in the weasel words. You can't change a tiger by whitewashing its spots. The men responsible for the first draft had changed little, if at all.

That conclusion can be substantiated by their actions in office. The abrogation of the anti-ballistic missile treaty, the vast buildup in military expenditures at the expense of those that the majority might consider more important, the installation of a worldwide system of regional defense commands, and the insistence on installing weapons of mass destruction in space.

It all adds up to an irrevocable resolve to maintain the U.S. status as the world's only superpower and to take whatever steps are necessary, including those that may not be necessary but which can be made to appear to be necessary, to that end.

One has to ask how such a small group of neo-conservative ideologues could take over the U.S. administration as a first step toward an expanded empire. In a stroke of good luck for them, and bad luck for nearly everyone else including the vast majority of the American people, George W. Bush chose Dick Cheney as his running mate. The die was cast.

Once the Supreme Court decided that George W. Bush would succeed Bill Clinton as the 43rd President of the United States, the President-elect put the former defense secretary in charge of his transition team. So Cheney slotted one after another of his Pentagon team for the New American Century into key posts to the point where they had the balance of power in the incoming administration. Overnight the long-standing tenet of defense being an extension of foreign policy was reversed.

It may have been relatively easy to persuade President Bush to abandon his stated policy of not getting America more deeply involved in international affairs, but persuading the American people would be more difficult. Sophisticated Americans would question such a giant sea change in policy.

The authors of "Rebuilding America's Defenses: Strategy, Forces and Resources for a New Century" recognized this difficulty from the outset because their document contained the following sentence. "Further, the process of transformation, even if it brings revolutionary changes, is likely to be a long one, absent some catastrophic and catalyzing event – like a new Pearl Harbor."[5]

Well, it wasn't too long before they got their catastrophic and catalyzing event. Terrorists struck the World Trade Center in New York, and the Pentagon in Washington.

September 11, 2001

I wept internally when the full impact of what was happening penetrated my consciousness. I was at the office when one of the staff said they had just heard on the radio that the World Trade Center in New York had been attacked. We turned on the TV and there it was – a spiral of flame and smoke escaping from one of the towers. It took a few seconds to absorb the fact that what we were watching was genuine and not some Orwellian computer creation. As we watched in silent horror we could only imagine how awful it really was.

It was a long day and night that no witness could ever forget – the reports of casualties followed by images of the dead and the dying – firemen trapped inside the buildings in the course of duty. Occasionally there was a good luck story of someone who had escaped or missed their train to be blessed by fortune.

Almost the whole world mourned. Canada mourned. The overwhelming majority of Muslims condemned the treacherous attacks. A vast crowd of 80,000 assembled on Parliament Hill in Ottawa in an outpouring of love and affection for our American friends and neighbors. Many of us attended special remembrance services in our respective churches as an expression of deepest concern and sympathy. A group of people from Toronto organized a weekend pilgrimage to New York to demonstrate their support and empathy.

My sympathy for the friends and families of the injured and dead was genuine and unwavering to this day. My sympathy for the U.S. government began to grow a bit thin, however, when I heard President Bush cite the reasons for the attack. "Why do they hate us?" he asked rhetorically in an address to the Congress. "They hate what they see right here in this chamber: a democratically elected government. Their leaders are self-appointed. They hate our freedoms: our freedom of religion, our freedom of speech, our freedom to vote and assemble and disagree with each other."[6]

I felt sad when I heard the President's words. I assumed that he believed what he was saying, but if that were true he was profoundly ignorant of the real thoughts and feelings of people in other parts of the world. If he wanted to hear the truth he should have listened to Osama bin Laden, leader of al-Qaeda, who was well-informed concerning the origins of the kind of fanatical hatred of the U.S. which had led to such treachery. This is his version of events.

"Every Muslim must rise to defend his religion. The wind of faith is blowing and the wind of change is blowing to remove evil from the Peninsula of Muhammad, peace be upon him. As to America, I say to it and its people a few words: I swear to God that America will not live in peace before peace reigns in Palestine, and before all the army of infidels depart the land of Muhammad, peace be upon him."[7]

That is clear enough. The dislike of America has nothing to do with democracy versus dictatorship, or wealth, or freedom of religion and assembly. It is directly related to American foot-dragging in stick-handling a just settlement of the Palestinian question while continuing to meddle in Middle Eastern affairs, including the stationing of troops on soil considered sacred to Islam. In short, American foreign policy was the root of the conflict.

You would think that someone in the State Department, the CIA or the FBI, if not all three, would have briefed the president on such critically important issues. Perhaps they did, but the American people were never let in on the secret. To do so would have created too much disillusionment. More important for the Bush administration, it would have undermined plans to implement the Project for a New American Century which rides roughshod over the sensibilities of all outsiders.

Months later the president was forced to admit that he had been forewarned of a possible al-Qaeda hijacking plot nearly a month before September 11, 2001. "U.S. National Security Adviser Condoleezza Rice acknowledged that the White House was alerted that 'something was coming' and that Mr. Bush was alerted to the possibility of hijackings in a written 'analytical' briefing delivered to him at his ranch in Crawford, Texas, on August 6."[8] She went on to insist that there was no information about the time, place or method of attack. This despite the fact that the word hijackings was used in the briefings.

One would have thought that the warning would have been sufficient for the U.S. forces to go on high alert and especially the two squadrons of fighter jets at Andrews Air Force Base assigned to defend the White House. There was another mystery. Why did the president pretend that he first learned of the attacks in that classroom, when he had actually been briefed as he left his hotel that morning?[9]

It is doubtful that the whole truth will ever be known and it has ceased to be relevant except to historians. What is relevant is the reaction to the attack and the brand of terrorism it represented. The administration was faced with three options. (a) It could accept the real reasons for the fanatical hatred and take the necessary steps to remove the causes of it. (b) It could accelerate the police and intelligence campaign necessary to locate and neutralize the very limited threat from a handful of al-Qaeda operatives. the active cooperation and assistance of just about everyone in the world including Muslim countries. (c) It could launch an all-out war on terrorism, the only option of the three that was destined to fail from the outset.

Not too surprisingly, option (c) was the administration's choice. An all-out war on terrorism was the only choice that fit the strategy of the military-industrial complex as reflected in the Plan for a New American Century. It is, unfortunately, a war that will never end until we see the end of the people who made the fateful and tragic decision to launch it.

Iraq – And the War of Lies

"In the councils of government, we must guard against the acquisition of unwarranted influence, whether sought or unsought, by the military-industrial complex. The potential for the disastrous rise of misplaced power exists and will persist."

Dwight D. Eisenhower

Most friendly observers could understand why a strike on the Taliban might be justified – despite pleas for mercy and reminders that it had been an ally of the U.S. in the Cold War – because it appeared to be essential, if only for domestic political reasons, to get at bin Laden. This despite a Taliban offer to turn bin Laden over if the U.S. could provide evidence of his complicity – an offer that was rejected out of hand.

The war against Iraq, however, was quite a different matter. It was not harboring al-Qaeda operations and it posed no imminent threat to the United States – the essential condition for a pre-emptive strike. None of this really seemed to matter. Iraq had been on the Defense Department's hit list for years and the final decision to attack was made within weeks of the September 11 tragedy.

Advance knowledge of the strike was voiced by Israeli Prime Minister Benjamin Netanyahu and published in the *World Tribune* in December 2001. "They have decided (on Iraq)," he told the annual Herzliya Conference on Israeli strategy. "It will not be in the long-term future." Netanyahu said Bush had decided that Iraq would be the U.S. next target in the U.S. war on terrorism."[10]

My first inkling occurred some months before any public announcement. I just happened to be listening to the radio and heard President George W. Bush use the term "weapons of mass destruction" eight or nine times in the course of three or four minutes.

"Oh, oh," I said to myself, "something's up; that is brainwashing."

It would be impossible to count the number of times that same quote was used by the president and his advisers in the weeks that followed. It didn't take long for everyone to get the point. Saddam Hussein and his Iraqi regime were the possessors of "weapons of mass destruction," and these posed a threat to the United States. Ultimately the majority in the U.S. and many others, especially in the English-speaking world, were convinced.

Apparently the administration had some difficulty in finding this plausible "reason" for the attack. Eventually they decided on "weapons of mass destruction" because, it seems, that was the one of several possibilities discussed that they could best agree on.[11]

Yet the administration knew, or should have known, that the Iraqis possessed no nuclear weapons and no capacity to produce them. Furthermore, any remnants of chemical or biological capability were of little, if any, consequence long before the war was launched. There had been a profound reduction in capability compared to that which existed before the Gulf War in 1990. At that time a team of scientists including Imad Khadduri, a former Iraqi nuclear scientist who later immigrated to Canada, was making good progress toward developing a nuclear capability. Following the Gulf War, however, funding was terminated and the team dispersed.

Prior to the war on Iraq, Khadduri insisted that Iraq had neither the scientific expertise nor the hardware to produce a nuclear bomb. This was in stark contrast to George W. Bush's claim that Iraq represented a credible nuclear threat – a claim Khadduri called "ridiculous."[12]

With respect to chemical and bacteriological weapons, the U.S. was on more familiar ground. Its knowledge of the Iraqis' capability had its roots in the U.S. A report of the United States Senate Committee on Banking, Housing and Urban Affairs included the following:

"We contacted a principal supplier of these materials to determine what, if any, materials were exported to Iraq which might have contributed to an offensive or defensive biological warfare program. Records available from the supplier from the period from 1985 until the present show that during this time, pathogenic (meaning 'disease producing'), toxigenic (meaning 'poisonous'), and other biological research materials were exported to Iraq pursuant to application and licensing by the U.S. Department of Commerce. Records prior to 1985 were not available, according to the supplier. These exported biological materials were not attenuated or weakened and were capable of reproduction."[13]

It is clear that the U.S. had been exporting the ingredients for biological warfare to Iraq prior to 1985. The list includes: Bacillus anthracis (anthrax); Clostridium bolulinum; Histoplasma capsulatum (causes a disease superficially resembling tuberculosis); Brucella melitensis (a bacteria which can cause chronic fatigue, loss of appetite, profuse sweating when at rest, pain in joints and muscles, insomnia, nausea, and damage to major organs); Clostridium perfringens (a highly toxic bacteria which causes gas gangrene). In addition, several shipments of Escherichia Coli (E. Coli) and genetic materials, as well as human and bacterial DNA, were shipped directly to the Iraq Atomic Energy Commission.[14]

Saddam Hussein used chemical weapons against Iran in 1983 and 1984 with the implicit approval of the U.S. An estimated 20,000 Iranians were killed by mustard gas and the nerve agents tabun and sarin. Later, Iraq used chemical weapons in its genocide campaign against the Kurds in September of 1988.[15]

In the fall of 2002 the London *Observer* reflected on the American attitude at the time. "As Iraq's use of poison gas in war and peace was public knowledge, the question arises: what did the United States administration do about it then? Absolutely nothing. Indeed, so powerful was the grip of the pro-Baghdad lobby on the administration of Republican President Ronald Reagan, that it got the White House to foil the Senate's attempt to penalize Iraq for its violation of the Geneva Protocol on Chemical Weapons to which it was a signatory. This made Saddam believe that the U.S. was his firm ally – a deduction that paved the way for his brutal invasion and occupation of Kuwait and the 1991 Gulf War.[16]

It was the Gulf War which led, ultimately, to Saddam Hussein's downfall. The U.N. imposed conditions for dismantling Iraq's nuclear, chemical, and biological capability, together with constant bombing by British and U.S. air forces, reduced Iraq's once formidable capability to near-total impotence. One has to assume, therefore, that U.K. and U.S. insistence that "weapons of mass destruction" remained a threat was primarily political propaganda without backing by any hard and credible intelligence.

The available intelligence was negative. Dr. Hans Blix and his team of U.N. inspectors could find no sign of current capability and begged for more time to reach an even more categorical conclusion. From a U.S. point of view, former Marine Corps intelligence officer and then U.N. weapons inspector, Scott Ritter, appeared to be a totally credible witness. A card-carrying Republican who voted for George Bush in 2002, he could not be accused of any political bias.

This is what he told CNN in London, England, in July 2002.

"Well look: As of December 1998 we had accounted for 90 to 95 percent of Iraq's weapons of mass destruction capability – 'we' being the weapons inspectors.

"We destroyed all the factories, all of the means of production and we couldn't account for some of the weaponry, but chemical weapons have a shelf life of five years. Biological weapons have a shelf life of three years. To have weapons today, they would have had to rebuild the factories and start the process of producing these weapons since December 1998."[17]

When asked how we knew this hasn't been happening, Ritter replied: "We don't, but we cannot go to war on guesswork, hypothesis and speculation. We go to war on hardened fact. So Tony Blair says he has a dossier; present the dossier. George W. Bush and his Administration say they know with certainty; show us how you know."[18]

The essence of Ritter's evidence was confirmed by the United Nations but this had no effect on the people who had already decided to go to war and they were only interested in conditioning public opinion to accept their word that there was a valid reason for it.

In fact the whole exercise of trying to get U.N. Security Council backing for the war was nothing but a charade – "process" – as we call it in politics. Tony Blair decided it would shore up his precarious position in the British Labour Party if the project carried U.N. approval. The reluctant Bush, desperate for support that would lend credibility to his proposed adventure, agreed.

The effort backfired when France, Germany and Russia, three of Europe's significant powers, rebelled. They realized only too well what the U.S. was up to and that the public reasons for the conflict were spurious. They also knew that the U.S. would be the principal beneficiary and that there would be no advantage for them. On the contrary, their relative advantage would be diminished. So, like the U.S., they played power politics.

It didn't really matter. The die was cast. The decision to attack Iraq had been made in the Pentagon years earlier at the time the PNAC had been written. So the Bush administration, which inherited the responsibility for implementing the plan, had to grasp at any available straw to justify an action so blatantly in contempt of international law. The one they chose turned out to be the short straw – the loser.

The war was launched. American forces marched toward Baghdad virtually unopposed. Later President Bush declared that the war had been won. There was some fleeting embarrassment when no weapons of mass destruction could be found, but with little more than a flick of an eyelash the rationale for the war was reformed. When insurgents in Iraq, and others from outside, refused to lay down their arms, the Iraqi conflict became an integral part of the global war on terrorism.

The war on terrorism, however, was lost the minute the first bombs rained down on Baghdad. Within a matter of a few weeks the small band of terrorists in the Arab world was being reinforced by literally thousands of young Muslims outraged by this further demonstration of American insensitivity toward them, their beliefs, and their sovereignty. Instead of dousing the flicker of international terrorism, the Iraqi war was the equivalent of pouring on gallons of explosive high octane fuel. One doesn't resolve conflict by stoking the fires of hate. On the contrary, conflicts are resolved when the two parties meet face-to-face, make an all-out effort to understand the other side's point of view, and reach a resolution.

South African terrorism ended when the evil apartheid was abandoned following face-to-face talks and months of negotiation between Nelson Mandela and the Afrikaaners responsible for the policy, who had been his persecutors. His way, including the subsequent Truth and Reconciliation Commission, avoided a bloodbath. The military wing of the Irish Republican Army laid down its arms when the Protestant majority in the north finally agreed to a sharing of power, and a principal cause of the conflict was eliminated.

Jewish terrorists in Palestine were transformed into upright citizens and international statesmen after their long struggle for independence resulted in the State of Israel. Similarly, the Palestinian terrorists and their sympathetic brothers and sisters in Hezbollah will cease their violence when there is a just settlement between Israel and its neighbors and a viable and vibrant Palestinian state is born. And there is no point in postponing serious negotiations until the violence ends, because the violence will never end as long as the provocation continues.

Tragically, peace and reconciliation are not the major thrusts of the Project for a New American Century. They are better summed up as unprecedented commercial and industrial arm-twisting backed by a massive military might.

Misguided Strategies

An overview of post-Cold-war developments leads one to the inexorable conclusion that virtually every major strategy has been badly flawed. The war on terrorism, for example, as soon as someone pretended that it could be won by military means. The war on Iraq has spawned more potential terrorists than the world has ever known. It should have been obvious to any thoughtful strategist that only by addressing the root causes of hate and substituting cooperation for conflict could produce the basis for reconciliation.

Economic globalization and the imposition of the "Washington Consensus" on threat of using the international banking system to destroy resisters was equally horrendous. It carried the mantle of a "politically correct" brand of international piracy. The elite clan running the U.S. and the world thought it was in their "best interests" but it has proved to be shortsighted and destructive of any sense of moral and economic justice.

An even greater mystery is why the U.S. would deliberately promote policies that would result in hundreds of North American factories being closed, and the massive transfer of manufacturing capacity to China, the world's fastest rising super-power. It seems like a perverse strategy when the U.S. appears to be subsidizing the industrial might of its successor.

It seems self-evident that the North American auto industry, too, will be sacrificed on the altar of free trade in the absence of either substantial tariffs on Chinese cars or the negotiation of some kind of a deal that would limit imports.

The most tragic wrong turn was to squander the peace dividend from the end of the Cold War on an unnecessary military buildup. Inevitably, other countries felt obliged to follow suit to some extent even in the face of much higher priorities. The result, as the quotation from General Eisenhower so eloquently states at the opening of this chapter, "This world in arms is not spending money alone. It is spending the sweat of its laborers, the genius of its scientists, the hopes of its children."

The Rekindling of Hope

My seemingly endless catalogue of errors, misjudgments, false gods, self-defeating strategies and elitist priorities all relate to past years and administrations. It appeared to many neutral observers that there was little hope for the United States and the world in the absence of an abandonment, followed by a total reversal of the whole list of current policies. Then when the landscape was most bleak, and all hope seemed lost, Barack Obama came on the political stage and hope was marvelously rekindled.

All partisan politics aside the election of Obama in November 2008 and his subsequent inauguration as President were the most positive developments to occur in many years. Not only does he have a much broader and enlightened worldview than his immediate predecessor, he is the first post-World War II president who is not significantly beholden to the elitists who have been influencing policy for their own benefit at the expense of the majority.

The new President has begun well. On the domestic front he has primed the economic pump which was absolutely essential to prevent a serious recession from sliding into an even more serious depression. An effort has been made to make health care available to the disadvantaged and underprivileged who have long been excluded from one of the basic necessities.

President Obama has moved America into the mainstream of world concern over global warming and the future viability of the planet. He has rejected the concept of presidential omnipotence and arbitrary power and is steering the U.S. back in the direction of the rule of law that so many of its brave men and women fought and died to uphold.

In this context the practice of torture has been suspended. Not only is it forbidden by international law, it is totally inconsistent with the word "civilized," as applied to nations. It is extremely doubtful that waterboarding ever saved any American lives, as a few of the neo-totalitarians suggest, but that is not all that is at stake. One should not forget the Golden Rule.

Suppose that the Taliban were to capture twenty or thirty members of the CIA, and remove them to an inaccessible place where they would be subject to continual torture including waterboarding. When the fact became known in the United States, can you imagine the ferocity of the reaction and some of the extreme retaliatory measures that would be suggested? It is wise to remember the truism that "As you sow, so shall ye reap."

It is one of these wider worldview issues where President Obama's initiatives have been so promising. In reaching out to the Muslim world he has taken the first step on the long road to peace and cooperation. A second essential step was to adopt a more even-handed approach to the Israeli-Palestinian conflict in stark contrast to the blatantly one-sided and biased policies of the Bush administration. There will be no peace on earth until there is a "just" peace in the Middle East.

Another olive branch that pleased me immensely was reaching out to the Russian people in the course of a July 2009 visit to the Kremlin. "America wants a strong, peaceful and prosperous Russia ... Look to the future that can be built if we refuse to be burdened by the old obstacles and old suspicions."[19]

Mr. Obama's "Reset" directions are "essentially reversals of recent U.S. policy" as John Bolton, former U.S. ambassador to the United Nations rightly pointed out in an Op-Ed piece in the Toronto *Globe and Mail*. They are, at the same time, exactly what the U.S. and the world need – a complete reversal of virtually all U.S. foreign policy of the 21st century to date.

It was heartwarming to read the following in a report of the President's Moscow visit. "As on some other foreign trips, Mr. Obama's remarks were modest for a U.S. leader, and avoided lecturing his audience or claiming he had all the answers.

"I think it's very important that I come before you with some humility," he tells opposition leaders. "I think in the past there's been a tendency for the United States to lecture rather than to listen. And we obviously still have much work to do with our own democracy."[20]

Dead on, Mr. President. Your "Reset" button produced an agreement to negotiate a new arms reduction treaty with Russia. That is a good start, but the goal should be dramatic cuts on both sides. Change will not come easily, however, due to the iron-fisted opposition of the civil and military bureaucracies that have little interest in reductions in armaments and sharply reduced defense expenditures. Defense Secretary Robert Gates was one of the first on the ramparts. "Pentagon procurement, he said, is plagued by a 'risk-averse culture, a litigious process, parochial interests, … and sometimes adversarial relationships within the Department of Defense.' "[21]

Nearly every one of the common-sense reversals of policy that President Obama has announced to date will be stoutly if not fiercely resisted by adherents to the status quo backed by an army of bureaucrats who provide the sinew.

Anyone unfamiliar with the political process may lament the fact that so many attractive promises don't result in real change. More often than not this is due to the constraints of the system rather than any lack of intent on the part of the politician. Some readers may have seen the British sitcom "Yes, Minister" in which the minister's chief bureaucratic adviser says "yes" to everything the boss suggests, and then proceeds to do whatever he and departmental officials decide is best.

I know from years of experience that there is more truth than fiction in this scenario. My book *Damn the Torpedoes: My Fight to Unify Canada's Armed Forces* is a case history in how difficult, bordering on impossible, it is to change anything of significance. This is directly due to the extraordinary power of what *Harper's* editor Lewis Lapham calls the "Permanent Government" that overshadows the ability of the "Provisional Government" (elected government) to implement its will.

The Permanent Government

It has been described in various ways at various times by various people but I thought Lapham summed it up well in one sentence as part of his "On Politics, Culture and the Media" keynote address to the Canadian Institute of International Affairs national foreign policy conference in October 1996. His definition: "The permanent government is the secular oligarchy that comprises the Fortune 500 companies and all their attendant lobbyists, the big media and entertainment syndicates, the civil and military services, the larger research universities and law firms."[22]

That pretty well sums it all up in a way that conforms with my sense of the real politic. The big supranational corporations with their lobbyists, public relations firms and lawyers, the international banks with their close ties to both the Fed and the Treasury Department, not to mention the IMF and World Bank, the close, almost incestuous relationship between

Bretton Wood institutions and the State Department, the information conglomerates that blur the lines between the manufacture of news and culture and its dissemination, these are all parts of the permanent government that holds the reins of real power. It is a power camouflaged by the diversions created by the antics of the politicians comprising the parallel provisional government.

"Just as the Catholic church was the predominant institution in medieval Europe, and the Roman legion the most efficient manifestation of organized force in the 1st and 2nd centuries BC, so also the transnational corporation arranges the affairs of the late 20th century. The American congress and the American president serve at the pleasure of their commercial overlords, all of whom hold firmly to the belief that all government regulation is wicked (that is, the work of the Devil) and that any impulse that runs counter to the manly interests of business is, by definition, soft, effeminate, and liberal. On behalf of the corporations that pay the campaign money, the politicians collect taxes in the form of handsome subsidies and congenial interest rates. The president performs the duties of a mendicant friar – sympathetic to the sufferings of the peasantry but alert to the concerns of the lords and nobles. Fortunately for the domestic tranquility of the United States, the American political system allows for the parallel sovereignty of two governments, one permanent and the other provisional.

"The permanent government ... hires the country's politicians and sets the terms and conditions under which the citizenry can exercise its right – God-given but increasingly expensive – to life, liberty, and the pursuit of happiness. Obedient to the rule of men, not laws, the permanent government oversees the production of wealth, builds cities, manufactures goods, raises capital, fixes prices, shapes the landscape, and reserves the right to speak to the customers in the language of low motive and base emotion.

"The provisional government is the spiritual democracy that comes and goes on the trend of a political season and oversees the production of pageants. It exemplifies the nation's moral aspirations, protects the citizenry from unworthy or unholy desires, and devotes itself to the mending of the American soul. Positing a rule of law instead of men, the provisional government must live within the cage of high-minded principle, addressing its remarks to the imaginary figure known as the thinking man, a superior being who detests superficial reasoning and quack remedies, never looks at *Playboy*, trusts Bill Moyers, worries about political repression in Liberia, reads and knows himself improved by the op-ed page of the *Wall Street Journal*.[23]

The Cabal

I have tried to make the case that our governments rather than being of, by and for the people, in accordance with the textbooks, are government by the elite for the benefit of the elite. Their dominance is maintained by an intricate network of interlocking private and public groups that control vast banking, commercial, including oil, and "news" distribution empires. Collectively, they are without doubt the most powerful unofficial conglomerate in the world.

Anyone who could stand the "shock and awe" of a more comprehensive reporting of their activities might want to read *The True Story of the Bilderberg Group* by Daniel Estulin[24] who has spent 15 years ferreting out the inside information "from behind closed doors and past the armed guards." I have mentioned these groups briefly in other books based on *Trilateralism: The Trilateral Commission and Elite Planning for World Management*, edited by Holly Sklar.[25]

Earlier in this book when I mentioned the three sisters, the Council on Foreign Relations, the Bilderbergers and the Trilateral Commission, I alluded to the possibility of a fourth. I was referring to what is called "the Cabal." This highly secret group is, in fact, a "shadow government" of the United States that has usurped powers of the Congress and of the president, and established itself as the ultimate arbiter of "American security interests."

It had its origin in the early post-World War II years when America and its armed forces were confronted with the fact of visitors from other planets. The U.S. forces were seriously non-plussed to be faced with the presence of visitors from other planets that were technologically light years more advanced than our best endeavors until that time. So following the retrieval of several crashed space ships the U.S. embarked on a top priority project of reverse engineering the technology that had come into their hands.

For reasons that will only be totally clear when "full disclosure" ultimately occurs, the whole subject of the extraterrestrial presence and technology was to be kept secret from the public. One possible reason was concern that the knowledge might cause a panic of the sort that followed Orson Welles' Halloween broadcast of "The War of the Worlds," in 1938. Another probably more serious concern, was the possibility that the Soviet Union might be embarked on a similar program and should they win the race, they might overtake the U.S. as the world's number one military power.

For whatever reason, the whole subject was assigned a classification higher than that for the hydrogen bomb, in a cover-up seldom if ever equaled. President Truman established a committee to oversee all related developments. It has become widely known as the MJ12, presumably because there were twelve members at the outset. That number has now increased to thirty-six, according to the late Dr. Michael Wolf, probably the most extensively involved member of the shadow community to come forward so far. Although reluctant to divulge names, he did confirm that former American Secretary of State Henry Kissinger, and father of the hydrogen bomb, Edward Teller, were members at the time of his interview with Chris Stoner.[26]

One can only wonder about projects so secret that secretaries of defense and even presidents are not cleared to know. According to Dr. Wolf, Ronald Reagan and George Bush Sr. were very knowledgeable about the ET reality – especially Bush, being former head of the CIA. "Bill Clinton was the least aware. He knows of Area 51 but not S4. Clinton has 'Above Top Secret' and 'Need to Know' clearances, but did not have the 'Umbra Ultra Top Secret Clearance' which gives access to upper level MJ12 secrets and 'Keystone Clearance' for information on ET research."[27]

In a speech to the X-Conference in Washington in April 2008, I asked the rhetorical question about what kind of democracy is the United States when the Commander-in-Chief is unaware of what the troops under his command are doing? The more that is revealed about the Special Access Programs, familiarly known as "black ops," the more one can understand why the cabal is not anxious for the light to shine in their dark corners.

While quite a few Americans and others interested in the ET subject have long been aware of Area 51 in Nevada, Dr. Wolf's brief description may be helpful in grasping the magnitude of what we are talking about. It is a sprawling city, the size of Rhode Island, which continues to grow and has a sister base S4, some twelve miles away, and another named Indian Springs. It employs hundreds of civilian and military personnel and has at least eight different underground black programs along with an annual $2 billion budget. There's intense security outside with martial law inside and it is patrolled by elite guards. Some of the visiting ET scientists live in their own magnificently designed apartments. There are also shopping malls, military-style shops and leisure areas including swimming pools, gymnasiums and basketball courts. The food is excellent.[28]

Dr. Wolf said that technology gained from the ETs include LEDs (light emitting diodes), superconductivity, computer chips, fiber-optics, lasers, gene-splicing therapy, cloning, night-vision equipment, stealth technology, particle beam devices, aerospace ceramics and gravity control flight. It comes as a surprise to some Americans I have met that many of these extraordinary innovations did not originate exclusively in the United States.

"Several different confederations of ETs are visiting us. They include *The Alliance* consisting of human looking beings from the Altair Aquilla and Pleiades star systems; *The Corporate* made up of various 'Grey' races from the Zeta Reticuli system; *The Federation of Worlds* which include an unspecified number of different ET groups from the universe; and the *United Races of Orion* which consist of various beings from that star system. These confederations are also inter-linked with each other."[29]

Some of the Star Visitors are very different in looks from the Greys who resemble the cartoon caricatures. A Pleiadian might walk past you on the street without being recognized as extraterrestrial. Still they do have a great deal in common. They are astounded by how badly we treat the Earth. They can't understand why we wish to destroy it; how multinationals can continually rape this planet through greed and avarice.

When they entertain such noble thoughts, one wonders why we don't embrace them, especially after they have done so much for us, and work in cooperation with the rest of the galaxy. Dr. Wolf explains:

"There is a group of xenophobic and paranoid generals, charged with the protection of American skies, who fear and hate the ETs and are waging war against them. Called the Cabal they use Star Wars weaponry including a neutral particle beam to shoot down ET craft and imprison survivors while attempting to extract information by force. 'The very technology the ETs gave us is now being used against them.' Despised by many within the satellite government, this Cabal also uses aggressive methods against those who try to end the UFO cover-up, a concern being that this aggression will intensify as the big announcement draws ever closer."[30]

This is precisely the reason that I decided to go public in 2005; since then the military universe is unfolding precisely as I had feared. The U.S. generals deeply resented the ETs interference with their nuclear installations and were willing to spend untold billions of U.S. taxpayers' money in a frantic effort to protect the means by which they could blow up the Earth and make it uninhabitable.

Although the generals have access to more ET information than anyone else, they absolutely refuse to listen to what the ETs say, i.e. "All worlds in the galaxy are interconnected. One Hiroshima atomic bomb can affect every different culture."[31] Little wonder that Star Visitors are concerned when we haven't got the common sense to take the essential steps for our own survival. We haven't properly catalogued the damage we have done from the atomic and hydrogen bombs that have already been detonated in the atmosphere let alone recognized and admitted the total insanity of even contemplating use of another one.

The Four Sisters?

While there is no direct connection between the Cabal, the Council on Foreign Relations, the Bilderbergers and the Trilateral Commission, there are enough indirect connections to be worrisome. Henry Kissinger is a long-standing member of the Majestic 12 and would have much inside knowledge of the secret works that have taken place over a very long period of time. Also, when the Majestic number was enlarged it is alleged that a number of European members were included. The public really has a right to know who they are, so that their interests can be assessed.

There are other Bilderbergers who have inside knowledge of what the U.S. has done in response to the ET presence and technology. One of these would be Paul Wolfowitz, former Deputy Secretary of the U.S. Department of Defense, and one of the key authors of the Project for a New American Century. The possibility of industrial links cannot be ignored, either. Remember that Nelson Rockefeller engineered the transfer of much of the responsibility for the UFO and ET files from government to private enterprise and more particularly to those who benefit from fear-based perpetual conflict.

So if all this sounds complicated, that is only because it really is. In this very large orchestra of unknown quality there are more bassoons and percussionists than violins, so the "music" can be deadening. Remember that Werner von Braun warned us that the military-industrial complex would find one excuse after another to justify perpetual conflict, vast military expenditures – first the communists, then the terrorists, and then the extraterrestrials.[32] The beneficiaries are the new totalitarians who have been running the United States and who wanted to extend their power and influence on a global scale.

At the end of World War II the United States brought a sizable group of Nazi scientists to America in order to prevent the Soviets, who had recruited a number of their own, from gaining military ascendancy. It was called Operation Paperclip. I have often wondered if some of their mentality hadn't rubbed off on important elements of the U.S. scientific and military communities with whom they worked. Dr. Wolf reports having worked on genetic experiments in one of the great secret underground labyrinths that are virtually identical to some of those that were performed by Hitler's Nazis in the 1930s. They are certainly experiments that are outside U.S. law and about which the majority of Americans would harbor grave reservations if they were aware. The fact that extraterrestrials have been drafted to assist with the experiments makes the practice all the more questionable.

I think of this when I see the way that the Star Visitors are sometimes portrayed in movies that are based on "leaked" information from the shadow government. The emphasis is on the grotesque and fearsome which would make us think of them as either real or potential enemies, rather than friends who would love to help us save our planet and then share more of their medical and other technology that would greatly enhance our quality of life. It is just one more of the grey (no pun intended) areas that can only be clarified with total disclosure – and I do mean total disclosure, and not just a few innocuous files of old sightings that some governments are now releasing to the public.

The most significant thing Dr. Wolf has told us is that the Cabal, with the help of the Star Visitors, has developed both zero point and cold fusion energy.[33] In other words the means of eliminating the necessity of burning fossil fuels already exists. But it is being kept secret by people who have put their own interests ahead of the survival of the planet.[34] The world has a right to know.

A good case can be made that the increased rate of visits by people from other planets is in some way opening a window of opportunity for our reconnection with the source of our creation whether He be known as God, Allah, the Great Spirit, the Creator, or the Forever. As Dr. Wolf pointed out, the ETs like many things about humans. They especially love our great imagination and creativity along with our ability to have profound dreams. But they would like to speed up our spiritual evolution. Whether a Zeta, Pheiadian, Altaran, Earthling, etc., we share the same God – we are all family.

One Major Inadequate Step

Of the major policy initiatives launched by the Obama administration in its first few months only one has failed the test of being progressive and insightful. That one is the plan to "reform" the banking and financial system.

On June 17, 2009 the U.S. Treasury released a White Paper, "Financial Regulatory Reform: A New Foundation," outlining the Obama administration's proposal for the most extensive reforms for the U.S. financial regulatory system since the Great Depression.

After reading all 85-pages of the document I am forced to conclude that the use of the word "reform" is a misnomer. It correctly states that the roots of the current crisis go back decades. It then continues by saying "Years without a serious economic recession bred complacency among financial intermediaries and investors," without any hint of what the root causes really were. There is no blunt admission that banks are far, far too highly leveraged and that the percentage of new money created by privately owned banks is much too high compared to that created by governments.

This omission is a passive acceptance of the so-called "capital adequacy" system and the private banks virtual monopoly on money creation. What is proposed, then, is a perpetuation of an unfair, unjust, basically silly and totally unstable system! Succinctly put it leaves Wall Street and the international banking clan in ultimate control of the financial fate of most nation states at the expense of the health and welfare of billions of innocent people.

208

This is a monumental disappointment to those of us who thought that the latest disastrous meltdown of stock market values, real estate and commodity prices could prove to be the best thing that has happened to the world in a long time provided our political leaders seize the opportunity to wrest control of our lives and future welfare from the bankers who have made life miserable for so many of us for so long. We accepted the necessity of the politicians scrambling around trying to patch up the old system as an emergency measure. An aid package here, some capital investment there, all designed to keep the banking system from collapsing completely – an outcome that had to be avoided at any cost because if we had not been able to pay our bills by check, or gain access to the small amount of cash we need on a daily basis, there would have been total chaos – a situation too dreadful to imagine.

These emergency measures have had a stabilizing effect though they have not compensated for the vast amounts of virtual money that disappeared when the banks called their loans in order to improve their balance sheets. The net result is continued high unemployment and underutilization of capacity.

I admit that the government document proposes a number of measures appropriate to the restoration of confidence in the existing system. What it does not say is that the system itself is hopelessly inadequate to meet the legitimate needs of the United States and the world in the years ahead. One would have hoped, therefore, that instead of proposing dozens of measures that remind one of welding a few new steel plates over the innumerable holes in the hull of an old and leaky ship, some visionary leader would have been yelling from the mountain tops "It's time to build a new ship compatible with the 21st century!" As long as the current highly-leveraged system remains in place the world economy and the fate and well-being of billions of people will be its hostage.

I do not hold President Obama personally responsible. He is a lawyer and in my whole long career I have only met a handful of lawyers who had even a rudimentary knowledge of the mysteries of money and banking. No, it is the President's financial advisers who are the authors of his first major misstep. They are deeply steeped in the old ways and some have been significant contributors to the entrenchment of the system that failed us.

The bottom line, however, is that the buck stops in the Oval Office. It is incumbent upon the President to learn the fundamentals of money and banking to the point that he has the confidence to overrule his advisers and effect real reform.

More rides on the outcome than one can easily imagine. Not only does the health and welfare of billions of people depend on the outcome in a very direct and literal way, the debt load of all countries will be determined by it.

It is possible that President Obama can achieve the distinction of being a great president without solving the rather simple riddle of the monetary scam. If he were to master it, and achieve what his predecessors have failed to do, he would be destined to be remembered as one of the greatest presidents in American history.

Chapter 9

ENDING THE WORLD FINANCIAL CRISIS

"Banking was conceived in iniquity and was born in sin. The Bankers own the earth. Take it away from them, but leave them the power to create money, and with the flick of the pen they will create enough money to buy it back again. However, take that power away from them and all the great fortunes like mine will disappear, and they ought to disappear, for this would be a happier and better world to live in. But if you wish to remain the slaves of Bankers, and pay the cost of your own slavery, let them continue to create money."

Sir Josiah (later Baron) Stamp, Director, Bank of England 1928-1941

THE WORLD NEEDS A MASSIVE REAL MONEY REFLATION

"Never again!" should be the rallying cry of real reformers all around the world. Never again should we have a banking system where a combination of greed and incompetence can doom billions of people to lives of misery and hopelessness. So the real issue is who is going to run the world? Will it be the politicians that we elect and pay to look after our health and welfare? Or will it be unelected, unaccountable bankers at all levels who have pretended to know what was best for us when in fact they were only interested in their own welfare, without concern for the money supply that they have been diluting indiscriminately.

Under the existing "capital adequacy" system banks are not only allowed to lend or invest their own money (capital), the rules (as interpreted) permit them to multiply the process nineteen (or more) times by simply creating the credit (virtual money) to do it. So when the market value of their total assets drops 5% or more, on average, their original capital is wiped out, and they are bankrupt. It is as simple as that.

An everyday life experience may be easier to understand. You buy a house for $200,000 and use your life savings of $10,000 as a 5% down payment. You assume a mortgage of $190,000 to cover the balance. Some time later you have to move to another city. Meanwhile the market value of your house has fallen below $190,000. When you sell the house you lose your entire capital of $10,000 and may not receive enough to pay off the outstanding mortgage. That is the position in which many banks found themselves.

In this latest meltdown there were some dramatic declines in the values of mortgages, and mortgage-backed financial instruments. Stock markets tanked, and the ensuing days of roller-coaster rises and declines wiped off as much as forty percent or more of their previous values when they reached their November 2008 and March 2009 lows. With losses on this scale some of the largest banks lost their entire capital base, or more, and that is the reason that the whole unstable system teetered on the brink of disaster.

The patchwork solutions that have been applied have at least restored some sense of order. Although banks are now being more selective in their risk assessments, and several are cracking down on their credit card customers, their doors are open again to credit-worthy borrowers. That will help some established businesses but will provide little relief to the people who need it most. Struggling entrepreneurs and undercapitalized initiatives of various kinds will be ignored and allowed to wither on the vine. So the availability of credit is welcomed by a small minority but provides no comfort to the vast majority.

A front-page story in the Toronto *Globe and Mail* of November 2, 2008 read as follows: "Universities eye 'painful cuts' in wake of crisis. With endowment funds taking a beating, student aid, scholarships, hiring and academic programs could all be on the chopping block."[1] Another headline in *The New York Times* of November 17, 2008 read "Facing Deficits, States Get out Sharper Knives – HUGE REVENUE DECLINE –

Deep Cuts, U.S. Loans, Hiring Freezes, Taxes are All on Table."[2] While the specific items vary from institution to institution these headlines captured the essence of the road ahead when city, state and provincial governments will be cutting back programs. Each of these actions tends to exacerbate and prolong the recessionary period.

To end the recession quickly all of these types of decisions that are a consequence of the meltdown have to be reversed. The common denominator in each decision is money – cash money. But where will it come from? In the case of universities, tuition fees, on average, are already too high for many middle class and working class students. So, too, are municipal, state and provincial taxes judged by what is politically tenable.

The only hope, then, lies with federal governments that have authority over money and banking and bear overall responsibility for the welfare of their citizens, and the economic climate that affects them so directly. Should governments incur deficits if they have none, or increase them if they are already in deficit as recommended by the late, great English economist John Maynard Keynes? Or are there other alternatives?

This dilemma leads to two more fundamental questions. Are recessions a fundamental facet of the system, and therefore we should expect our economic tsunami every so often as suggested by former Chairman of the Federal Reserve System Alan Greenspan? Or are they the result of faulty economic theory, as I will argue? Two other questions are related to the first. What is money? And where does it come from?

But first, the multi-trillion dollar question. Why should a national or world economy that has all of the machinery and labor required to run smoothly and produce as much as it had done previously, suddenly start producing less? It doesn't make any sense! The problem, on analysis, is insufficient gas – gas in this case being money.

What is Money?

What is money? It is a good question for which there is no easy answer. It has meant different things to different people in different cultures at different times. In early cultures money usually meant copper, iron, silver or gold coins, although there were many innovative exceptions such as cattle, sea shells, beads and playing cards to meet extenuating circumstances.

A dual system of metallic coins and barter acted as the principal financial instruments worldwide for centuries. With the advent of the Industrial Revolution, however, the volume of commerce became so great that the widespread use of paper money became essential. Sometimes the paper money was convertible into gold or silver and sometimes it was not, but that is too long a story to include here.

In any event the practice of convertibility into gold was ended by U.S. President Richard Nixon in 1971 when the market value of gold rose above the exchange rate and some foreign governments were taking advantage of a profit-making opportunity. Incidentally, of all the ideas being floated around today perhaps the worst is a return to some kind of gold standard. It would be one more millstone around the neck of international commerce.

Besides, most of us don't really care how much gold we can buy with our money. We do care very much, however, how many groceries, and other goods and services of all kinds that we can purchase. It is the "basket" of our day-to-day needs that concerns us – our total range of needs and wants as measured in the consumer price index.

Our current monetary system is quite complex. In addition to a few coins we have three major sources of "money." The bills we carry are known as *fiat money* that Webster's Dictionary defines as "paper currency that has value only by law and is not backed by gold or silver." This kind of money is created by governments or their agents – usually a central bank – and can be called government-created money, or GCM, for short.

Another kind of money is virtual money, or phantom money, as I call it. This money is created by privately owned banks and can be called bank-created money, or BCM. A third important source is the money that is "created" by the issuance of credit cards. Let's call it CCM. A retired chief economist of one of Canada's largest banks summed it all up this way. "Money is what is generally accepted in exchange for goods and services." That is as good a definition as any.

Without in any way underestimating the importance of credit card money for which some kind of regulation appears to be highly desirable, my examination relates primarily to government-created money and bank-created money, and especially the quantity of each that determine our financial destiny. It is essential to take a closer look at the relationship between the two, and the advantages and disadvantages of each. If readers are similar to most of my friends these are matters that have not been given as much thought as they deserve.

Where Does Money Come From?

When I was writing my first book on the subject, which was called *Funny Money*, even though there wasn't anything very funny about it, I asked scores of my friends and acquaintances – not including my circle of economist friends, some of whom are well versed in the subject, while the majority is not – the leading question that is the heading for this section.

My sample included doctors, lawyers, dentists, accountants, newspaper editors-in-chief, newspaper publishers, financial page columnists and scores of ordinary common-sense people. I asked each one the same question. "Do you know where money comes from?" Some were a little hesitant about the question but, when pressed, they all said that the government prints it. When I asked the follow-up question of what percentage of the new money "printed" each year the government created, the answers ranged from 60% to 100 percent. No one came up with a number smaller than 60 percent. If that were true we would have a very different system from the one that actually exists. Not one of my samples had what you might call a working knowledge of the monetary system, yet these are the kinds of people who tell governments how they should be running things.

In fact, most of the new money added to the money supply each year (printed, manufactured or put into circulation, if you prefer – it's all the same) is created by privately owned banks. In his book *"Money, Whence it came, Where it went,"* the late economist John Kenneth Galbraith said, "The process by which banks create money is so simple the mind is repelled. When something so important is involved, a deeper mystery seems only decent."[3]

The fact that private banks "print" money is extremely difficult for many of my friends to accept. Most of them believe the bankers' myth that the money they lend you today is money that I or someone else deposited yesterday. The odds of that being true are infinitesimal. Usually banks are fully lent so when you go in for a loan they have to create the money for you.

This is the way it works. Suppose that you want to borrow $35,000 to buy a new car. So you visit your friendly banker and ask for a loan. He/she will ask you for collateral – some stocks, bonds, a second mortgage on your house or cottage or, if you are unable to supply any of these, the co-signature of a well-to-do friend or relative. When the collateral requirement is satisfied you will be asked to sign a note for the principal amount with an agreed rate of interest.

When the paperwork is complete, and the note signed, your banker will make an entry on the bank's computer and, presto, a $35,000 credit will appear in your account which you can use to buy your car. The important point is that seconds earlier that money did not exist. It was created out of thin air – so to speak.

The banking equation is a kind of double-entry bookkeeping where your note becomes an asset on the bank's books, and the new money that was deposited to your account is a liability. The profit for the bank comes from the difference between the low rate of interest, if any, you would be paid on your deposit if you didn't spend the borrowed money immediately, and the much higher rate you would be obliged to pay on your note – the technical term is "the spread."

An even more striking illustration of how the system works is to consider someone in the building business who borrows $200,000 to build a house. This money is used to pay the people who dig clay from a pit and make bricks, the bricklayers who lay the bricks, the woodsmen who cut trees to make lumber, the carpenters who use it to build the frame, the miners who extract the metals for the hardware, and the manufacturers who turn out the plumbing, wiring and fixtures. But when they are all finished, it is the bank that owns the house.

The bank did little more than create the "money" which acted as the intermediary to facilitate construction. Nevertheless, because it was created as debt, all of the money has to be repaid when the house is sold because there may be the equivalent of a lien on it that has to be discharged by the bank. Consequently, the builder has to sell the house at a price that will allow him to repay the bank and, if he is lucky, leave a little over to reward him for the work he has done and the risk he has taken. If he can't, and there is a shortfall, he will have to make up the difference to prevent the bank from liquidating part or all of the collateral pledged to get the loan.

In reality, the banks have turned the world into one humongous pawn shop. You hock your stocks, bonds, house, business, rich mother-in-law or country and the bank(s) will give you a loan based on the value of the collateral. Still there is an element of uncertainty in dealing with the banks that doesn't apply with legitimate pawn shops. The latter don't phone you and ask for their money back if the price of silver or gold goes down after they have given you cash for your gold watch or silver candlesticks.

The banks, on the other hand, often change the terms of the deal with little warning. If the market value of your collateral goes down, they phone and insist that you either provide additional collateral, which you may not have, or give them their money back. That isn't always easy or convenient for you to do – especially on short notice.

That is exactly what happened when the crisis began in the fall of 2007. As the market value of assets that banks were holding as collateral for loans began to fall, the banks demanded increased collateral or the repayment of part or all of their loans. Many borrowers had to sell stocks into a falling market – a dizzying downward spiral that the economists call de-leveraging. This would not have been necessary if the banks themselves were not so highly leveraged. They have loaned or invested twenty times as much money as they actually have on the basis of collateral that was no longer adequate for the amount that was loaned.

Bank Leverage: The Banks Are Never Satisfied!

"I believe that banking institutions are more dangerous to our liberties than standing armies. If the American people ever allow private banks to control the issue of their currency, first by inflation, then by deflation, the banks and corporations that will grow up around the banks will deprive the people of all property until their children wake-up homeless on the continent their fathers conquered."

Thomas Jefferson, 1802

Although European banking can be traced back to Roman times, I will begin my story of the gradual increase of bank leverage with the creation of the Bank of England over three hundred years ago. The Bank of England was conceived as a solution to a dilemma. King William's War, 1688-1697, had been extremely costly and this resulted in much of

England's gold and silver going to the continent in payment of debt. As a result the money supply was sorely depleted and something had to be done to keep the wheels of commerce turning. Someone got the bright idea that establishing a bank might help to fill the void.

At the time the Bank was chartered the scheme involved an initial subscription by its shareholders of £1,200,000 in gold and silver which would be lent to the government at 8 percent. That seems fair enough, although the interest rate was more than ample for a government-guaranteed investment. It was only the beginning, however, because in addition to a £4,000 management fee, the Bank of England was granted an advantage only available to banks and bankers. It was granted authority to issue "banknotes" in an amount equal to its capital and lend the notes into circulation. This was not the first case of paper money issued by private banks in the modern era but it was the first of great and lasting significance in the English-speaking world.[4]

It was the same system that had been developed by the goldsmiths of Lombard Street, in London. By lending the same money twice the Bank could double the interest received on its capital. Nice work if you can get it and you can get it with a bank charter. It is not too surprising, then, that discussions of this advantage encouraged some members of parliament to become shareholders in the Bank. Money lenders learned early, and have never forgotten, that it pays to have friends in parliament.[5]

In the slightly over three hundred years since the Bank of England began with a leverage of two-to-one (in effect, lending twice the amount of its subscribed capital), the deal has been sweetened many times. In the early years of the 20th century, federally chartered U.S. banks were required to have a gold reserve of 25 percent. They could lend four times as much as they had gold in their vaults, though they always required some redeemable asset as collateral. State chartered banks were subject to less restraint and there were some shocking examples of excess.

With the introduction of Central Banks, the Federal Reserve System in the U.S. and the Bank of Canada north of the border, the system changed in form though not in substance. Banknotes issued by private banks were phased out and replaced by a uniform, legal tender, currency. In the U.S., Federal Reserve Notes became predominant, while in Canada, the Bank of Canada was given a monopoly on the creation of legal tender paper money. In the process banks were required to keep cash, legal tender, reserves against deposits instead of gold.

Consequently, in Canada, when I was younger, the cash reserve requirement for banks was 8% which allowed them to lend up to twelve and a half times that amount. Today the cash reserve requirements in the U.S. are 3% for current accounts, 0% for savings accounts and 0% for Eurodollar accounts. In Canada, the reserve requirement is 0%, period! You are lucky if your bank has a cent, or a cent-and-a-half, in cash, for every dollar you think you have in the bank. The only reason they can get away with this is the time-honored one of knowing from experience that only a handful of depositors are likely to ask for cash at any one time. If for any reason depositors' confidence was shaken, and they began a "run" on the bank, they would be out of luck because their "money" doesn't exist in real form. Their only hope would be a massive intervention by the Federal Reserve in the U.S. or the Bank of Canada in Canada to monetize (print legal tender money to buy) the bonds and other assets held by the banks.

It was Prime Minister Brian Mulroney who eliminated the requirement for Canadian banks to hold cash reserves. The Bank Act of 1991 phased them out. This was a gift worth several billion dollars a year to the banks, at taxpayers' expense. The banks were allowed to spend their reserves to purchase bonds and treasury bills on which we, the taxpayers, pay several billions a year in interest payments.

A Change in System

In effect the phasing out of cash reserve requirements marked the beginning of an entirely new system known as "capital adequacy." Banks are allowed to own assets that are equal to several times their paid up capital. Regulations have varied but for Canadian banks the permitted limit has been twenty times and most large U.S. banks have been operating at similar multiples, while some merchant banks have scaled the heights to much higher numbers.

The new system is quite inferior to the old one of cash reserves because in practice it is pretty well tantamount to total deregulation. It is a system that the Bank for International Settlements (BIS), with its headquarters in Basel, Switzerland, has foisted upon an unsuspecting world. It is a part of the plan to switch the world banking system to 0% reserves in accord with the theories of the late Professor Milton Friedman.

The Current Chaos is the Legacy of Milton Friedman and the Chicago School

In 1996, the first chapter of my book *Surviving the Global Financial Crisis: The Economics of Hope for Generation X*, was entitled "Monetarists and the Chicago School Blew It!" The first two paragraphs read as follows.

"Let's face it, the monetarist counter-revolution of the last twenty years has been one monumental flop. This was inevitable because monetarism is a hothouse plant bred and nurtured in the esoteric garden of the Academy. It was never suitable for transplanting directly into the real economy where, despite its cosmetic innocence, it would have the same smothering effect demonstrated by the purple loosestrife when transported from Europe to the swamps of North America. It crowded out everything traditional and worthwhile.

"It is true that 'practical monetarism,' as former Federal Reserve Board Chairman Paul Volcker called the variety that he planted in the real world, reduced the level of inflation substantially and dampened the inflationary expectations that had raised their ugly head. But at what cost? The implementation of monetarism has created more financial turbulence than we have seen at any time since World War II. It has induced two horrendous recessions, slowed economic growth, produced unconscionable levels of unemployment and raised the debt burden to the point where the world economy is set on a collision course with disaster. Thanks to 'practical monetarism' the world financial system is headed for a meltdown."[6]

It would have been nice if that prediction had proved to be wrong. But the cards were stacked from the beginning. Professor Milton Friedman and his colleagues made several cardinal errors in their analyses. The first was the attempt to make a science of something that is really more of a combined art and science that used to be described as political economy. In the process Friedman and his colleagues produced complex mathematical models that are good fun for mathematicians, but which don't relate to the real world where there are an almost infinite number of variables.

Another fundamental error was Friedman's misdiagnosis of the inflation of the late '60s and early '70s. He claimed that it was classic inflation, defined as "too much money chasing too few goods." He couldn't have been more wrong. The supermarkets were crammed with goods, and small stores were going bankrupt every day for lack of customers for their wares. The facts refuted Friedman's thesis, but that didn't matter to the Chicago School.

Friedman sold his theory to thousands of students on the basis of his research which had showed that for a hundred years in a hundred countries prices had risen in direct proportion to the amount of money created. While it may be true that figures don't lie, they don't always reveal the whole truth either. In this case Friedman's observations are about as helpful as the discovery that for a hundred years in a hundred countries summer followed winter.

That, too, is true but it doesn't tell you whether the summers were too hot and dry, too cool and wet, or just about the right balance for abundant crops. The devil is in the details and Friedman completely overlooked a new phenomenon that had profoundly influenced prices in the '60s and '70s. For the first time in recorded economic history nominal wages in Western countries had risen two or more times faster than productivity for twenty-five consecutive years.

It had been this disconnect between wages and productivity that had been primarily responsible for the inflation of those years. True, there were a couple of blips caused by increases in oil prices when the Organization of Petroleum Exporting Countries (OPEC) got its act together. But this was never responsible for more than a small fraction of the inflation of that period. Nor was the Vietnam War the culprit, as most orthodox economists insisted.

The data from fifteen Organization for Economic Co-operation and Development (OECD) countries shows clearly that the principal cause of inflation in the '50s, '60s and '70s was nominal wages rising faster than productivity. The average of averages for fifteen countries showed that prices rose by the difference between the average increase in nominal wages, and the average increase in real output per member of the labor force, within one-quarter of one percent, which is about as close as you can get in economics.

The arithmetic is simple. If each of us, on average, produces less than 2% more goods and services than we did the year before, as was the case in the United States and Canada from 1964 to 1991, how large a real wage increase can we have? The answer is, less than 2%, on average. Anything more than that creates inflation – of the cost-push variety.

The problem with misdiagnosis in economics, as in medicine, is that prescribing the wrong medication can produce excruciatingly painful results. So when Friedman's disciple Paul Volcker, Chairman of the Federal Reserve Board in the United States, Gerald Bouey, Governor of the Bank of Canada, and other central bankers restricted the money supply in 1981-82, their actions caused the worst recession since the Great Depression of the 1930s. Economies were strangled, growth rates plummeted, government revenues fell dramatically and deficits soared; these were rolled over into debt which compounded at the artificially high interest rates, and headed to heights that put the world in hock to the money lenders.

The ratio of total public and private debt to GDP in the United States had fallen from slightly above 165% in 1946, to a low of 134% in 1951, and then remained more or less constant in the 135-145% range for thirty years until 1981. It was only when the Fed adopted the monetarist "theology," and its consequent high interest rates, that the ratio began to rise again to a level of approximately 200% of GDP – well above the 1946 peak.[7]

The totally disastrous recession of 1981-82 not only put millions of people out of their jobs, their homes, their businesses, and off their farms, it was the beginning of a new era of high debt for governments, both domestic and foreign, that has never been brought under control, and never will be as long as the present system continues. About 95% of all the new money created every year is created as debt. The debt load just keeps getting bigger and bigger until the balloon bursts and recession sets in.

Sadly, just as we were beginning to recover from that smashing blow, the central bankers induced another recession in 1990-91, and the world economy is still reeling from the cumulative effects.

Perhaps the saddest commentary of all, is that almost twenty years later central bankers, steeped in the Friedman dogma, still don't see the real nature of the problem or the appropriate policy mix necessary to cope.

The third and probably most disastrous of Friedman's errors related to his views on the necessity for banks to maintain cash reserves against deposits.

The Bank for International Settlements (BIS)

In 1974 the Bank for International Settlements, the central bankers' bank, endorsed Friedmanism. As a result, the central banks of the western world changed the rules that, however inadequate, had kept the system afloat since the end of World War II. It has been downhill for the world system ever since.

Central banks drastically reduced their holdings of government bonds, that had filled the function of interest-free loans. This was a big loss to taxpayers because their governments then had to borrow from private banks and pay interest at market rates. More subtle, yet more profound, the economy began to split into two parts – an increasingly complex financial economy and an increasingly neglected real economy. The financial economy was soon recognized as the place where easy money could be made. The people who printed money and played with money became the exorbitantly paid high rollers who eclipsed most – though not all – of the visionaries who developed new products and new services.

Bright mathematicians created exotic financial instruments that were so complex that they were not fully understood even by financial managers charged with assessing the risk. There were significant underlying unknowns that were downplayed in order to keep the risk within the limits imposed by "capital adequacy," the new regulatory jargon adopted by the BIS that proved to be "capital inadequacy."

Inevitably, in an industry that was to all intents and purposes self-regulated, greed that knew no bounds trumped both prudence and common sense. The system collapsed once again in 2008 and taxpayers were asked to ride to the rescue one more time.

Periodic meltdowns are integral to a system that is so heavily dependent on bank-created credit. It's like blowing up a balloon. The balloon keeps getting bigger and bigger until someone sticks a pin in it. Then the system looks like a deflated balloon and it takes a long while to reflate it.

It should be self-evident that the boom-bust system that has plagued humankind for so long must end. Propping up the existing system must be what Albert Enstein had in mind when he wrote, "*The definition of insanity is doing the same thing over and over again and expecting different results.*"

My Proposal: A New Economics

"All the forces in the world are not as powerful as an idea whose time has come."

Victor Hugo

First I would like to list just a few important points for you to think about as you contemplate the major change in direction that national economies must take in order to secure your future and that of your children and their children.

- In former times monarchs exercised the sovereign right to issue the currency of the realm.

- In modern times federal politicians have inherited the sovereign control of money and banking on behalf of all the people.

- Instead of exercising that right on behalf of the people, federal politicians, except in a few rare cases, have granted licenses to privately-owned banks and allowed them to create most of the nation's money supply.

- These same politicians, when they are short of money, often borrow from the private banks and pay them interest on money that they could have created for themselves, interest free. Can you think of anything more ridiculous?

- The chartered (privately-owned) banks now create approximately ninety-five percent of all the new money created each year.

- All of this money is created as debt – debt on which interest must be paid.

- No one creates any money with which to pay that interest.

- Consequently the only way we can collectively pay the interest on bank-created money is to borrow more and go deeper in debt in the process.

- If the average interest rate on the debt is higher than the growth in gross domestic product the debt rises faster than GDP until eventually the debt burden is too heavy for the system to sustain.

- The system collapses!

- Everyone scurries around trying to repair the unseaworthy ship so that the cycle can start all over again.

What I am proposing is a new economic regime based on a fairer and more stable sharing of the money-creation function between governments, who control the patents on behalf of the people, and the private banks, the licensees who have benefited so enormously as a result of their right to "print" money.

In theory governments should create all the new money as a function of their sovereignty. If they did, however, they would have to set up new institutions to ration some of it out to meet the needs of industry and commerce and that is a function that is more suitable to privately-administered enterprise. So any long-term solution should be designed to meet the needs of governments, on the one hand, and business enterprise on the other.

In a couple of earlier books, including one in the Jubilee year at the turn of the century, I proposed that private bank leverage allowing them to own assets equal to twenty or thirty times their invested capital be reduced to assets equal to twice their paid up capital including retained earnings.

On reflection, however, I think that may be a bit Draconian. In addition it should be self-evident that the system of capital adequacy should be abandoned altogether as a principal control mechanism. It is time to turn our backs on an experiment that didn't work satisfactorily in favor of one that definitely will and that results in the transfer of power over the economy from private banks to duly elected officials.

So I am now proposing a return to the cash reserve system as the regulator of private banks money creation. It is not really a new system but rather a re-introduction of the one that existed prior to 1974 when central banks adopted Friedmanism. What would be new is that banks, near banks and deposit-taking institutions of all kinds would not be allowed to create assets in excess of three times the cash reserves in their vaults or on deposit with the central bank. It will take time to implement the changeover as I will explain later. It is a solution, however, that meets three important criteria.

First, it allows banks about the same maximum ratio of debt that a bank would consider prudent in making a commercial loan to industry. (Bank deposits are debts that banks owe to their depositors.)

Second, there would be virtually no chance that a bank could fail and, consequently, the need for a periodic government (taxpayer) bailout would be eliminated.

Third, and most important from a humanitarian and world view, governments of nation states would be able to create enough new money each year to balance any kind of realistic budget without resort to excessive taxation.

The figures are really impressive. For the years 2004 and 2005 in Canada, the average increase in the money supply (M2+) was about $43.3 billion. The government's share under the proposed formula would have been $14.29 billion a year. In 2006 and 2007 the gross increase was much higher and averaged $76.9 billion. The government's share would have been just over $26 billion.[8] Extrapolating to the United States the figures would be more than ten times greater. In both cases the extra cash available without resorting to higher taxation would be enormously helpful.

The banks would still have ample capacity to meet the core needs of business, industry and consumers – the sole justification for their licenses to print (create) money. Commercial banks should not be allowed to finance leveraged buyouts, the purchase of stocks on margin (a major cause of instability in times of crisis), to lend money to hedge funds or play Russian roulette with exotic derivatives. In other words, the divorce between the financial and real economies should end with reconciliation and remarriage.

Implementation Phase I – Jump Start the World Economy

How much government-created money will be required to jump start the world economy? A lot of it! Any number is just a guess because there is no formula for a rescue operation of this magnitude, but let's say ten trillion dollars, or equivalent, worldwide, to start, and more as needed until the desired result is achieved.

The cash infusion could be coupled with a short-term tax holiday for families of low and medium incomes and/or a modest across the board tax cut for those same income groups. Once the augmented source of government funds is established the number of permutations and combinations is very large.

It would be nice if the G20 group of nations agreed to implement the policy simultaneously. But this is not essential and any country or group of countries can act on their own. It is highly desirable, however, that the United States take the lead because it was the meltdown of U.S. institutions that spread like a virus around the world.

In its case the new Obama administration's opening salvo of close to a trillion was probably appropriate but may need to be followed up by additional stimulus until the sleeping giant shows unmistakable signs of resuscitation, followed by a quick return to full health and vigor. Much of the new money should be made available for under-funded projects at every level, including health care, education and infrastructure. In the case of the latter, however, commitments should be of an order that can be guaranteed for a three or preferably four-year minimum. There are few experiences more frustrating than making plans and then having to cancel before the construction or installation is complete as a result of changing economic conditions.

Each country or union of countries will have to work out the legalities of its own solution. All will be required to establish or re-establish cash reserve requirements for privately-owned banks. This is the answer to a former governor of the Bank of Canada who, when it was suggested that government-created money be used to escape from a particularly bad economic situation, said "But who will hold the government-created cash? Will people keep it under their mattresses or in their attics?" The banks will hold it governor, that should be an essential part of their mandate.

Implementation Phase II – A Permanent Stable System

Before this section was written I talked to an American banker who had been referred to me by a mutual friend. I asked him how long he thought that the current recession might last and he replied two or three years but it could be as long as six or eight. I offered to send him a copy of one of my old books where I argue that recessions are unnecessary and that there is a simple answer to the instability.

I become very upset when I hear former Fed Chairman Alan Greenspan and former Secretary of the Treasury Henry Paulson make it sound as though the 2008 experience has been a very rare event and, by implication, we should just accept it as inherent to the system and be prepared to muddle through. They remind me of my economics professors who could never give me a straight answer when I asked them if recessions and depressions were necessary.

Economic history tells us that there have been a number of "panics," more than we recall. And for sixty years since I first discovered what went wrong I have been of the strongly held view that none of them was necessary. Not one! Furthermore, even one more is one too many!

So what I am proposing is a system where bank leverage is so sensibly limited that it will be almost impossible for them to get in trouble; and where federal governments everywhere will have enough debt free income that they will be able to balance their budgets without taking on additional debt. In fact, changing the system would be a heaven-sent opportunity to reduce their debt somewhat and perhaps pay off most or all of Third World debt as well.

The money (cash) required to revitalize the U.S. and other national economies will be insufficient to allow banks to meet their 34% reserve requirements so governments should take advantage of the opportunity to monetize enough of their debt (buy back their bonds with cash they print) to achieve that goal. It would also be the opportunity for the industrialized world, collectively, to use some of the proceeds to pay off most, if not all Third World and developing world debt and still have enough left over to reduce their own indebtedness significantly.

There has been much talk of paying off Third World debt, a great deal of which can be considered "odious" by any just and moral standard.[9] So far, however, that is almost all it has been – just talk. And to be fair to political leaders, it would be virtually impossible for them to increase taxes to the extent necessary to accomplish the job that must be done.

To give the banks the privilege of financing it, however, as part of the de-leveraging process, would be a kind of just penance – a kind of reparations – for the part they have played in the whole dismal game of debt accumulation as well as the multi-trillion dollar losses due to the 2008 meltdown. This is not only politically desirable, it would be applauded by millions who want to see the poorest of the poor given a bit of a leg up in their struggle to achieve the most basic of needs.

This massive de-leveraging is just what the world desperately needs. Leverage has been the key contributor to the increasing gap between rich countries and poor countries and to the widening income spread between rich and poor within countries.

Even the banks will win in the long run because they will be perceived more favorably by most of us, their dutiful customers; and they will become more stable, reliable members of the world economic family to boot.

In *Funny Money* and its U.S. version, *Surviving the Global Financial Crisis: The Economics of Hope for Generation X*, I referred to econometric simulations that had produced amazing results. The most significant new input, of course, was the addition of modest amounts of government-created money to federal government revenues. There was another assumption that contributed positively. It was the imposition of mandatory wage and profit guidelines in cases where monopoly or market power resulted in arbitrary wage and price increases. The policy only applied to monopolies and oligopolies, but it did theoretically limit the wage price spiral that had led to inflation and then stagflation.

The principle is based on the philosophy of the English political philosopher John Stuart Mill, who stated that the freedom of any person or group ends at the point where it trespasses on another person or group. If the new money created each year is distributed vertically, through higher wages for the already employed and consequently higher prices for existing output, it will not be available to finance additional employment and increased output. If there is any one thing that must be learned in order to understand the failure of monetarism it is this. To the extent that the increase in the money stock – translated into income – is distributed vertically, in excess of increases in productivity, it contributes to higher wages and prices rather than increased output. Unless wage increases to the already employed are limited to the average increase in real output, inflation will continue; and if inflation continues interest rates will be higher than necessary because lenders will continue to demand a premium as a hedge against the anticipated inflation. This has negative implications for governments and for the economy as a whole. It is the people who must bear the extra burden.

The other great advantage of continuous low inflation is that it permits a significantly higher level of employment. If there is one benefit which tops the list from a humanitarian point of view it is the availability of jobs for people who want to work. This has been the over-riding motive in my life-long obsession with economics because I think the need to contribute to the common well-being is fundamental to one's feeling of self worth. Finally, it should be noted, negligible inflation protects the value of savings for everyone.

There are alternatives for anyone for whom any type of regulation is anathema. One is a social contract – an agreement by both big business and big labor to accept voluntary restrictions. Another is to use taxing power to make it unprofitable to exceed voluntary guidelines. Either is theoretically workable but experience would lead one to believe that there is no long-term substitute for guidelines as a substitute for rigorous enforcement of anti-trust principles.

The Fed Must be Replaced by a Publicly Owned Central Bank of the United States

Anyone familiar with the history of the Fed and the real reasons for its birth would shout Halleluiah at its demise. The whole sordid story of its beginning is told in *The Creature from Jekyll Island* by G. Edward Griffin where the summary of the first chapter begins as follows.

"The basic plan for the Federal Reserve System was drafted at a secret meeting held in November 1910 at the private resort of J.P. Morgan on Jekyll Island off the coast of Georgia. Those who attended represented the great financial institutions of Wall Street and, indirectly, Europe as well. The reason for secrecy was simple. Had it been known that rival factions of the banking community had joined together, the public would have been alerted to the possibility that the bankers were plotting an agreement in restraint of trade – which, of course, is exactly what they were doing. What emerged was a cartel agreement with five objectives: stop the growing competition from the nation's newer banks; obtain a franchise to create money out of nothing for the purpose of lending; get control of the reserves of all banks so that the more reckless ones would not be exposed to currency drains and bank runs; get the taxpayer to pick up the cartel's inevitable losses; and convince Congress that the purpose was to protect the public. It was realized that the bankers would have to become partners with the politicians and that the structure of the cartel would have to be a central bank. The record shows that the Fed has failed to achieve its stated objectives. That is because those were never its true goals. As a banking cartel, and in terms of the five objectives stated above, it has been an unqualified success."[10]

Griffin goes on to explain in great detail how the wool was pulled over the eyes of the politicians who ultimately approved the scheme very much as it was first drafted by its promoters. Little did they realize that they were enshrining into law a Machiavellian plot to legalize one of the biggest heists in history.

William Jennings Bryan, who acted as Democrat whip, and is credited with a major effort in getting the Federal Reserve Act of 1913 passed, later said: "In my long political career, the one thing I genuinely regret is my part in getting the banking and currency legislation (FR Act) enacted into law."[11] Senator Carter Glass, one of the original sponsors of the Act of 1913, said on June 7, 1938: "I never thought the Federal Bank System would prove such a failure. The country is in a state of irretrievable bankruptcy."[12]

An early view from the Oval Office sounds the same note. President Woodrow Wilson, just three years after passage of the Act wrote: "A great industrial nation is controlled by its system of credit. Our system of credit is concentrated (in the Federal Reserve System). The growth of the nation, therefore, and all our activities are in the hands of a few men.... We have come to be one of the worst ruled, one of the most completely controlled and dominated governments in the civilized world."[13] It is a moot point as to why succeeding presidents and congresses have not remedied the mistake.

No one who is familiar with the Fed's dismal record of failures that include the Great Depression of the 1930s and every recession since, including the present disastrous one, could possibly justify giving it additional powers as some have suggested. On the contrary it is beyond redemption and must either be converted into or replaced by a new Bank of the United States (BUS), a publicly owned central bank to be responsible for the day to day implementation of federal government policy. The governor of the Bank should be directly responsible to the secretary of the treasury and take direction from him or her. There should be a provision in the law that in the event of a disagreement between the two, the secretary, or minister of finance as the case may be, takes precedence but is required to make his or her instructions to the governor public.

This should effectively end the spectacle of central banks pursuing monetary policies that are totally at odds with the fiscal stance of the government of the day. I still burn when I recall the recession of 1980-81 when Paul Volcker in the U.S. and Gerald Bouey in Canada adopted policies that resulted in putting hundreds of thousands of people on the breadlines while governments struggled valiantly to re-employ a few of them.

It was especially annoying when there was a better alternative. A twelve month freeze of wages and prices – except for the harvests of farm and sea and internationally traded commodities – would have reduced inflation much closer to zero than the monetarily-induced recession achieved, and the lower inflation would have been possible without a single job being lost.

Then if an incomes policy had followed the freeze, inflation would have remained low and we would have been spared the spectacle of central bankers following interest rate policies that made them look like neophyte pilots. First they would pull the stick back too far too fast and then overcorrect in the opposite direction when the economy began to stall.

The notion that there are no measures available to fight inflationary tendencies other than a universal increase in interest rates is both shortsighted and erroneous. If real estate prices are escalating too fast in one area, minimum equity requirements can be raised to cool the market before a bubble forms. If a general inflation appears on the horizon, minimum monthly payments on credit cards can be increased to dampen consumption. The bottom line is that there are options other than a high interest rate policy.

The era when ultimate control over the economic welfare of a nation is exercised by unelected, unaccountable bankers must end. Control must be exercised by the people who are elected for that purpose. If their policies fail they can be held accountable at the next available election.

One final consideration is only relevant when the BUS is up and running. It is a technical point of primary interest to economists and bankers who fret about such matters. It should interest politicians too.

It is quite a while since I read the story of how the Fed assisted the U.S. government in financing World War II. I think it was similar to the Canadian system that I remember well. The Bank of Canada deposited cash to the government account in exchange for Government of Canada interest-bearing bonds that the Bank booked as assets against the liability of the money created.

The government paid the BOC interest on the bonds. Then the Bank gave it back in the form of dividends – deducting only enough to pay for the cost of administration. To all intents and purposes, however, they were interest-free loans. Still the bonds appeared on the government's books as debt.

Today, however, in a world overwhelmed in debt, cosmetics are important and what every country needs is an infusion of "debt free" money. So instead of governments giving central banks bonds to fill the function of assets on their books, they should use non-convertible, non-transferable shares in the country. The shares could be given a nominal value of, say, one share equals $10 billion in the U.S. For a smaller country like Canada, perhaps one share equals $1 billion would be more appropriate. But these are details. The aim is to provide governments with some cash that does not wind up on their books as debt. They all have much too much of that already.

The Pros and Cons

Whenever government-created money (GCM) is mentioned in polite circles you can expect the knee-jerk reaction, "It would be inflationary." This is a substitute for reasoned analysis on the part of economists and editorial writers who put it forward in all seriousness. In fact government-created money is no more inflationary than bank-created money if the amount is not excessive and the private banks' share is reduced proportionately. It is the total amount of money created that influences prices, not who creates it.

What the objectors are really saying is that they don't trust politicians, and would prefer to leave the most powerful of all economic tools in the exclusive hands of unelected, unaccountable bankers. They won't come clean and say that they don't believe in democracy, because that would be politically incorrect! Still, that is the inevitable, hard rock, core of their beliefs.

One of America's genius inventors, Thomas Edison, put the whole question of bonds, bills and national credit in perspective. "If the nation can issue a dollar bond it can issue a dollar bill. The element that makes the bond good makes the bill good. The difference between the bond and the bill is that the bond lets money brokers collect twice the amount of the bond and an additional 20 percent. (Total of principal and interest by the time the bond is paid off.) Whereas the currency, the honest sort provided by the constitution, pays nobody but those who contribute in some useful way. It is absurd to say our country can issue bonds but cannot issue currency. Both are promises to pay, but one fattens the usurers and the other helps the people. If the currency issued by the people were no good, then the bonds would be no good, either."[14] Edison said it well.

Graham Towers, the first and in my opinion the brightest of Bank of Canada governors, said: "Banks manufacture money the same way that steel companies manufacture steel, that is their business." He made no attempt to disguise the nature of money. "It is nothing but a book entry; that is all it is," he said. If he were alive today he would say: "Money is nothing but a computer entry; that is all it is."

More than half-a-century ago I raised the subject of GCM with Governor Towers during a recess when he was appearing as a witness before the House of Commons Finance and Commerce Committee. His reply explained both the advantages and the dangers in a nutshell. "It would be something like this," he said, "Drinking a bottle or two of Coca Cola from time to time can be quite refreshing. If you were to drink a whole case at one time it would kill you."[15] Towers analogy was his way of saying that judicious use of government-created money could be a good thing, whereas too much would be highly inflationary. Can you think of a more intelligent approach to the use of government-created money?

This is about the point during my lectures on the subject when someone will ask if there is anywhere in the world where the theory has been successfully translated into practice. "Not often enough," I reply, "but there are some noteworthy examples." The ideas are not new! They have been around for generations but they have been too long ignored at inestimable cost in human wellbeing.

As Curtis P. Nettles points out: "Paper currency issued under government auspices originated in the thirteen colonies; and during the 18th century they were the laboratories in which many currency experiments were performed."[16] There were no banks at that time in any of the thirteen colonies so all the paper money was created under the authority of the colonial legislatures. In all there were about 250 separate issues of colonial notes between 1690 and 1775 and the system worked just fine when they avoided over or under issue. It also had distinct advantages over bank or coin money. The legislature could spend, lend or transfer the money into circulation, while banks could only lend (or spend their interest earnings back into circulation) and the coin money was always leaving the colonies to pay for imports.

There is no doubt that the thirteen colonies were the Western pioneers in the creation of "funny money," the label many skeptics and cynics apply to government-created money. Why they consider it any funnier than the phantom money banks create I will never understand. Perhaps they just suffer from a peculiar sense of humor.

A more recent and continuing case is the Guernsey Experiment. When skeptics ask for an example in real life where government-created money has been utilized consistently and effectively for an extended period it is only necessary to look at the history of the Isle of Guernsey, beginning in the early 19ᵗʰ century. At that time the island boasted natural beauty but little else. There was nothing to attract visitors or to keep residents from moving to the mainland. There was no trade or hope of employment for the poor. The market was open to the elements and needed a roof, and the shores were eroding due to the sorry state of the dykes. What to do? Why set up a committee, of course.

"Finally," as Olive and Jan Grubiak report in *The GUERNSEY Experiment*, "after grave deliberation, the Committee reported in 1816 with this historic recommendation – that property should be acquired and a covered market erected; the expenses to be met by the Issue of States Notes to the value of £6000."[17] The story, as related by the Grubiaks in their well-documented pamphlet, is well worth reading for anyone interested in the subject.

The experiment had its ups and downs as the banks made an intense, but in the end unsuccessful, effort to put an end to the practice. Consequently, it has persisted to this day with the result that the island has modern infrastructure, no unemployment to speak of, very low taxes and no debt. If you contrast this extremely successful policy with that of the United Kingdom with its enormous debt, and taxpayers still paying interest on money borrowed to fight the American colonists in the War for Independence more than 200 years ago, it will be hard to escape the conclusion that there is a better system and that we should be well advised to adopt it.

Lincoln and Government-Created Money

Although Abraham Lincoln was not a proponent of government-created money, he certainly recognized its usefulness in time of emergency. In his December 1862 message to Congress, Lincoln made the following reference to greenbacks: "The suspension of specie payments by banks soon after the commencement of your last session, made large issues of United States Notes [greenbacks] unavoidable. In no other way could the payment of the troops, and the satisfaction of other just demands, be so economically or so well provided for. The judicious legislation of Congress, securing the receivability of these notes for loans and internal duties, and making them a legal tender for other debts, has made them a universal currency; and has satisfied, partially, at least, and for the time, the long-felt want of an uniform circulating medium, saving thereby to the people immense sums in discounts and exchanges."[18]

There was some Congressional support for adopting the system on a permanent basis. Representative Thaddeus Stevens, first elected to Congress as a Whig and later as a Republican, in speaking during the spirited debates over the first of the Legal Tender Acts prior to the enactment of the legislation authorizing the printing of greenbacks, said: "The government and not the banks should have the profit from creating a medium of exchange."[19] Another booster was Alexander Campbell, a mining engineer and entrepreneur, elected to Congress from Illinois in 1874 for a single term on a Democrat-Independent ticket. In *The True Greenback* he wrote: "The war has resulted in the complete overthrow and utter extinction of chattel slavery on this continent, but it has not destroyed the principle of oppression and wrong. The old pro-slaver serpent, beaten in the South, crawled up North and put on anti-slavery clothes, and established his headquarters in Wall Street where ... he now, through bank monopolies and non-taxed bonds, rules the nation more despotically than under the old regime. ... I assert ... that an investment of a million dollars under the National Banking Law, or in non-taxed government securities, will yield a larger net income to its owner than a like amount invested in land and slaves employed in raising cotton and sugar did in the South in the palmiest days of the oligarchy."[20]

A Time for Statesmanship

It is a crime against humanity in the literal sense of those words for millions of people to suffer due to the lack of something that can be manufactured in twenty-four hours or less.

That is the truth! Worse, we are all guilty of being accessories after the fact. Over the generations we have allowed the private banks to connive, manipulate, bribe and cajole us into allowing them to usurp our heritage – the right to create our own money. The process has been incremental so very few of us were aware of what was actually taking place. Like the proverbial camel that first stuck its nose into the tent to get warm and then wriggle its way in bit by bit until it took over the whole tent, the banking fraternity has managed to acquire a virtual monopoly in the exercise of one of our most fundamental of rights. The result has been that it has become our master and we have become its slaves.

The banking fraternity was responsible for the crash of 1929! During the Great Depression it exercised its powers ruthlessly in foreclosing on farms and homes. Its rights always superseded any human rights. The great recessions of 1981-82 and 1990-91, while not on a scale comparable to the Great Depression, again put vast numbers of people off their farms after many generations, bankrupted many promising businesses, and put millions of people out of work and on the bread lines.

This latest example of the meltdown of 2007 and 2008 is but the latest and most horrendous since the Great Depression. By right, the people of the world should be launching a class action suit for trillions of dollars against the banks responsible for the meltdown. Instead, due to the economic pickle (dependency) in which we have found ourselves, we are in the unhappy position of having to lend the banks money, and buy their questionable assets, in order to restore their ability to continue the scam which can only be properly described as legal grand larceny.

This latest disaster, because that is what it is, has caused indescribable hardship in poor countries around the world, as well as unnecessary and unacceptable hardship in the more advanced countries that have developed safety nets in response to the earlier cases of banking system failure. So we absolutely must take back at least part of our inalienable right to create money and start undoing some of the damage that has been done to the human species worldwide.

This will not be easy because in an earlier book I said that the next world war would be a war between the people and the banks. They will fight ferociously to safeguard their monopoly in the hope of keeping us all on a short leash in perpetuity. Should they succeed, they will do it to us again sometime down the road. That must never happen!

The final straw was an article in the July 31, 2009 edition of the *New York Times* entitled "Bankers Reaped Lavish Bonuses During Bailouts."

According to the article "Nine of the financial firms that were among the largest recipients of federal bailout money paid about 5,000 of their traders and bankers bonuses of more than $1 million apiece for 2008."[21] It is particularly galling that they take such a large slice of the financial pie when their contribution to the production of real wealth is so small.

As I said at the beginning of the chapter the world needs a massive infusion of real money, and quickly, to speed the recovery. At the same time the system must be changed fundamentally, and forever. Already we see the monstrous situation where banks that have been bailed out with taxpayers' money have regained the strength to buy government bonds and reward taxpayers by charging interest. If that isn't the most blatant case of double-dipping possible I don't know the meaning of those words.

To end this nonsense America needs a man who can stand tall in the shoes of Abraham Lincoln, print the money necessary to free the slaves – black and yellow, red and white – from the helplessness and hopelessness of an economic collapse due entirely to a faulty banking system long entrenched for the benefit of an elite minority.

The world will salute the man brave enough to confront the elitists and win the victory of economic freedom on behalf of all people everywhere!

N.B. Anyone interested in a more comprehensive background of the economics in support of this proposal might like to get a copy of *A Miracle in Waiting: Economics that Make Sense* that is being published in tandem with this book.

CHAPTER 10
A POLITICAL AGENDA

It is impossible to save the world literally, as opposed to metaphorically, without massive, fundamental and immediate changes in policy. No amount of fine-tuning such as a slow and incremental reduction in the use of fossil fuels will work. Planet Earth is in crisis mode and the only hope of reversing its trajectory toward long-term uninhabitability is a mobilization on a scale comparable to a war for survival, in the historical context. It's a case of all, or nothing at all, because nothing less than an all-out effort will achieve the essential miracle.

I have made a list of some of the reforms required to save the planet and then to make it a more peaceful and happier place for all humankind. I have categorized some of the reforms necessary to achieve these goals as (a) Absolutely Essential, (b) Essential, (c) Highly Desirable, (d) Desirable, in order to provide some sense of where to start.

ABSOLUTELY ESSENTIAL

End the Press Embargo on Truth

A good place to begin would be for the press to end its embargo on truth. There are three topics that appear to have been subject to either a deliberate or simply *de facto* embargo for reasons that have never been made clear. They are: (a) The extraterrestrial presence and technology, opening up a new and wider reality of our place in the cosmos. After sixty years, national security is no longer an excuse, especially when global security is at stake and takes precedence. (b) Monetary theory and how the privately-owned banks have acquired a near monopoly in money creation. (c) The dark side of globalization and the extent to which it reduces people to ciphers rather than living, breathing, thinking, feeling, flesh and blood individuals. The world's best newspapers and electronic media should commission one or more of their most experienced investigative reporters to probe incessantly into each of these subject areas until the truth is fully exposed.

Full and Complete Disclosure of the ET Presence and Technology

This project, without doubt, will be extremely difficult. It isn't easy to demand full disclosure of information about unidentified flying objects (UFOs) and their occupants, extraterrestrial biological entities (EBEs) or (EBENS), when the official position of the United States government has been that they don't exist. After sixty years of lies and deceit, in what has been the most expensive and one of the most if not the most effective cover-up in history, the time is long since past to peel back the multiple layers of hidden information. It should no longer be necessary to make liars of some of America's highest-ranking citizens, both civil and military.

There have been some controlled leaks over the years. Bits of information have been passed along to selected movie and TV producers in order to condition the public to some of the concepts of the broader reality. And recently the official debunkers – the people who attend UFO conferences in order to disparage the information being made public by those who have been demanding full disclosure for many years – have changed their tunes. They now admit that UFOs are real, because to deny their existence would be laughed at by all those who know better, but then go on to say that the subject is of no particular interest to the United States government in what must be one of the most monstrous untruths imaginable. For more than sixty years these subjects have been of profound interest to succeeding governments – or alternative governments (shadow governments) – as they have become known, and to the "Cabal," the hard inner core, and most highly secretive group within the alternative government.

It is absolutely essential that the people of the United States – Republicans, Democrats and Independents – wrest control of their country from the iron grip of the shadow government, the Cabal, and the "Three Sisters," discussed in earlier chapters – as it is inevitable that there are some connections between them – and re-establish some semblance of government of, by and for the people as envisaged by the fathers of their country. The situation is now so bad that when Sarah McClendon, a White House reporter, asked President Clinton why he didn't demand disclosure of the UFO phenomena he replied: "Sarah, there is a government within the government, and I don't control it."[1]

What about civilian control of the military over which there have been so many battles? In the U.S. there has been a quiet coup as ultimate power has been seized by a small Cabal accountable to no one but themselves.

Only the Congress can launch and win the counterattack to re-establish democratic control of the United States. For decades politicians have been turning a collective blind eye to the fact that they were providing billions of dollars for secret projects – the black ops – of which they were unaware. This total abrogation of responsibility under the Constitution was somehow rationalized on the basis that it was essential for national security – as vaguely and totally inadequately sketched to some committee chairman who had to stickhandle the mechanics of the illegal expenditures.

As the Congress bears the primary responsibility for allowing the illegal system to develop and persist, it must take the initiative to restore the primacy of the Constitution. The task cannot be left to any president. It is far too dangerous for any individual to take the risk alone. And there is no sense trying to talk to the Cabal because that would be like talking to a Sphinx – especially when so few names of the inner circle are actually known. Only the Congress has control of the heavy artillery that can penetrate the underground bunkers and closed minds – "money" is the name of its arsenal.

The Congress will have to seriously threaten and if necessary actually cut the appropriations for the armed forces to the basic minimum necessary to pay for salaries, food and fuel to get to and from work until the Cabal surrenders. When that happens, as it soon would when the money dried up, I think there would be a sense of general relief among most of the members of the alternative government, many of whom have been lobbying for disclosure only to be overruled by the Cabal, the real diehards.

Once the Congress has caught their attention with the most convincing of weapons available to it, there will still be the problem of getting individuals to talk freely and honestly. A necessary precursor will be to repeal the National Security Act of 1947 and/or the legislative grant of a complete amnesty for everyone who is called to testify. It would be a brand of truth and reconciliation commission. Why is it necessary? Simply because the alternative government has broken about every law in the book – coercion, character assassination, premature termination of employment, misappropriation of funds, illegal experiments, and worse. So the offenders would be unlikely to talk if they were going to spend the rest of their lives in jail for it.

The necessity for amnesty, that seems so self-evident, was one of the ideas that was given to abductee Jim Sparks by the Star Visitors. They know, far better than we do, the variety and extent of the crimes that have been committed. So in the interests of full disclosure, which is absolutely vital in assessing strategies to save the planet, and for full cooperation in the parallel initiatives necessary to establish a greater degree of justice between rich and poor nations and rich and poor people, the extraordinary team of scientists, organizers and industrial leaders who have been flouting the law will have to be conscripted to help build the better world we all talk about, but do so little to realize.

There should be a whole series of interesting disclosures made public including the genetic experiments, the diabolical weapons development, the extent to which the UFOs have been replicated and if, as alleged, progress has been significant, to what purpose the space vehicles will be put. But when it comes to saving the planet for the congenial use of future generations, these extraordinary feats, all based on extraterrestrial technologies, pale in significance to the development of zero point energy and cold fusion both of which can help eliminate the use of fossil fuels at a rapid pace. As I mentioned earlier, the late Dr. Michael Wolf said both had been developed.[2]

This information has been confirmed by other reliable sources who choose to remain anonymous. And even if the information should prove to be a little optimistic, there is no doubt in my mind that the Star Visitors would give us the technology necessary to save the planet if we asked them to, if only we would stop trying to shoot them down when they arrive, and welcome them as visiting cousins. They, too, are deeply concerned about the future of Earth as a "live" member of the family of habitable planets. With their help, or the technology that has already been developed but kept secret from the world, we should be able to convert from an oil economy to a zero point or fusion economy within a decade – give or take a year or two.

That should be soon enough to save us, whereas to set your own rules and hope for the best approach adopoted at Copenhagen certainly will not, and anybody who talks in those terms rates an "A" for *naiveté*, or is quietly working for the oil industry, one or the other. That is just one more reason for immediate disclosure. There is a strong suspicion that the oil industry has connections to the Cabal, and that it is wittingly or otherwise willing to sacrifice the planet in the interests of its own short-term financial gains.

It is interesting to know how many secret patents have been filed in the period since Earthlings began to replicate or adapt extraterrestrial technology. Dr. John Reed, treasurer of the Society for Scientific Exploration, filed an application to the U.S. Patent Office under the Freedom of Information Act. He was staggered by what they disclosed. There were 10,158 Secrecy Orders issued by the U.S. Patent Office from 1942-1993 and there were about 6,000 still in effect in 1993. Dr. Reed wonders how many more may have been issued since 1993.[3] Congress should pass a law authorizing the review of all these patents by a highly qualified scientific panel with authority to make public any patents that would be of significant benefit to the future welfare of mankind, including clean forms of energy, and so on. The panel should also have the power to determine the financial arrangements under which the patents could be used, taking into account factors such as the origin of the technology and how much, if anything, the development had depended on taxpayer financing. No secret should be sacrosanct if the health and/or welfare of humankind could be improved by its release. There have to be limits when it comes to intellectual property rights.

Failure to disclose a clean energy alternative to fossil fuels, if there is one, is worse than a crime against humanity. It is a crime against creation and the Creator!

Essential Changes to the Monetary and Banking Systems

There are several excuses given for maintaining secrecy about the ET presence and technology. These include religious concerns. Dr. Wolf said that the Vatican had requested more time to condition Catholics and to say that man was not created to look like God, but that it is our souls that are created in the image of God. People might panic if they knew the truth. The U.S. has to maintain its near monopoly respecting some of the sophisticated technology. And, finally, that switching quickly from an oil to a clean fuel economy would cause too great an economic disruption and that the system would collapse.

None of these is reason enough for withholding the truth. But of the four, the one that is most scary to bankers, businessmen and politicians is the potential economic disruption, the extent of which cannot be accurately calculated. And, of course, the owners of trillions of dollars in oil-based assets are greatly concerned. There are steps that can be taken to ease the transition, and the most important of these is changing the monetary system, reinstating the requirement for significant cash reserve requirements for banks and giving governments access to enough government-created money (GCM) that they can prevent an economic downturn throughout the adjustment period, and forever thereafter.

A significant infusion of GCM would allow the kind of "demand management" essential to steady, uninterrupted growth. It could be used to subsidize individuals and businesses converting from dirty to clean energy in conformance with tight time schedules. It could also be used to offset extremely generous tax write-offs of new capital expenditures by the oil and arms industries as they adjust to the new reality.

A ten-year adjustment period should prove adequate for both the oil industry and the military-industrial complex to switch to new products that are compatible with a green and peaceful world of cooperation. The range of medical products and facilities is virtually without limit as is reconstructing cities to new and greener standards and the construction of new ones that would be comparable to paradise on earth. Cities of several million people built on the modular rather than linear basis so that each module of ten or twelve thousand would have its own range of essential services, as well as easy access to the city centre recreational and other common areas that are integral to large population centers. All of this

244

plus a transportation system that would allow travel from any one place to any other place within twenty minutes or half an hour at most – thus eliminating all the gridlock and fume-filled commutes that have become part of our daily lives.

A Just Israeli-Palestinian Peace Agreement

He has shown you, O man, what is good
And what does the Lord require of you
But to do justly,
To love mercy,
And to walk humbly with your God?

Micah 6:8[4]

If there is one certainty in world politics it is this: there will be no peace on Earth until there is a just settlement of the Israeli-Palestinian conflict. Consequently, a just resolution – and I emphasize the word just – should be at the top of the list of priority considerations for the new U.S. administration.

It seems apparent to an outside observer that Israeli strategy since the 1976 war has been one of gradual encroachment on those areas that remained in Palestinian hands after the United Nations awarded Israel the lion's share of the land at the time the state came into existence in 1948.

The implementation of this strategy has resulted in a policy of constant and sometimes cruel harassment of those Palestinians living in the occupied territories and Gaza. One suspects that this may have been an unspoken attempt to make life so difficult for the Palestinians that many more of them would abandon their lands and find refuge or start a new life elsewhere.

On balance the strategy has not worked, nor will it, ever. Palestinians have dug in their heels and fought back in a desperate effort to regain autonomy over the small area that the U.N. had left under their ownership. The root of the conflict can be found in a fundamental disagreement over who really owns the land – on both sides of the Israeli border.

I decided to read *Whose Promised Land: Israel or Palestine?* by Colin Chapman as additional background to that which I knew from the Bible. At the end I thought that both sides may have an equal claim to all the land but on very different premises. The Palestinian claim is based on hundreds of years of possession. The Israeli claim is based on the Bible and a covenant God made with Abraham. At this point in history there is no acceptable solution other than to share the land in two adjoining autonomous states. I would like to quote a few paragraphs from a piece written by my Messianic Jewish Zionist friend Gavriel Gefen who takes the path of love and compassion that is also, in my opinion, the practical approach of live and let live.

"We are told that God promised Abraham to give his physical children the land that extends from the river of Egypt to the Euphrates River. Egypt is where Africa meets the Arabian subcontinent. The Euphrates flows through southern Turkey and passes through Iraq to the Persian Gulf. This vast territory is the heart and the bulk of the Middle East. Who lives there today? Exactly the descendants of Abraham – the children of Ishmael and Isaac, and the children of Esau and Jacob. It is just as we were told it would be.

"Tragically, the three great Abrahamic faiths of Judaism, Christianity, and Islam have all developed religious traditions that interpret the Abrahamic covenant exclusively, leaving out the other children in one way or another. Judaism sees in the Hebrew Scriptures that Isaac and Jacob inherited the promises of the covenant, and assumes that it is to the necessary exclusion of the other brothers. Christianity interprets the covenant as now being spiritual and belonging exclusively to the Church. Islam holds that Ishmael received the inheritance.

"Some Jewish and Christian fundamentalists embrace a joint Judeo-Christian worldview that excludes Muslim descendants of Abraham. They have visions of a Greater Israel that would encompass all of the territory between the Euphrates and Egypt. This is complete insanity. What do they plan to do with the millions of people already there? Drive them out? Rule over them? Kill them all? It is madness.

"Each time the Israeli government enters into serious negotiations with Palestinian leaders, Jewish and Christian fundamentalists accuse Israel of "dividing God's land." Dividing it with whom? With her Abrahamic brothers who are also heirs of the same father? How is that "dividing God's land"? It isn't. It is rightfully seeking how to share a common heritage."[6]

Gavriel's words reflect great wisdom. That is because they flow from a God of love, a God of mercy, a God of justice as revealed by Micah,

Zechariah, and the other prophets. It is the fundamentalists in all camps who are the stumbling blocks obstructing peace with justice.

They should remember that God's covenant with Israel was always conditional and that it was the failure to fulfill their part of the contract that resulted in their being expelled from the "promised land" on more than one occasion. It is only through God's good grace that they have been given back more of the land than they have occupied at any time since the Kingdoms of David and Solomon.

So compromise will have to be the order of the day. A small commission led by someone of the stature of Jimmy Carter should be established. It must represent all the major players including Iran and Syria. It is only realistic that Hamas and Hezbollah be involved in the negotiations because substantial agreement and compliance by their supporters is key to a genuine peace.

It should be remembered that Jewish terrorists, later respected citizens, were key to the establishment of the state of Israel. Palestinian "terrorists," who perceive themselves as "freedom fighters," are key to the establishment of a state of Palestine. I urge every Jew and every evangelical Christian who only see their side of the situation to read *Blood Brothers*[7] by Elias Chacour. They are likely to be shocked, as I was, by the extreme treatment meted out by overzealous Zionists.

Negotiations must not be allowed to fail. The U.S. will have to confront its Jewish lobby and the wrath of fundamentalist evangelicals and adopt an even-handed approach to the resolution of the dispute. Canada, too. If it is impossible for the two sides to reach agreement on all points a solution that is considered just by the majority of players on both sides will have to be imposed. Failure is not an option.

At a Bar Mitzvah that I had the pleasure of attending in January 2009 the Rabbi asked the congregation to pray for Israel. I took him at his word and have been doing just that though perhaps not in the words he intended. I have been praying that Israel change its strategy; that it give up its occupation of its neighbors' land after more than forty years and allow a viable Palestinian state to be born – a state where the two nations can live side by side in peace and cooperation with neither physical nor psychological walls between them.

I don't think the Israelis have any real conception of the depth of hate they have rekindled with their last two dreadful attacks first on Lebanon and then on Gaza. Nor do they comprehend the extent of healing that will be necessary to convince both their neighbors and the world at large that their intentions are worthy of respect and support.

Their extreme right-wing elements should, in this context, abandon their fantasies of a new Jewish Temple on Temple Mount. Destroying the Dome of or on the Rock and/or the mosque of Al Asqua would bring on World War III for sure. The Mosque is a House of the God of Israel and, with the kind of peace that must be pursued, the day might come when Jews and Christians would be invited by its owners to share its use as a place of worship being "People of the Book" as the Qur'an describes those of us who worship the God of Abraham, Isaac, Ishmael, Jacob and Esau. Isn't that too far-fetched to be taken seriously, you ask? Nothing is impossible with God working through men and women of goodwill who worship Him.

The moderate Muslims we meet in the Middle East are willing to listen. They might prefer a state where Jews and Arabs enjoy a common citizenship, but they have accepted the existing reality. The state of Israel is here to stay and God, with the help of the United States and its allies, will not let anyone drive the Jews into the sea. Now it is time for the Palestinians to have a state of their own.

It is our turn to meet them half way. They will not accept any settlement that is less than just, nor should they. A just settlement, that includes large-scale international financial support to help the Palestinians build a homeland they can be proud of, is the only way to end the Intifada against Israel and its protector, the United States. Osama bin Laden made this very clear in the aftermath of September 9, 2001, but the U.S. administration of the day chose not to listen.

No more time should be lost. The fortress mentality of erecting fences that, in the end, will protect no one, must be abandoned. Hate must be replaced with love and compassion. It is the only hope of a world where both anti-Semitism and anti-Americanism subside and the welcome mat is extended equally to all of God's children. That kind of world is possible if we would all treat others as we, ourselves, would want to be treated.

Save and Protect the Rain Forests

One of the major concerns of the Star Visitors is our careless and callous attitude toward the environment. And a principal element of this concern is the continual destruction of the rain forests that form an integral element of the earth's ecology. Yet despite all the warnings about global warming, the vast majority of Earthlings continue to allow one of our most precious environmental assets to be destroyed. We have even allowed the World Bank to finance projects to convert rain forests into pasture to satisfy our passion for red meat.

An article in the *New York Times* of November 11, 2009 by Thomas L. Friedman underlines the almost incomprehensible immensity of the problem. "Imagine if you took all the cars, trucks, planes, trains and ships in the world and added up their exhaust every year. The amount of carbon dioxide they collectively emit into the atmosphere is actually less than the carbon emissions every year that result from the chopping down and clearing of tropical forests in places like Brazil, Indonesia and the Congo. We are now losing a tropical forest the size of New York State every year and the carbon that releases into the atmosphere now accounts for roughly 17 percent of all global emissions contributing to climate change."[8]

The sacrilege has got to stop. This is part of the message that abductee Jim Sparks was given. Jim was so impressed that he started a foundation to raise money to save a slice of the rain forests. Three cheers for him and his initiative, and those of others. These need to be supplemented by a massive program that will stop, totally, any further deliberate destruction, and provide the economic alternatives for those whose livelihood may be negatively affected by the change in policy.

The United States should take the lead, but it should recruit a consortium of the major economic powers to pledge the money necessary to make it happen. It doesn't matter how much it might cost in dollar terms, the cost of not doing anything is ten times higher, and could soon be irreversible. So immediate action is required! The plan should be even more comprehensive than just the rain forests. Some poor Africans are forced to cut down any tree in sight because they can't afford any other fuel for cooking and warmth. The plan must include subsidized clean energy fuel sources that provide an economically acceptable alternative to tree harvesting.

These two steps should be implemented at once, but there is a complementary long-term initiative that must follow in train. The whole world must embark on the most extensive reforestation in history. No country should be exempt. And those that literally cannot afford the small cost of growing the seedlings should be included, but subsidized by the well-to-do countries to the extent required to make the plan work quickly and efficiently. Some years down the pike the extent of the reforestation required can be assessed in light of the progress being made toward stabilizing the planet's ecology.

Massively Reduce Stockpiles of Atomic Weapons

In the course of a brief encounter I had with Dr. Hans Blix, chairman of the Weapons of Mass Destruction Commission, he recommended their report of 2006 as the best source of information on the subject of disarmament in the weapons of mass destruction (WMD) categories. He was good enough to send me a copy with his compliments.

Just leafing through it is enough to give one nightmares. To look more closely raises the question of why one of the most important subjects in the world is receiving so little attention. There have been discussions, negotiation and this excellent commission, but progress has been minimal measured by the seriousness that these threats actually pose.

I will just quote one of the many recommendations of the commission, i.e. number 19 under "Nuclear Weapons."

"Russia and the United States, followed by other states possessing nuclear weapons, should publish their aggregate holdings of nuclear weapons on active and reserve status as a baseline for future disarmament efforts. They should also agree to include specific provisions in future disarmament agreements relating to transparency, irreversibility, verification and the physical destruction of nuclear warheads."[9]

That is a very modest beginning. It should be followed by an immediate reduction of stockpiles of 10% a year for five years. Then the remaining 50% should be reduced by 10% a year for five years. At that stage negotiations should take place to see how much further nations would be willing to go and the absolute minimum to be retained as a protection against cheating.

Any nation refusing to cooperate should be subject to severe sanctions like a 10% tariff on all its exports to be increased each year of non-compliance. The existence of atomic weapons is a threat to the viability of the planet itself and any person or nation that even contemplates circumstances under which they might be used should be the subject of universal condemnation.

A similar plan should apply to biological and chemical weapons.

Massively Reduce Defense Expenditures Worldwide

One of the most depressing articles I have read since the November 2008 U.S. election was one that claimed that the election of a new administration would have no effect on the Military-Industrial Complex. The inference was that the perverted priorities are permanent. Tell me it isn't so!

Surely the United States, after sixty years of concentration on the weapons of war, is ready to change its worldview and shift its priorities to the salvation of the planet and the well being of all its inhabitants including Americans. It is time to concentrate on life, abundant life, rather than death.

So at long last it should heed President Eisenhower's warning and start cutting military expenditures while inviting all other countries to do the same. All military budgets worldwide should be reduced by 10% a year for five years. I would make a plea for a two year reprieve for the Canadian Armed Forces because, unlike the U.S., they have been grossly underfunded for more than thirty years. The grace period would barely keep them mobile.

Not only should expenditures for armaments be reduced by half in five years, the major arms exporters should be teased, cajoled or ordered to stop selling weapons that are used to launch or maintain the many ethnic and tribal conflicts that are inflicting so much misery on millions of people around the globe. Let the manufacturers of weapons start making sophisticated energy devices to emancipate the hundreds of millions of people in desperate need of electricity for heat, light and water. The profit could be comparable and the moral satisfaction ten times greater.

ESSENTIAL

Afghanistan

It would require the wisdom of King Solomon to know how to cope with the military and moral quagmire in Afghanistan. For that reason I was never critical of President Obama for taking his time before reaching a decision. On the contrary, I applauded him for attempting to develop a cohesive strategy rather than act hastily as some had been urging.

One can understand their impatience. Assessments by senior diplomats and top military commanders had indicated that the war was not going well and that in fact the Taliban was gaining ground. The demand for immediate reinforcements carried echoes of the war in Vietnam. There, too, it was hoped that superior military power alone would prevail but time proved that it could not.

President Obama has correctly assessed that the Afghanistan insurgency is a much more complicated kettle of fish and the absolute best that military power can achieve is enough time and tranquility for the other complex pieces of the puzzle to be put in place. What is ultimately at stake is an Afghan government blessed with a modicum of honesty and efficiency and a population that is generally supportive and increasingly sympathetic to the aims and objectives of the United States and its NATO allies.

Is this possible? Heaven only knows. The plan announced by President Obama on November 30, 2009 is probably as good a shot as the U.S. can afford to take, but there is no guarantee that it will be successful. It would have been if the initial air assault of October 2001 had been followed up when both the Taliban and al Qaeda were on the run. Hot pursuit could have ended in victory.

But then the U.S. failed its own test by launching the futile and senseless war against Iraq. In the process it shifted the emphasis from the real "war on terror," allowed the Taliban to regroup and created more potential terrorists worldwide than the world has ever known. The present is an unprecedented mess bequeathed to the world by the Bush administration. So far from being Obama's war, the Afghan "surge" is an integral part of a heroic effort to escape from the quagmire he inherited.

While one hopes and prays for success the odds are not great. A new book titled *A Woman Among Warlords*, written by a young female activist who was elected to the new Afghan parliament in 2005, but suspended two years later for condemning top government officials as warlords, is highly suspicious of the west's motives, the Karzai government, and NATO's methods of operation. She would like to see all foreign troops withdraw now.[9]

Malalai Joya (not her real name) says that the situation for women is as catastrophic today as it was under the Taliban, that you can't really believe in democracy when relying on warlords for support. "Foreign powers occupy Afghanistan through the warlords under the banner of democracy and women's rights. Their only interest is a geopolitical one. They want easy access to the gas and oil of the Central Asian Republics. They are not there for my people. They are there for themselves."[10]

Reading the young lady's cynical views of the west underlined for me that absolute truth that winning the hearts and minds of activists like her is every bit as important as military operations, and perhaps even more so. They want us to walk the talk. Three important opportunities come to mind.

I heard Ms. Joya say that they are tired of fighting the Taliban on the ground and the U.S. from the air. Every time a bomb kills innocent civilians the support of a village or community is lost and hatred of the invaders is enhanced. So a good strategy would be to end all aerial bombardment except perhaps in the remote mountainous border areas where the presence of civilians is highly unlikely.

In the *Globe and Mail* interview she said, "My message to peace-loving activists is to educate my people. My message to Canada is to build schools, shelters, literacy courses, build hospitals."[11] That reminded me of one of the best books I have read recently – *Three Cups of Tea* by Greg Mortenson and David Oliver Relin.

This incredible story of a mountain climber turned school builder reads like an action thriller – because that is what it is. It begins with a promise to build one school in a remote Pakistani village and this leads to a life commitment of building schools in Pakistan and later in Afghanistan.

The hero, Greg Mortenson, is a unique individual who had no motive except to help the children of remote areas and this kept him alive and well. He succeeded because he made no attempt to proselytize or propagandize. A good allied strategy would be to recruit the few hundred or a thousand "would be" Greg Mortensons to go into the villages of Afghanistan and help supervise a worthwhile project. Taking a leaf from Mortenson no project would be launched without the full backing and support of the local elders.

Action on this front should be as speedy as the deployment of troops because one is unlikely to succeed without the other. Each volunteer, or a designated assistant, would be responsible for handling the funds so there would be no bureaucratic delays, bribes or payoffs.

Finally, it will be very difficult to resolve a situation where both the Taliban and various warlords flourish from the illegal drug trade. Poppy growing in the south of Afghanistan is still the major source of income. To win the cooperation of the farming population it is absolutely essential that they have an alternate income to replace the $2.7 billion a year that constitutes one-third of Afghanistan's gross domestic product.

John Polanyi, Nobel laureate and member of the Department of Chemistry at the University of Toronto, has written the only rational solution.[12] In effect, it would be for the International Narcotics Control Board to licence Afghan growers as it does in France, India and Turkey. The entire Afghan output could be usefully used as a painkiller for the rapidly growing number of cancer patients worldwide.

The most hopeful aspect of the conflict is that President Barack Obama appears to understand that the so-called war on terrorism cannot be won by military means and it is unlikely that it will end until all U.S. and allied troops are out of Iraq and then Afghanistan. A prolonged war might suit some segments of the Military-Industrial Complex but it would be counter-productive for the vast majority of Americans and all of the rest of us who believe that the top priority should be relations between the United States and the Muslim world. That may require a negotiated solution.

All of the principal players have to be involved. And there can be no preconditions. If Mohammad won't come to the mountain, then the mountain should go to Mohammad. There are problems, of course, as to who speaks for the Muslims. Al-Qaeda represents a very small minority, and is almost as unpopular with moderate Muslims, as is the U.S. Yet it is doubtful that it can be ignored. In the longer run, however, Muslim fundamentalists will have to be tamed by Muslim moderates as will be the case with other religions both spiritual and secular.

At the top of all U.S. briefing papers there should be a line saying: Remember the Golden Rule, and that the policy is designed to generate respect, and perhaps even Agape love, where there has been vitriolic hate.

This cardinal rule should be the cornerstone of all U.S. foreign policy in this century. The U.S. should set a standard of conduct that would earn it the reputation as world leader for Team World working in cooperation to bring about universal peace and well-being everywhere. It is a noble pursuit, but it is also in America's long-term interests in the kind of world in which we live. It would be the best hope for security at home and admiration abroad – the kind of scenario where wearing the American flag on one's knapsack would generate a smiling positive response.

In the course of writing a book just before the tragic attack of September 11, 2001, I quoted President George Bush from his inaugural speech. "We will build our defenses beyond challenge, lest weakness invite challenge. We will confront weapons of mass destruction, so that a new century is spared new horrors." Those are brave words, Mr. President, but what you are promising is impossible. The reality is that there is no such thing as security in today's world, and there never again will be. So to suggest otherwise is really misleading. Potential enemies already have atomic technology and it is certain that someone can and will sneak a bomb into the United States if the level of hate is high enough. The only protection is the kind of world where no one would want to do that. Such a world is possible, but not without a revolution of the mind and heart.

That is the reason that the U.S. should be the world leader in mobilizing a worldwide joint effort to reduce the disparity between nations, and not rest until all Earthlings have a roof over their heads, clothing adequate to their climactic conditions, potable water to drink, good food to eat, adequate health care and access to enough education that their full potential is capable of realization. It can be done, and it can be financed by diverting military expenditures to development expenditures and by using enough government-created money to increase world GDP by the extra one percent or more that would flow from operating all economies at a higher level of capacity.

Roll the World Trade Organization Back to a General Agreement on Trade and Tariffs

The lead editorial in the *Toronto Star* on July 31, 2008 read "Doha trade talks fail world's poor." So what else is new? I thought, almost every policy put in place for decades has disadvantaged the poor. The World Trade Organization itself was not intended to help the poor. It was designed to enhance and consolidate the power of the elite at the expense of the poor nations and poor people. It, too, has transferred far too much sovereignty from nation states to unelected, unaccountable bureaucrats working under rules actually written by, or at the behest of, the chief executive officers of multinational corporations.

The concept of a rules-based system is great in theory. It sounds very reasonable. But surely not just one set of rules applying to all countries equally?

The World Boxing Federation has fifteen classes including fly-weight, lightweight, middleweight and heavyweight. I would guess that the world's many different countries could be classified in as many as fifteen different categories. Certainly not just one! The WTO rules were written by or on behalf of the heavyweights for the benefit of heavyweights. The result is a trade regime under which everyone else is going to be clobbered.

The second objection is, as I said, the loss of democracy. The WTO exercises *de facto* executive, judicial and legislative powers equivalent to that of a world government. These powers were transferred to it without the advice or consent of the peoples affected. Apologists for the WTO say that consent was granted when people elected the governments which did the deal. But that is a cop-out. The governments neither told their electors what was involved nor asked their opinion about it. Needless to say this was deliberate policy on the part of governments attempting to serve two masters.

The resulting loss of sovereignty is not acceptable. It is extremely offensive that the rights and prerogatives of nation states should be decided by unelected, unaccountable three-person panels. How does that square with the concept of democracy? It doesn't! It is all part of the plot to end popular democracy as we used to know it, and substitute a corporate plutocracy in its stead. Everything that men and women fought and died for is being taken away by stealth.

The only satisfactory remedy is to abolish the WTO and go back to the General Agreement on Tariffs and Trade (GATT) from which it sprang. From there we can build a trade regime which preserves the essential powers of nation states, recognizes the different needs of countries based on size, population and state of development, and provides the flexibility for cooperative rather than coercive relationships. For want of a better description I call them the "Marquess of Queensberry" Rules of Trade.

The Marquess of Queensberry Rules for Trade and Investment

- Fair trade, not "free trade." There is no such thing as genuine free trade, as Canada has found in its relationship with the U.S.

- Every country should have the right to protect some of its infant industries. If it doesn't, they will never grow to adulthood.

- Every country has the right to determine the conditions under which direct foreign investment is welcome.

- Every country has the right to impose controls on the movement of short-term capital in cases of emergency.

- Every country has the right to determine the limits of foreign ownership in each area of economic activity.

- Every nation state should have the right to decide what trade concessions it will put on the table in exchange for others as was the case under the GATT.

- Every country should have control over its own banking system including majority ownership.

- Every country has the right to use its own central bank to assist in the financing of essential services and to keep the economy operating at or near its potential at all times.

- Rich countries should be encouraged to license the use of their technology by poor countries at modest cost.

- Every country should be obligated to cooperate with other countries in the protection of the oceans, their species, the ozone layer and in all ways essential to protect the ecosystem for the benefit of future generations.

- Every country should be encouraged to maintain some control of its own food supply, to the extent practical, and not become dependent on patented seeds and products.

- Every country should be encouraged to pass a law amending corporate charters in a way that would require directors to consider the interests of all stakeholders and not just those of shareholders when making decisions.

- Every country should have the right, and should be encouraged, to develop and maintain a significant degree of self-sufficiency in the production of goods and services for the use and enjoyment of its own people. The objective should be to reduce its vulnerability to the vagaries of decisions made by people far away who think of foreigners in terms of economic digits rather than as human beings.

Some may say that I am proposing a return to a "protectionist" world. Let me put it another way. I am proposing a system where the rights and interests of billions of people are protected from the predators – so the rich barons do not have unrestricted license to poach on other people's estates.

The New World Order is a gigantic hoax. It has much more to do with investment and centralized ownership than it has with trade. The former has increased much more rapidly than the latter. In fact, globalization is a greed-driven monster which gains credibility from an economic theory based on academic abstractions far removed from the real world and real people.

Fundamentalist economics is a numbers game, in which people are digits. They are counted, sorted, exploited when useful, and abandoned when surplus. It would be numerically inefficient to treat them otherwise. The system I am proposing is one where human beings are entitled to a status greater than inanimate objects – one where they will have some control over their own lives and destiny. Such a system would be closer to the model of nature, where babies and children are protected until they reach maturity and can compete on their own. Even then, there are physical and intellectual differences between adults that must be taken into account.

What I am proposing is the transformation of a system that is immoral and inefficient, into one that is fundamentally moral and much more efficient – a system where everyone, everywhere, can hope for better things to come. To accomplish this will require some very major changes, including one or two new institutions to fill some of the functions now being performed by the old.

A New World Dollar to Replace the Euro and U.S. Dollar as Reserve Currencies

If I say that establishing a new world currency to replace the U.S. dollar and the euro as reserve currencies is one of the most urgent problems facing the world today, many of you are likely to raise an eyebrow. The chances are ten to one that you haven't read or heard very much about it and that the subject is very low on your priority list of concerns. This is not a case, however, of what you don't know won't hurt you. Quite the contrary!

For many years the U.S. has been getting a free ride with its huge balance of payments deficits. It has been buying a lot more from the world – much of it oil – than it has been selling. Normally that would result in a substantial devaluation of the U.S. dollar so exports would increase and imports become more expensive; or the U.S. would have to sell its assets as poor countries are required to do.

The U.S., however, has enjoyed a privilege not available to others. When it went off the gold standard, and refused to redeem U.S. dollars in gold, it obliged the world's central banks to finance its balance-of-payments deficit by using their surplus dollars to buy U.S. Treasury bonds, whose volume quickly exceeded America's ability to pay. All of the dollars that wind up in the world's central banks have no place to go other than into the U.S. treasury. So the U.S. got the oil and other goods while the world wound up holding a lot of financial paper of questionable worth.

The U.S. "credit card" extravaganza might have gone on forever, or at least as far ahead as the eye can see, had it not been for the creation of the euro. Despite its slow start it has become a fast-growing giant on the world financial scene, and has altered its geopolitics on a scale comparable to World War II or the collapse of the Soviet Union.

In offering governments and central banks a real choice of reserve currencies, the euro has become a direct threat to the U.S. money monopoly.

As William Thomas points out "Washington laughed when Saddam [Hussein] took the world's second biggest oil fields off the dollar standard and began demanding payment in euros in October, 2000. The seemingly dim-bulb dictator also converted his $10 billion UN reserve funds to euros – just as that fledgling currency hit a historic low of 82 cents. The laughter stopped abruptly when the euro's value crouched, then leaped 30%."[13]

Although the Pentagon planners running the U.S. had targeted Iraq as far back as 1992, Saddam's decision in 2000 increased the urgency of the project. "According to Aussie analyst Geoffrey Heard, the second brutal war against Iraq was intended to return Iraq's oil reserves to the dollar, intimidate other oil producers considering passing on the buck, and sabotage other potential Middle East players."[14]

Carleton University economics professor, and head of the Centre for Research on Globalization, Michel Chossudovsky, says that the war on Iraq was more than just the U.S. taking over the oil reserves, it was intended to cancel the contracts of rival Russian and European oil companies, "as well as exclude France, Russia and China" from a Middle East/Central Asian region containing more than 70% of the world's reserves of oil and natural gas.

"No kidding" says William Thomas. "A $40 billion Iraq-Russia contract to hunt oil in Iraq's western desert is now scrap paper. Ditto the rights of the French oil company TotalFinaElf to develop the huge Majnoon field, near the Iranian border, which may contain up to 300 billion barrels of greenhouse-goosing carbon."[15] Perhaps if President Bush had told the American people what was really at stake in Iraq, they might have been a bit more understanding of the French and Russian reluctance to assist.

Washington's greatest fear is that the shift from the dollar to the euro will spread. Iran and Saudi Arabia, between them, have the power to do incredible damage. Partly to retaliate against Bush's Axis of Evil rhetoric, Iran shifted most of its central bank reserves to euros, and a move to use that currency as its oil standard appears to be in the cards. So far Saudi Arabia has remained faithful to the U.S. dollar but sniping from Washington has not gone unnoticed – a change could come.

What is going on now is a new "war" for financial dominance of the world. It is a "war" on many fronts – diplomatic, financial and military. The more any country dislikes or feels aggrieved by the U.S., the more likely it is to take the only action a non-military power can take against a superpower. It can switch sides in the financial "war" and win a moral victory.

The average person on the streets may not really care too much whether it is the United States or Europe that gets the free ride – the open ended credit card. Or even if Japan should try something similar in the Pacific region. But it's not right. No country or region should be able to buy goods and services from their neighbors on endless credit. They should be required to balance their books just as their neighbors do. Short-term credit to meet emergency circumstances is quite acceptable. But indefinite, and virtually unlimited credit, is not.

A World Bank and A World Dollar

The solution, that would put the U.S. dollar, the euro, the yen and all other currencies on an equal footing, is a new world bank with a new world dollar. It could be called "The Universal," or "Uni," for short. It would be the currency of traveler's checks and of central bank reserves. It would be, in effect, the universal world currency in which all international transactions were denominated.

The new world bank should be publicly owned, by the people of the world, under a formula that would prevent undue influence from any country or region. Its assets would comprise very large deposits of all world currencies and gold. Each would be convertible into any other at market prices, as the bank would be the *de facto* bank of international settlements, replacing the highly secretive existing Bank for International Settlements (BIS).

The establishment of such a bank would be a major change to the world landscape. It would require a Herculean effort. But compare that to the alternative which will be continuous diplomatic, financial and shooting wars over possession of the endless supply of golden eggs.

The Elimination of Third World Debt

I don't think there is much hope for billions of the world's poorest people unless they can get out from under the crushing burden of debt which makes them virtual slaves of the money lenders. In all too many cases poor countries pay most of their income from foreign sources just to pay the interest on their international debts.

And there is no light at the end of that tunnel. Just paying the interest on their debt is a bigger burden than most poor countries can bear. So there is nothing left over for principal repayments. In fact the principal owing continues to rise. Total external debt of low and middle-income countries rose from $1.458 trillion in 1990 to $2.491 trillion in 2000.[16] So the only hope is debt forgiveness on a massive scale and the repeal of all conditions imposed by the IMF and World Bank.

Debt forgiveness by the rich countries, to date, has been picayune. Worse, there are often conditions attached. Poor countries are required to "reform" their economic systems, which really means adopting the Washington Consensus and opening their economies to rapacious exploitation by the big-hearted donors.

There are two very important reasons for paying off all Third World and most of the developing country debt. The first is that a substantial part of the debt qualifies as "odious."[17] The World Bank, the IMF, private foreign banks and the Wall Street banks have all been major contributors to what has become an impossible situation.

The World Bank and private international banks lent far too much money to poor countries, often for projects that did not generate enough income to repay principal and interest. Paul Volcker and the Federal Reserve made a bad situation impossible when interest rates were raised to intolerable 18% levels. The debt compounded. Then the IMF, and later the World Bank, exacerbated the situation by providing new loans so the poor countries could pay the interest on what they already owed, and the international banks could remain solvent. Sure, some of the Third World leaders borrowed the easy money with the fervor of kids in a candy store. But the lenders were equally, if not more, culpable. So the wealthy Western world must be held responsible for a bad situation it could have prevented.

The second reason is enlightened self-interest. There is no doubt that paying off Third World debt is the moral thing to do. It is akin to admitting paternity and accepting financial responsibility for the consequences. But there is a bright side that cannot be ignored. Freed from the shackles of debt, the young economies will grow much faster and become stronger, more reliable trading partners in the years ahead.

What I am suggesting would be politically impossible if the $2.5 trillion had to be raised through taxes. Even the most warm-hearted citizens of the G8 might balk if they had to pay higher taxes for Third World debt relief at a time when their own essential services are being downgraded. Fortunately there is a much easier, painless way to accomplish the miracle.

All that is needed is for the governments of the rich countries to require all banks and deposit-taking institutions to increase their cash reserves to the 34% that I have recommended, and for the governments themselves to create the money (cash) to make that possible. More than enough money would be created to pay off the entire Third World and developing country debt and contributing countries would be able to substantially reduce their own internal debt at the same time. Individual rich countries' contributions to Third World debt would be proportional to their country's GDP, in U.S. dollars as a percentage of the total GDP, in U.S. dollar equivalent, for the total list of contributor countries.

A Tobin Tax

The Tobin Tax, named after the economist James Tobin, is another idea whose time has come. The idea is to tax every exchange of one country's currency for another. The purpose is to slow down short-term speculation in currencies. For a number of years about two trillion a day has been involved.[18] The imposition of a small cost – it was originally to be 1% but even a smaller levy of, say, 0.25% might be enough to make the gamblers pause before making their overnight bets.

While the rationale for a tax of this kind is primarily to create greater stability in financial markets – a worthy cause as we have learned to our total dismay – a secondary benefit would be a steady stream of income that could be earmarked for the U.N. High Commissioner for Refugees at a time when the need for support has never been greater.

Reducing the Central Intelligence Agency Budget 10% a Year

This is a priority that should be undertaken immediately. The Central Intelligence Agency (CIA) has become an organizational and public relations liability for the United States. In my opinion both the U.S. and the world would be better off if it were disbanded completely. But that isn't going to happen, so the best that can be hoped for is that it have its wings clipped sufficiently that it becomes a lesser menace to world peace and stability.

The CIA, unfortunately, was modeled on the Soviet KGB in the early years of the Cold War and managed to adopt all of the latter's bad habits of meddling in other people's business on a worldwide scale. Look for a left-wing leader anywhere, one who in theory at least was elected to serve the best interests of the citizens of his country, and the CIA will have been there trying to destabilize or overthrow his or her regime in America's "interests," which means in the interests of U.S. financial and commercial organizations.

Apart from the extremely dubious moral questions surrounding attempts to thwart the democratic will of other nation states, the means and methods employed require the organization to operate well outside the law, and this becomes a habit, as it was for the KGB before it. It was a matter of profound regret when President George W. Bush reinstated their right to assassinate "unfriendlies" without fear of being accountable under any law. It would be wise to re-read the Ten Commandments.

Spying and intelligence gathering is supposed to be the CIA's business. Regrettably it spies on friend and foe alike, and extends it operations to include allies like Canada and Great Britain. Still it was unable, in concert with its fellow agency, the Federal Bureau of Investigation, to prevent the dastardly attack on the World Trade Center and the Pentagon in September 2001.

Of more urgent concern to an outsider, is the assumption of its new role as an armed force in situations like Iraq and Afghanistan. One would think that the United States Navy, Army, and Air Force, plus the Marines, would be more than enough armed forces for one country. A fifth is about as necessary as a fifth teat on a cow. One has to assume that the reason for the addition is to facilitate operations that are outside the internationally recognized rules of engagement.

We have seen evidence of this in the establishment of secret prisons where torture is allowed. Also, reports of kidnapping individuals without so much as "by your leave" and flying them off to an undisclosed destination in an unmarked plane. Routinely they have lied to the friendly countries over whose territory they fly as to the reason for the flights, their ultimate destinations, or their passenger list – contrast that with U.S. requirements.

Persons who have survived these ordeals say that the object was to torture them in a way that would be unacceptable in the continental United States. It is the kind of moral double standard that our American friends might want to consider when the CIA appropriations are being considered by Congress. Long-term and present policies certainly justify a sharp reduction in the amount of public funds voted for such nefarious practices to the dishonor of the United States.

A Limit on Executive Salaries

Fifteen years ago – in the early '90s – CEO's salaries were about forty times the average salary of their employees. Since then they have escalated to 237 times (one report says 433) on average – ratios that cannot be justified by any economic or moral standard.

Inevitably it will be argued that big bonuses are warranted as a reward for extraordinary corporate results. It is an argument for which there is a counter argument. Doing a good job is what CEOs are paid for and their principal satisfaction should be in a job well done. Rewarding short-term results has often resulted in short-term planning at the expense of a longer-term vision. Equally perverse, the culture of exorbitant rewards has become so all-pervasive that it extends even to mediocre results and separation agreements.

This example of greed and avarice is totally unacceptable. How can you ask union leaders to accept increases of 2% or less – to narrow the gap between money wages and productivity increases – when executives set such a bad example.

So executive compensation including salary, bonuses, stock options and retirement benefits should be limited to fifty times the average for their employees and any excess should be subject to a 100% excess profit tax in order to end the abuse of privilege.

HIGHLY DESIRABLE

Sometimes with these major projects it is difficult to differentiate between what is essential and what is highly desirable. Often, both designations apply. It is really a question of prioritizing initiatives between those that must be launched immediately, if there is to be any hope of saving the planet as an ecologically viable unit, and those that could be postponed for a year or two, or three until the top priorities have been undertaken and firmly established.

Reorganize and Streamline the United Nations Organization

This one is not new and much work has already been done in anticipation of a more streamlined United Nations. Agreement for action, however, is still pending. So change, especially where there are so many disparate interests involved, does take time.

Probably the most important reform is in reference to the Security Council, and the single country veto. Obviously this has to be replaced with some sort of majority decision-making formula. It is not my task to suggest what the formula should be, but a decision should require a substantial majority, as opposed to unanimity. Giving each of the big powers an absolute veto is as unrealistic as giving every shareholder of a large, publicly traded company the right to overrule management. The principle, which is a recipe for stalemate, is wrong. The majority must rule having in mind, as always, the interests of those who are opposed for one reason or another.

The principle of a United Nations to carry out many of its existing functions, and perhaps some new ones, is sound. In any streamlining, however, it has to be kept in mind that some of its original proponents were less than altruistic toward the plan. The Council on Foreign Relations saw the new organization as a cover for a new kind of colonialism, one that provided the advantages of colonial rule without the corresponding responsibilities.

The U.N. has not always worked to the Council's liking. On more than one occasion it has exercised its independence to the annoyance of the United States. Sometimes the Congress has been sufficiently irritated that it has held back part of the U.S. share of funding in a not too subtle effort to get its way. This, of course, is contrary to the spirit of community that was envisaged by most of the founders.

One new area of U.N. involvement should be in establishing diplomatic relations and channels of communication with visitors from other planets and galactic federations. The U.N. is the obvious choice for negotiations rather than any single nation. It is a development that may be stoutly resisted by that small group of Americans who have enjoyed privileged access to much alien technology, and have used some of it in ways that might not meet the approval of either American or world citizens.

Again we will have to ask the Congress of the United States to take the high road under a new policy of cooperation, rather than confrontation, and insist that valuable technology be made available for the benefit of humankind, and that the existing Cabal surrender its power to make life and death decisions concerning our treatment of, and relations with, our cosmic cousins.

In recent years I have been impressed by the wonderful humanitarian aid being provided by the United Nations Children's Fund (UNICEF), United Nations Human Rights Council (UNHRC) and other U.N. agencies. Also, U.N. leadership in promoting important treaties for the benefit of all humankind is precisely the kind of initiative one would expect and hope for from such a body. To be even more effective, some major powers should be prepared to drop their opposition to some proposals that their military view as impediments to their war-making capabilities such as land mines and cluster bombs. The war-making capabilities, as well as the reliance on military force, should be phased out of plans for the future!

Convert NATO to a Permanent U.N. Force

The North Atlantic Treaty Organization was intended to be a defensive alliance. I was already involved in politics when a group of nations decided to band together in a collective effort to deter an attack on any one of them by the Soviet Union. They feared a repeat of the situation that existed in the late 1930s when a highly-armed Germany tried to conquer Europe piecemeal until general war became inevitable. In theory collective defense might have been a function of the United Nations but it was considered impotent to act. So NATO was born.

It was never intended to be used as an attack force, however, despite efforts by the U.S. as far back as the Vietnam War to persuade some of its members to get involved. They all refused, and for good reason.

President Bush's invocation of the charter for his war against terror was really a perversion of its intent. Little wonder, then, that member countries have been reluctant to get involved in wars that were more offensive than defensive.

Another highly questionable American initiative has been the expansion of NATO into Eastern Europe as a kind of "in your face" to Russia at a time when cooperation, rather than confrontation, is essential for the peace of the world. The U.S. should remember how indignant Americans were when the Soviet Union began installing missiles in its back yard in Cuba. It was not to be tolerated! Still the U.S. is treating Russia the same way including the audacious installation of anti-ballistic missile systems in its back yard.

For years now a case has been made for a standing U.N. army ready at any and all times to intervene in situations authorized by the Security Council. The dream has never materialized because member nations were never willing to commit the necessary troops. Converting the standing NATO force into a U.N. force would reduce tensions between the U.S. and Russia and provide the muscle that had been needed but not available in several critical situations where U.N. action was really called for.

Most important of all, it would restore the principle of multilateralism as a welcome relief from the unilateralism of recent years.

DESIRABLE

Universal Health Insurance

A fast read of newspaper clippings in both countries convinced me that neither the U.S. nor Canadian systems are considered adequate. The American style leaves too many citizens without coverage, and quite a few who do have insurance find themselves victims of the fine print.

Canada's universal Medicare started out well in the early years when it was adequately funded. Later, however, cutbacks resulting from the induced recessions of 1981-82 and 1990-91 created funding deficits that persist. The net result has been a slow but inexorable transition to a two-tier system where Medicare still works well most of the time but long delays in gaining access to specialists and backlogs in non life-threatening surgical procedures have encouraged the wealthy to seek alternative sources of attention at their own expense.

The trend is sufficiently disturbing that it is time to look at the fundamentals of what needs to be accomplished and how best to achieve it. As a senior member of the Canadian cabinet that approved Medicare in 1966, I think it is time to review the alternative that we discussed and that all of my colleagues and I considered a superior system. The minister promoting Medicare while agreeing that the alternative was a "better plan," insisted that "it wouldn't be politic." He had Prime Minister Pearson's support so common sense was abandoned in the name of political expediency.

Before giving you a very brief précis of the alternative I would like to state the principles under consideration. Prior to Medicare, if someone in the family was stricken with cancer or some other affliction they could, and often did, incur medical and hospital bills that would exhaust all of the family's financial assets and leave them penniless – in extreme cases even homeless. What we were concerned about was a kind of insurance that would save them from financial disaster.

Somehow, in the process of public debate, the nature of the problem got lost in an avalanche of philosophical and rhetorical discourse and ended up in a government funded system that would pay a prescription for Aspirin when the dispensing fee was greater than the over-the-counter price of the product.

The greatest weakness in Canadian Medicare, however, has been the rigidity of centralized planning that is quite incapable of grasping the subtle differences in need from one community to another. The one shoe fits all approach is both frustrating and inefficient, as has been proven in other areas of economic activity. Marry rigidity to underfunding and you have a recipe for a functional breakdown.

The alternative plan would solve nearly all the problems in both the American and Canadian systems. Implementation in either or both countries would be far from easy! In the U.S. it would be bitterly opposed by the powerful insurance lobby that would probably be willing to spend millions attempting to prove that white is black. In Canada the change would be bitterly opposed by left-wing ideologues who still suffer from the quaint notion that bureaucrats are omnipotent and can somehow outguess the decisions of professionals on the front lines.

Nothing ventured nothing gained, however. So here is the alternative plan for politicians, philosophers and the sick, who are either waiting in queues or lacking any kind of health insurance, to chew on. Space restrictions limit me to the principles only.

Universal Government Funded Health Insurance

The criteria on which the plan was based are these: equal access to the best medical care for rich and poor alike, minimum red tape, and the least incentive for people who can well afford their own routine "throat checks" to take advantage of the system and demand services just because they are "free."

Each individual person would be free to go to the doctor and/or hospital of their choice, and all would be responsible for their own medical bills up to a limit of two percent of their gross income. It has to be gross rather than net income because some well-to-do people have business losses or other adjustments that result in a low net. Medical expenses in excess of two percent would be 100% insured.

This means that someone with a gross income of $100,000 would pay their own bills up to $2,000. Those earning $30,000 would pay up to $600.00, while people with no income would pay nothing. No one would be subjected to financial hardship as a result of medical expenses because the burden would be proportionate to their ability to pay.

At the same time, the fact that the majority would pay most of their expenses in a normal year would relieve governments of the responsibility of collecting and then disbursing billions in routine transactions and would eliminate much of the abuse experienced by the British, Swedish and Canadian systems.

To ensure that a temporary lack of cash would not deter anyone from seeking medical attention, and also to guarantee that doctors and hospitals would be promptly reimbursed for services provided, everyone would have a health card. They would then have the option of paying by cash or credit card, when appropriate to the circumstances, or of using their health card that would transmit the bill electronically to the insurer, a government agency, for immediate payment and subsequent adjustment in income tax evaluations. Expenses might be averaged over two or three years to discourage people from "storing" medical problems for the specific purpose of incurring major expenses in one taxation period. Apart from that, and a few technical details, there is no fine print to detract from the simplicity and efficacy of the plan.

One additional benefit, if the system worked as well as it should, it would be possible to add dental care at some stage by simply raising the deductible – perhaps to something around 3% of gross income.

Casinos

A very visible symptom of the post-World War II breakdown in moral and spiritual values has been the proliferation of casinos, lotteries and gambling outlets. As a former CEO of what was then the Canadian Foundation on Compulsive Gambling, I have witnessed firsthand the negative impact on people's lives.

I have never seen an unhappier group than the habitués of casinos. Far worse is the certainty that a small but significant percentage will become problem or compulsive gamblers – a disease that results in them losing first their own money, and then what they are able to borrow or steal from family or employers. The end of the road for far too many is taking their own lives.

Some years ago I saw a study indicating that there was no net benefit to governments from gambling revenues. It is just that seeing so much money in one easy pot has become totally seductive. What is overlooked are the huge costs of rehabilitation, jail time and lost work.

It is my hope that when federal governments have access to government-created money, and are no longer so financially strapped that they have to postpone or abandon many worthwhile causes, that they will find a way to compensate junior levels of government that make an effort to phase out their dependence on gambling revenues.

◆ ◆

There are myriad other subjects I would love to comment on but this tome has to end somewhere. The pursuit of individual, corporate and political righteousness, in the sense of doing right and making right and moral decisions is a monumental challenge in which each of us as individuals has a part to play.

NOTES

Chapter 1: We are Hell Bent Toward the Extinction of the Human Species

1. James Lovelock, "We're all doomed! 40 years from global catastrophe – and there's NOTHING we can do about it, says climate change expert," April 2008. http://www.dailymail.co.uk/pages/live/articles/news/news.html?in article id=541748&in page id=1770
2. *Ibid.*
3. *Ibid.*
4. Peter Gorrie, "Grim prognosis for Earth: The world in 2050," *Toronto Star*, January 3, 2007.
5. Peter Calamai, "Breeding Perfect Storms," *Toronto Star*, June 1, 2006.
6. Lead Editorial, "The sky-high cost of global warming," *Globe and Mail*, October 31, 2006.
7. Jessica Leeder, "Huge chunk snaps off storied Arctic ice shelf," *Globe and Mail*, July 29, 2008.
8. Kenneth Chang, "Study Finds New Evidence Of Warming in Antarctica," *The New York Times*, January 22, 2009.
9. Paul Krugman, "Enemy of the planet," *The New York Times*, April 17, 2006.
10. Gillian Wong, "Public misled, Gore says," *Toronto Star*, August 8, 2007.
11. Andrew C. Revkin, "On Climate Issue, Industry Ignored Its Scientists," *The New York Times*, April 24, 2009.
12. Associated Press, "Greenhouse gases rise to record levels," *Toronto Star*, November 24, 2009.
13. John M. Broder, "5 Nations Forge Pact on Climate; Goals go unmet," *The New York Times*, December 19, 2009.
14. Philip J. Corso, *The Day after Roswell*, (New York: Pocket Books, 1997).
15. An e-mail from Pierre Juneau, February 11, 2008.
16. Noel Cooper, *Language of the Heart. How to Read the Bible: A User's Guide for Catholics*, (Ottawa: Novalis Publishing Inc., 2003).

Chapter 2: Exploring the Middle East – 2006

1. Kent Hotaling journal, April 5, 2006.
2. Kay Hotaling journal, April 9, 2006.

3. As confirmed in an e-mail from Gavriel Gefen, June 19, 2008.
4. Kay Hotaling journal, April 10, 2006.
5. Holy Bible, New King James Version, Mark 4:35.
6. Paul Hellyer diary, April 11, 2006.
7. Kent Hotaling journal, April 12, 2006.
8. *Ibid.*, April 19, 2006.

Chapter 3: We Are Not Alone in the Cosmos

1. Don Schmidt and Thomas J. Carey, *Witness to Roswell: Unmasking the 60-year cover-up*, (Franklin Lakes: New Page Books, 2007), p. 38.
2. *Ibid.*, p. 39.
3. Paul Hellyer interview with Leo Pearce, January 6, 2008.
4. E-mail from Stan Fulham, October 31, 2007.
5. Nickolas Evanoff e-mail to Ray Stone, July 13, 2007.
6. "Description and Performance of Unidentified Flying Objects from 1947-1967," as taken from newsstand sources. Compiled by Malcolm McKellar, Vancouver, Canada, 1968. Hellyer papers, Toronto.
7. Senator Daniel K. Inouye at the Intra-Contra public hearings 1987. Chaired the Senate Select Committee on secret military assistance to Iran and the Nicaraguan opposition.
8. Dwight Eisenhower Presidential Departure Speech, January 17, 1961.
9. Steven M. Greer, *Disclosure: Military and Government Witnesses Reveal the Greatest Secrets in Modern History*, "Testimony of Brigadier General Stephen Lovekin," (Crozet: Crossing Point Inc., 2001), p. 235.
10. Paola Harris, *Connecting the Dots: Making Sense of the UFO Phenomenon*, (Mill Spring: Wild Flower Press, 2003), p. 47.
11. Timothy Good, *Need to Know: UFOs, the Military and Intelligence*, (London: Sidgwick & Jackson, 2006), p. 209.
12. Downgraded to Confidential, September 15, 1969. Hellyer papers, Toronto.
13. Wilbert B. Smith, "What we are doing in Ottawa," an address to the Vancouver area UFO Club, March 14, 1961.
14. Wilbert B. Smith, "The Philosophy of the Saucers." Hellyer papers, Toronto.
15. The 5th Annual Prufos Police Report 2006. The complete list is available at www.prufospolicedatabase.ca.uk
16. Robert Chapman, *UFO Flying Saucers over Britain?*, (London: Mayflower Books, 1969), pp. 13-15.
17. Robert Salas, *Faded Giant*, (North Charleston: Booksurge Llc, 2005), pp. 167-169.

18. From tape recording of interview with Lieutenant Colonel (Ret.) Charles I. Halt, February 2, 2007.
19. E-mail from "George," October 17, 2005. Hellyer papers, Toronto.
20. Hellyer diary, May 11, 2006.
21. *Ibid.*, May 18, 2006.
22. From a transcript of the dinner conversation at the Hellyer condo, July 7, 2006.
23. Jim Sparks, *The Keepers: An Alien Message for the Human Race*, (Columbus: Wild Flower Press, 2006), pp. 167-171.
24. As related by Leslie Kean, *Prescott Daily Courier*, interview with Arizona Governor Fife Symington III, March 18, 2007.
25. Chris Stoner in an interview with Dr. Michael Wolf, former U.S. National Security Council's Special Studies (UFO) Group and Jim Sparks in *The Keepers*.
26. *Ibid.*
27. Col. Philip J. Corso with William J. Birnes, *The Day After Roswell*, (New York: Pocket Books, 1997), p. 4.
28. Jim Sparks, *The Keepers*, op. cit., pp. 14-17.
29. John E. Mack, M.D., *Passport to the Cosmos: Human Transformation and Alien Encounters*, (New York: Crown Publishers, 1999), p. 276.

Chapter 4: The (Political) Gospel of John

1. Holy Bible, New International Version, John 6:41.
2. *Ibid.*, John 6:52.
3. *Ibid.*, John 18:36.
4. Karen Armstrong, *The Bible: The Biography*, (London: Atlantic Books, 2007), p. 69.
5. *Ibid.*, p. 68.
6. *Ibid.*, p. 56.
7. *Ibid.*, p. 57.
8. *Ibid.*
9. *Ibid.*
10. Holy Bible, op. cit., Acts of the Apostles 6:8.
11. *Ibid.*, Acts 7: 54-60.
12. *Ibid.*, Acts 11:25.
13. *Ibid.*, Acts 15:28-29.
14. Fr. Fréderic Manns, *John and Jamnia: How the Break Occurred Between Jews and Christians C.80-100 A.D.*, (Jerusalem: Franciscan Printing Press, 2002), p. 23.
15. *Ibid.*, p. 25.
16. *Ibid.*

17. *Ibid.*

18. *Ibid.*, p. 26.

19. Karen Armstrong, *The Bible*, op. cit., p. 65.

20. Bart D. Ehrman, *Lost Christianities: The Battles for Scripture and the Faiths We Never Knew*, (New York: Oxford University Press, 2003), p. 109.

21. *Ibid.*, p. 112.

22. Martin Goodman, *Rome and Jerusalem: The Clash of Ancient Civilizations*, (London: Penguin Books, 2007), p. 535.

23. Karen Armstrong, *The Bible*, op. cit., p. 102.

24. Elaine Pagels, *Beyond Belief: The Secret Gospel of Thomas*, (New York: Random House, 2003), p. 81.

25. *Ibid.*, p. 85.

26. *Ibid.*, pp. 85-86.

27. *Ibid.*

28. Holy Bible, op. cit., Mark 1:10-11.

29. *Ibid.*, Mark 1:24.

30. *Ibid.*, Mark 8:27-29.

31. *Ibid.*, Mark 9:2-7.

32. *Ibid.*, Mark 10:17-18.

33. *Ibid.*, Mark 13:32.

34. *Ibid.*, Mark 14:36.

35. *Ibid.*, Mark 15:34.

36. Mark D. Siljander, *A Deadly Misunderstanding: A Congressman's Quest to Bridge the Muslim-Christian Divide*, (New York: HarperCollins, 2008).

37. *Ibid.*, p. 144.

38. Holy Bible, The New King James Version, John 1:14.

39. *Ibid.*, Genesis 6:1-4.

40. *Ibid.*, Job 1:6.

41. *Ibid.*, Psalm 2:7.

42. *Ibid.*, Matthew 5:9.

43. Holy Bible, New International Version, Matthew 27:25.

44. *Ibid.*, John 14:6.

45. *Ibid.*, Matthew 25:34-46.

46. *Ibid.*, John 1:46.

47. Karen Armstrong, *The Bible.*, op. cit., p. 53.

48. Fr. Fréderic Manns, *John and Jamnia*, op. cit., p. 9.

49. *Ibid.*, p. 10.

50. Holy Bible, op. cit., Mark 12:29-31.

51. *Ibid.*, Matthew 5:44.

52. Ethan Bronner, "Ancient Tablet Ignites Debate On Messiah and Resurrection," *The New York Times*, July 6, 2008.

53. *Ibid.*

Chapter 5: Writing History Years after the Events Occurred

1. Senator Keith Davey, *The Rainmaker: A Passion for Politics*, (Toronto: Stoddart Publishing Co. Limited, 1986), pp. 23-24.
2. Walter L. Gordon, *A Political Memoir*, (Toronto: McClelland and Stewart, 1977), p. 91.
3. Michael Arnheim, *Is Christianity True?: A critical re-examination of the evidence*, (London: Prometheus Books, 1984).
4. In an e-mail from Beatrice Orchard to the author dated July 6, 2007.
5. John H. Heller, *Report on the Shroud of Turin*, (Boston: Houghton Mifflin Company, 1983).
6. John C. Iannone, *The Mystery of the Shroud of Turin*, (New York: Fathers and Brothers of the Society of St. Paul, 1998), p. 170.
7. PBS Home Video, 2004.
8. *Ibid.*
9. Fr. Peter Rinaldi, *When Millions Saw the Shroud: Letters from Turin*, (Don Bosco Publishers, 1979), p. 137.
10. Ariel David, "Shroud of Turin a medieval fake, Italian debunkers say," *Globe and Mail*, October 6, 2009.
11. Siabhan Roberts, "Ancient plants, grains prove Shroud is real, botanist says," *National Post*, August 3, 1999.
12. John Shelby Spong, *Born of a Woman: A Bishop Rethinks the Birth of Jesus*, (New York: HarperCollins Publishers, 1992).
13. John Shelby Spong, *Resurrection: Myth or Reality?*, (San Francisco: HarperCollins, 1994).
14. John Shelby Spong, *Born of a Woman*, op. cit., p. 50.
15. *Ibid.*
16. Tom Harpur, *For Christ's Sake*, (Toronto: Oxford University Press, 1986). In referring to the resurrection, however, he says it was not the physical body but presumably some higher form that was not always recognized by Jesus' followers.
17. Tom Harpur, *The Pagan Christ: Recovering the Lost Light*, (Toronto: Thomas Allen Publishers, 2004).
18. Bart D. Ehrman, *Truth and Fiction in The Da Vinci Code*, (New York: Oxford University Press, 2004).
19. *Ibid*, p. 106.
20. Linda Moulton Howe, *Glimpses of Other Realities, Volume II: High Strangeness*, (Jamison: LMH Productions, 2001), p. 141.
21. Elaine Pagels, *The Origin of Satan*, (New York: Vintage Books, 1995).

22. David Van Biema, "Secrets of the Nativity," *Time* magazine, December 13, 2004, p. 48.
23. *Ibid.*, p. 47.
24. E.M. Blaiklock, *Quirinius*, The Zondervan Pictorial Encyclopedia of the Bible, Volume 5, Merrill C. Tenny (gen. ed.), (Grand Rapids: Zondervan Publishing House, 1976), p. 6.
25. Jim Sparks, *The Keepers: An Alien Message for the Human Race*, (Columbus: Wild Flower Press, 2006), p. 15.
26. Holy Bible, op. cit., I Kings 18:38-39.
27. Bard D. Ehrman, *Misquoting Jesus: The Story Behind Who Changed the Bible and Why*, (New York: HarperCollins, 2005).
28. John Shelby Spong, *Born of A Woman*, op. cit., p. xvi.

Chapter 6: A Religious Agenda

1. Stuart Laidlaw, "War in religion's name denounced," *Toronto Star*, September 13, 2006.
2. *Ibid.*
3. Associated Press, "Monks wield sledgehammers in ungodly battle," *Toronto Star*, December 21, 2006.
4. John O'Sullivan, "The Irish 'Troubles' continue," *National Post*, August 3, 2007.
5. Matthew Campbell, "Barbarians of suburbs target French Jews," *U.S. News Today*, April 2, 2006.
6. Mitch Potter, "Israel bombs bridges, sends tanks into Gaza," *Toronto Star*, June 28, 2006.
7. Barbara Amiel, "Finally, someone who cares about Christians," *Maclean's* magazine, October 9, 2006.
8. Associated Press, Reuters, Canadian Press, "Malaysia PM fans flames after remarks cause storm," *Toronto Star*, October 18, 2003.
9. Rod Mickleburgh, "One dead in shooting at U.S. Jewish centre," *Globe and Mail*, July 29, 2006.
10. Sam Dagher and Mudhafer Al-Husaini, "Bomber at Iraqi Shrine Kills 40, Including 16 Iranian Pilgrims," *The New York Times*, January 5, 2009.
11. Timothy Williams and Atheer Kakan, "Concealed By Potatoes, Bomb Kills 10 In Baghdad," *The New York Times*, May 7, 2009.
12. Chip Cummins, Ben Lando and Peter Spiegel, "Deadly Blasts Test Iraq's Grip," *Wall Street Journal*, August 20, 2009.
13. Holy Bible, The New King James Version, Genesis 5:1-2.
14. Holy Bible, The Deeper Life Edition, Exodus 20:13.
15. Desmond Tutu to a convocation at the University of Toronto as reported in the *Toronto Star*, February 18, 2000.

16. Denise Chong, *The Girl in the Picture: The Kim Phuc Story*, (Toronto: Penguin Books Canada Ltd., 1999), p.363.
17. Michael Rubinkam, "Amish relying on faith to cope with slaying of schoolgirls," *Globe and Mail*, October 5, 2006.
18. CBC News Online, April 27, 2004.
19. An account written by Samir Kreidie and sent to the author August 28, 2008.
20. Mark D. Siljander, *A Deadly Misunderstanding: A Congressman's Quest to Bridge the Muslim-Christian Divide*, (New York: HarperCollins, 2008.)
21. Holy Bible, op. cit., Leviticus 19:18.

Chapter 7: Mammon Rules the World

1. Daniel Estulin, *The True Story of the Bilderberg Group*, (Walterville: Trine-Day LLC, 2007), pp. 92-93.
2. Memorandum E-A10, 19 October 1940, Council on Foreign Relations, War-Peace Studies, Baldwin Papers, Box 117.
3. Memorandum E-A17, 14 June 1941, CFR, War-Peace Studies, Hoover Library on War, Revolution and Peace.
4. Memorandum T-A25, 20 May 1942, CFR, War-Peace Studies, Hoover Library on War, Revolution and Peace.
5. *Ibid.*
6. J.H. Retinger, The European Continent, London's Hodge, 1946.
7. "The Crisis of Democracy: Report on the Governability of Democracies to the Trilateral Commission," New York University Press, 1975.
8. Holly Sklar (ed.), *Trilateralism: The Trilateral Commission and Elite Planning for World Management*, (Boston: South End Press, 1980), pp. 199-209.
9. *Ibid.*
10. Daniel Estulin, *The True Story of the Bilderberg Group*, op. cit., p. 33.
11. John R. MacArthur, *The Selling of "Free Trade": NAFTA, Washington and the Subversion of U.S. Democracy*, (New York: Hill and Wang, 2000).
12. As reported in the *Toronto Star*, October 22, 1987, in an article "More signs the U.S. believes it beat Canada." Yeutter denied making the statement but *Star* reporter Bob Hepburn added: "However, the U.S. sources, who asked not to be named, are considered impeccable. They were heavily involved in the talks, are extremely close to U.S. Treasury Secretary James Baker and were privy to confidential conversations and documents." I believe Yeutter did, in fact, make the statement because it sounds like him and what he said would have been what any forward-thinking U.S. negotiator would have thought and said privately when they were not expecting to be reported.

13. Based on Michael B. Smith's recollection of the meeting aboard Smith's 34-foot Sabre Sloop, *Wind*, as recorded in *Building a Partnership: The Canada-United States Free Trade Agreement*, Mordechai Kreinin (ed.), (East Lansing: Michigan State University Press, 2001), p. 7.
14. Greg Palast in an interview with *Acres USA*, June 2003.
15. Susan George, "Winning the War of Ideas: Lessons from the Gramscian Right," originally published in *Dissent*, Summer 1997.
16. *Ibid.*
17. Joseph E. Stiglitz, *Globalization and its Discontents*, (New York: Norton Trade, 2003), p. 71.
18. William Finnegan, "The Economics of Empire: Notes on the Washington Consensus," published in *Harper's* magazine, May 2003.
19. An excerpt from an article by Greg Palast, "Failures of the 20th Century: See Under I.M.F.," *The London Observer*, October 8, 2000.
20. William Finnegan, "The Economics of Empire," op. cit.
21. "World Bank Secret Documents Consumes Argentina," Greg Palast in an interview with Alex Jones, March 4, 2002.
22. *Ibid.*
23. *Ibid.*
24. Joseph E. Stiglitz, *Globalization and its Discontents*, op. cit., p. 231.
25. Economic Report of the President, 1991, 1994 and OECD.
26. Source: OECD.
27. Greg Palast, "Failures of the 20th Century," op. cit.
28. William Finnegan, "The Economics of Empire," op. cit.
29. Richard A. Lester, "Currency Issues to Overcome Depressions in Pennsylvania, 1723 and 1729," *The Journal of Political Economy*, Volume 46, June 1938, p. 338.
30. Adam Smith, *Wealth of Nations*, (New York: P.F. Collier and Son, 1909), p. 266.
31. Remarks by George Soros, "The Crisis of Global Capitalism: Open Society Endangered," December 10, 1998.
32. Steve Lohr, "In Bailout Furor, Wall St. Pay Becomes Target for Congress," *The New York Times*, September 24, 2008.
33. David Olive, "Time for CEOs to pay piper," *Toronto Star*, July 26, 2009.
34. Dan Seymour, "An industry of dizzying paycheques," *Toronto Star*, April 17, 2008.
35. Greg Farrell, "Court ruling ends pay case against Grasso," *USA Today*, July 2, 2008.
36. Excerpt from an article by Barrie McKenna, "Enron's Lay snubs Congress," *Globe and Mail*, February 4, 2002.

37. Excerpt from an article by Stephen Labaton, "MCI Agrees to Pay $500 Million in Fraud Case," *The New York Times*, May 20, 2003.
38. *Ibid.*
39. Excerpt from an article by Stephen Labaton, "10 Wall St. Firms Settle with U.S. in Analyst Inquiry," *The New York Times*, April 29, 2003.
40. Excerpt from an article by Brian Miller, "There's little repentance on Wall Street these days," *Globe and Mail*, April 28, 2003.
41. Donald Day, *Will Rogers: A Biography*, (New York: David McKay Company, Inc., 1962), p. 285.
42. Henry C. Simons, *Economic Policy for a Free Society*, (Chicago: University of Chicago Press, 1948), p. 80.
43. Milton Friedman, in a footnote reply to a letter from William F. Hixson, November 9, 1983.
44. Milton Friedman, in a letter to Professor John H. Hotson, February 3, 1986.
45. *Ibid.*
46. Paul A. Volcker, Statement by Chairman, New Board of Governors of the Federal Reserve System, before the Joint Economic Committee of the U.S. Congress, January 26, 1982.
47. Rita Trichur, " 'Watershed moment' for American banking," *Toronto Star*, July 15, 2008.
48. Sinclair Stewart, "Black days in July," *Globe and Mail*, July 16, 2008.
49. David R. Henderson (ed.), *The Fortune Encyclopedia of Economics*, (New York: Warner Books, Inc., 1993), p. 174.

Chapter 8: Unless We Repent and Change our Ways, We are Doomed

1. Michael Lind, "The Weird Men Behind George W. Bush's War," *New Statesman*, April 12, 2003.
2. "American Century," Pentagon Document on Post-Cold-War Strategy, February 18, 1992.
3. As reported in *The New York Times*, May 24, 1992.
4. *Ibid.*
5. "Rebuilding America's Defenses: Strategy, Forces and Resources for a New Century. A Report of the Project for the New American Century, September 2000."
6. From the text of U.S. President George W. Bush's address to a joint meeting of Congress, September 20, 2001.
7. From a translated text of Osama bin Laden's broadcast taken from *The New York Times*, October 8, 2001.
8. Excerpt from an article by Barrie McKenna, "Bush faces furor over knowledge of attack," *Globe and Mail*, May 17, 2002.

9. Excerpt from an article by Michele Lansberg, "Conspiracy crusader doubts official 9/11 version," *Toronto Star*, May 11, 2003.

10. As reported in *World Tribune*, Middle East Newsline, December 20, 2001.

11. See Special Report, "The Path to War," *Vanity Fair* magazine, May 2004, p. 228.

12. Excerpt from an article by Kevin Donovan, "How Saddam plotted to get A-bomb power," *Toronto Star*, January 31, 2003.

13. A Report of Chairman Donald W. Riegle, Jr., and Ranking Member Alfonse M. D'Amato of the Committee on Banking, Housing and Urban Affairs with Respect to Export Administration, United States Senate, 103rd Congress, 2nd Session, May 25, 1994.

14. *Ibid.*

15. Excerpt from an article by Estanislo Oziewicz, "United Nations weapons inspectors weren't thrown out of Iraq," *Globe and Mail*, April 4, 2003.

16. Excerpt from an article by Vilip Hiro, "When US turned a blind eye to poison gas," *The Observer*, September 1, 2002.

17. Scott Ritter speaking in London, England to CNN's Fionnuala Sweeney, July 17, 2002.

18. *Ibid.*

19. Jeff Mason and Michael Stott, "Obama praises democracy, blasts graft," *Globe and Mail*, July 8, 2009.

20. *Ibid.*

21. Mark Thompson, "Taming the system," *Time* magazine, February 23, 2009, p. 31.

22. Lewis Lapham, "Pax Iconomica," in *Behind the Headlines*, Vol. 54, No. 2, Winter 1996-97, p. 9, in his 'On Politics, Culture and Media' keynote address to the Canadian Institute of International Affairs national foreign policy conference in October 1996.

23. *Ibid.*, p. 8.

24. Daniel Estulin, *The True Story of the Bilderberg Group*, (Walterville:TrineDay, 2007).

25. Holly Sklar (ed.), *Trilateralism: The Trilateral Commission and Elite Planning for World Management*, (Boston: South End Press, 1980).

26. "Chris Stoner Interviews Dr. Michael Wolf – Former NSA Consultant." http://exopolitics.org.uk/ark%11hive/docs/chris-stoner-interviews-dr-michael-wolf-%11-former-nsa-consulant/

27. *Ibid.*

28. *Ibid.*

29. *Ibid.*

30. *Ibid.*

31. *Ibid.*

32. Quote from Dr. Carol Rosin who worked closely with Werner von Braun.

33. "Quantum mechanics predicts the existence of what are usually called 'zero-point' energies for the strong, the weak and the electromagnetic interactions, where 'zero-point' refers to the energy of the system at temperature T=0, or the lowest quantized energy level of a quantum mechanical system." As quoted in an article "Zero Point Energy and Zero Point Field," Calphysics Institute.

34. "Chris Stoner Interviews Dr. Michael Wolf," op. cit.

Chapter 9: Ending the World Financial Crisis

1. As reported in the *Globe and Mail*, November 2, 2008.

2. As reported in *The New York Times*, November 17, 2008.

3. John K. Galbraith, *Money, Whence it Came, Where it Went*, (Boston: Houghton Mifflin Company, 1975), p. 18.

4. William F. Hixson, *Triumph of the Bankers: Money and Banking in the Eighteenth and Nineteenth Centuries*, (Westport: Praeger Publishers, 1993), p. 46.

5. *Ibid.*, p. 60.

6. Paul Hellyer, *Surviving the Global Financial Crisis: The Economics of Hope for Generation X*, (Toronto: Chimo Media, 1996), pp. 1-2.

7. Source: Flow of Funds Accounts, Table L2 through 4, U.S. Federal Reserve Bulletin, from many issues.

8. Data published in the Bank of Canada Banking and Financial Statistics approximately 30 calendar days after each end of reference month.

9. Patricia Adams, *Odious Debts: Loose Lending, Corruption, And the Third World's Environmental Legacy*, (London: Probe International, 1991).

10. Griffin, G. Edward, *The Creature from Jekyll Island: A Second Look at the Federal Reserve*, (Westlake Village: American Media, 2009), p. 23.

11. Jack Metcalf, *The Two Hundred Year Debate: Who Shall Issue the Nation's Money*, (Olympia: An Honest Money for America Publication, 1986), p. 91.

12. *Ibid.*

13. *Ibid.*, p. 92.

14. Thomas Edison, American Inventor (Feb. 11, 1847-Oct. 18, 1931).

15. Graham F. Towers, first Governor of the Bank of Canada from 1934-1954.

16. Curtis P. Nettles, *The Money Supply of the American Colonies before 1720*, (New York: Augustus M. Kelley, 1964), p. 265.

17. Olive Grubiak and Jan Grubiak, *The GUERNSEY Experiment*, (Hawthorne: Omni Publications, 1988), p. 7.

18. John G. Nicolay and John Hay (eds.), *Abraham Lincoln: Complete Works*, (New York: The Century Co., 1907), p. 264.
19. William F. Hixson, *Triumph of the Bankers*, op. cit., p. 135.
20. Alexander Campbell, *The True Greenback*, (Chicago: Republican Books, 1868), p. 31.
21. Louise Story and Eric Dash, "Bankers Reaped Lavish Bonuses During Bailouts," *The New York Times*, July 31, 2009.

Chapter 10: A Political Agenda

1. Steven M. Greer, *Hidden Truth, Forbidden Knowledge: It is time for you to know*, (Crozet: Crossing Point, Inc., 2006).
2. Chris Stoner interviews Dr. Michael Wolf – Former NSA Consultant. http://www.exopolitics.org.uk/ark%11hive/docs/chris-stoner-interviews-dr-michael-wolf-%11-former-nsa-consultant/
3. An e-mail from Dr. John Reed to Paul Hellyer January 7, 2009. Statistics based on Freedom of Information Act (FOIA) Request No. 94-14.
4. Holy Bible, The New King James Version, Micah 6:8.
5. Colin Chapman, *Whose Promised Land: Israel or Palestine?*, (Oxford: Lion Publishing plc, 1992.)
6. E-mail from Gavriel Gefen to author May 21, 2007.
7. Chacour, Elias, *Blood Brothers*, (Grand Rapids: Chosen Books, 2003).
8. Thomas L. Friedman, "Save the Rainforest," *The New York Times*, November 11, 2009.
9. Dr. Hans Blix, WMDC Report "Weapons of Terror," June 1, 2006, p. 94.
10. Sonia Verma, "Young activist wants Canadian troops out now," *Globe and Mail*, November 20, 2009.
11. *Ibid.*
12. John Polanyi, "There's a way to end Afghanistan's and the world's pain," *Globe and Mail*, September 23, 2006.
13. William Thomas, "The Bucks Stops Here: The End of the Dollar and Just About Everything Else," www.willthomasonline.net
14. *Ibid.*
15. *Ibid.*
16. Source: International Financial Statistics Yearbook, 2002.
17. Patricia Adams, *Odious Debts: Loose Lending, Corruption, And the Third World's Environmental Legacy*, (London: Probe International, 1991).
18. Niall Ferguson, *The Ascent of Money: A Financial History of the World*, (London: Penguin Books, 2008).

BIBLIOGRAPHY

Adams, Patricia, *Odious Debts: Loose Lending, Corruption, And the Third World's Environmental Legacy*, (London: Probe International, 1991).

Armstrong, Karen, *The Bible: The Biography*, (London: Atlantic Books, 2007).

Arnheim, Michael, *Is Christianity True?: A critical re-examination of the evidence*, (London: Prometheus Books, 1984).

Bartlett, Donald L. and James A. Steele, *America: What Went Wrong?*, (Kansas City: A Universal Press Syndicate Company, 1992).

Beverley, James A., *Understanding Islam*, (Nashville: Thomas Nelson Publishers, Inc., 2001).

Bose, Shonali, *Amu*, (New Delhi: Penguin Books, 2004).

Cahill, Thomas, *How the Irish Saved Civilization: The Untold Story of Ireland's Heroic Role from the Fall of Rome to the Rise of Medieval Europe*, (New York: Anchor Books, 1996).

Caldicott, Helen, *The New Nuclear Danger: George W. Bush's Military-Industrial Complex*, (New York: The New Press, 2002).

Caner, Ergen Mehmet (gen. ed.), *Voices Behind the Veil: The World of Islam Through the Eyes of Women*, (Grand Rapids: Kregel Publications, 2003).

Carter, Jimmy, *Palestine: Peace not Apartheid*, (New York: Simon & Schuster, 2006).

Carter, Jimmy, *Our Endangered Values: America's Moral Crisis*, (New York: Simon & Schuster, 2005).

Chacour, Elias, *Blood Brothers*, (Grand Rapids: Chosen Books, 2003).

Chandler, Paul-Gordon, *Pilgrims of Christ on the Muslim Road*, (Plymouth: Cowley Publications, 2007).

Chapman, Colin, *Whose Promised Land? Israel or Palestine?*, (Oxford: Lion Publishing plc, 1992).

Chapman, Robert, *UFO Flying Saucers over Britain?*, (London: Mayflower Books, 1969).

Cooper, Noel, *Language of the Heart. How to Read the Bible: A User's Guide for Catholics*, (Ottawa: Novalis Publishing Inc., 2003).

Corso, Col. Philip J. with William J. Birnes, *The Day After Roswell*, (New York: Pocket Books, 1997).

Currer-Briggs, Noel, *The Shroud and the Grail*, (New York: St. Martin's Press, 1987).

Danaher, Kevin (ed.), *50 Years is Enough: The Case Against the World Bank and the International Monetary Fund*, (Boston: South End Press, 1994).

Davey, Senator Keith, *The Rainmaker: A Passion for Politics*, (Toronto: Stoddart Publishing Co. Limited, 1986).

Dawood, N.J., *The Koran*, Translated with Notes, (New York: Penguin Books, 2003).

Day, Donald, *Will Rogers: A Biography*, (New York: David McKay Company, Inc., 1962).

Ehrman, Bart D., *Misquoting Jesus: The Story Behind Who Changed the Bible and Why*, (New York: HarperCollins, 2005).

Ehrman, Bart D., *Truth and Fiction in The Da Vinci Code*, (New York: Oxford University Press, 2004).

Ehrman, Bart D., *Lost Christianities: The Battles for Scripture and the Faiths We Never Knew*, (New York: Oxford University Press, 2003).

Estulin, Daniel *The True Story of the Bilderberg Group*, (Walterville: TrineDay, 2007).

Ferguson, Niall, *The Ascent of Money: A Financial History of the World*, (London: Penguin Press, 2008).

Galbraith, J.K., *Money, Whence it Came, Where it Went*, (Boston: Houghton Mifflin Company, 1975).

Gard, Richard A. (ed.), *Buddhism*, (New York: George Braziller, Inc., 1961).

Glasbeck, Harry, *Wealth by Stealth: Corporate Crime, Corporate Law, and the Perversion of Democracy*, (Toronto: Between the Lines, 2002).

Good, Timothy, *Need to Know: UFOs, the Military and Intelligence*, (London: Sidgwick & Jackson, 2006).

Goodman, Martin, *Rome and Jerusalem: The Clash of Ancient Civilizations*, (London: Penguin Books, 2007).

Gordon, Walter L., *A Political Memoir*, (Toronto: McClelland and Stewart, 1977.)

Greer, Steven M., *Hidden Truths, Forbidden Knowledge: It is time for you to know*, (Crozet: Crossing Point, Inc., 2006).

Greer, Steven M., *Disclosure: Military and Government Witnesses Reveal the Greatest Secrets in Modern History*, (Crozet: Crossing Point, Inc., 2001).

Griffin, G. Edward, *The Creature from Jekyll Island: A Second Look at the Federal Reserve*, (Westlake Village: American Media, 2009).

Harpur, Tom, *The Pagan Christ: Recovering the Lost Light*, (Toronto: Thomas Allen Publishers, 2004).

Harpur, Tom, *For Christ's Sake*, (Toronto: Oxford University Press, 1986).

Harris, Paola Leopizzi, *Exopolitics: How Does One Speak To A Ball of Light?*, (Bloomington: AuthorHouse, 2007).

Harris, Paola Leopizzi, *Connecting the Dots…Making Sense of the UFO Phenomenon*, (Mill Spring: Wild Flower Press, 2003).

Heller, John H., *Report on the Shroud of Turin*, (Boston: Houghton Mifflin Company, 1983).

Hellyer, Paul, *The Evil Empire: Globalization's Darker Side*, (Toronto: Chimo Media, 1997).

Hellyer, Paul, *Surviving the Global Financial Crisis: The Economics of Hope for Generation X*, (Toronto: Chimo Media, 1996).

Hellyer, Paul, *Damn the Torpedoes: My Fight to Unify Canada's Armed Forces*, (Toronto: McClelland and Stewart Inc., 1990).

Heydarpoor, Mahnaz, *Love in Christianity and Islam: A Contribution to Religious Ethics*, (London: New City, 2002).

Hitchens, Christopher, *God is not Great: How Religion Poisons Everything*, (Toronto: McClelland & Stewart, 2007).

Howe, Linda Moulton, *Glimpses of Other Realities, Volume II: High Strangeness*, (Jamison: LMH Productions, 2001).

Humber, Thomas, *The Sacred Shroud*, (New York: Pocket Books, 1977).

Iannone, John C., *The Mystery of the Shroud of Turin: New Scientific Evidence*, (New York: Fathers and Brothers of the Society of St. Paul, 1998).

Jeffrey, Grant R., *Creation: Remarkable Evidence of God's Design*, (Toronto: Frontier Research Publications Inc., 2003).

Keyhoe, Donald E., *Flying Saucers from Outer Space*, (New York: Henry Holt & Co., 1954.)

LaMarsh, Judy, *Memoirs of a Bird in a Gilded Cage*, (Toronto: McClelland and Stewart, 1969).

MacArthur, John R., *The Selling of "Free Trade": NAFTA, Washington and the Subversion of U.S. Democracy*, (New York: Hill and Wang, 2000).

MacLaine, Shirley, *Sage-ing While Age-ing*, (New York: Atria Books, 2007).

Mack, John E., *Passport to the Cosmos: Human Transformation and Alien Encounters*, (New York: Crown Publishers, 1999).

Mander, Gerry and Edward Goldsmith (eds.), *The Case Against the Global Economy: And a Turn Toward the Local*, (San Francisco: Sierra Club Books, 1996).

Manns, Fr. Fréderic, *John and Jamnia: How the Break Occurred Between Jews and Christians C.80-100 A.D.*, (Jerusalem: Franciscan Printing Press, 2002).

Marchetti, Victor and John D. Marks, *The CIA and the Cult of Intelligence*, (New York: Dell Publishing Co. Inc., 1974).

Marrs, Jim, *Alien Agenda: Investigating the Extraterrestrial Presence Among Us*, (New York: HarperPaperbacks, 1997).

McGrath, Alister E., *Studies in Doctrine: Understanding Doctrine, Undertaking the Trinity, Understanding Jesus, Justification by Faith*, (Grand Rapids: Zonderval Publishing House, 1997).

Nouwen, Henri J.M., *Life of the Beloved: Spiritual Living in a Secular World*, (New York: The Crossroad Publishing Company, 1992).

Pagels, Elaine, *Beyond Belief: The Secret Gospel of Thomas*, (New York: Random House, 2003).

Pagels, Elaine, *The Origin of Satan*, (New York: Vintage Books, 1995).

Palast, Greg, *The Best Democracy Money Can Buy: The Truth about Corporate Cons, Globalization, and High-Finance Fraudsters*, (New York: Penguin Putnam, 2002).

Perkins, John, *Confessions of an Economic Hit Man*, (New York: Plume, 2006).

Pope, Nick, *Operation Lightning Strike*, (London: Simon & Schuster, 2002).

Rachlis, Michael and Carol Kushner, *Second Opinion: What's Wrong with Canada's Health Care System and How to Fix it*, (Toronto: Collins Publishers, 1989).

Ramadan, Tariq, *Western Muslims and the Future of Islam*, (Oxford: Oxford University Press, 2004).

Roy, Arundhati, *The Algebra of Infinite Justice*, (London: HarperCollins, 2002).

Salas, Robert, *Faded Giant*, (North Charleston: Booksurge Llc, 2005).

Salla, Michael E., *Exopolitics: Political Implications of The Extraterrestrial Presence*, (Tempe: Dandelion Books, 2004).

Schmidt, Don and Thomas J. Carey, *Witness to Roswell: Unmasking the 60-year cover-up*, (Franklin Lakes: New Page Books, 2007).

Scully, Frank, *Behind the Flying Saucers*, (New York: Henry Holt & Co., 1950).

Siljander, Mark D., *A Deadly Misunderstanding: A Congressman's Quest to Bridge the Muslim-Christian Divide*, (New York: HarperCollins, 2008).

Simone, Rob, *UFO's in the Headlines: Real Reporting on a Real Phenomenon*, (Lafayette Hill: Headroom Publishing, 2007).

Simons, Henry C., *Economic Policy for a Free Society*, (Chicago: University of Chicago Press, 1948).

Sklar, Holly (ed.), *Trilateralism: The Trilateral Commission and Elite Planning for World Management*, (Boston: South End Press, 1980).

Smith, Adam, *Wealth of Nations*, (New York: P.F. Collier and Son, 1909).

Sparks, Jim, *The Keepers: An Alien Message for the Human Race*, (Columbus: Wild Flower Press, 2006).

Spencer, John, *The UFO Encyclopaedia*, (London: Headline Book Publishing, 1991).

Spong, John Shelby, *Resurrection: Myth or Reality*, (New York: HarperCollins Publishers, 1995).

Spong, John Shelby, *Born of a Woman: A Bishop Rethinks the Birth of Jesus*, (New York: HarperCollins Publishers, 1992).

Stevenson, Kenneth E. and Gary R. Habermas, *Verdict on the Shroud: Evidence for the Death and Resurrection of Jesus Christ*, (Ann Arbor: Servant Books, 1981).

Stiglitz, Joseph E., *Globalization and its Discontents*, (New York: Norton Trade, 2003).

Walton, Travis, *Fire in the Sky: The Walton Experience*, (New York: Marlowe & Company, 1997).

Wilson, Barrie, *How Jesus Became Christian*, (Toronto: Random House, 2008).

Winston, Robert, *The Story of God: A Personal Journey into the World of Science and Religion*, (London: Bantam Press, 2005).

Wood, Ryan S., *Majic Eyes Only: Earth's Encounters with Extraterrestrial Technology*, (Bloomfield: Wood Enterprises, 2005).

Yancey, Philip, *What's so Amazing about Grace?*, (Grand Rapids: Zondervan, 1997).

INDEX

ABOUT THE AUTHOR

Paul Hellyer is one of Canada's best known and most controversial politicians. First elected in 1949, he was the youngest cabinet minister appointed to Louis S. St. Laurent's government eight years later. He subsequently held senior posts in the governments of Lester B. Pearson and Pierre E. Trudeau, who defeated him for the Liberal Party leadership in 1968. The following year, after achieving the rank of senior minister, which was later designated Deputy Prime Minister, Hellyer resigned from the Trudeau cabinet on a question of principle related to housing.

Although Hellyer is best known for the unification of the Canadian Armed Forces and for his 1968 chairmanship of the Task Force on Housing and Urban Development, he has maintained a life-long interest in macroeconomics. Through the years, as a journalist and political commentator, he has continued to fight for economic reforms and has written several books on the subject.

A man of many interests, Hellyer's ideas are not classroom abstractions. He was born and raised on a farm and his business experience includes manufacturing, retailing, construction, land development, tourism and publishing. He has also been active in community affairs including the arts and studied voice at the Royal Conservatory of Music in Toronto. His multi-faceted career, in addition to a near-lifetime in politics, gives Hellyer a rare perspective on what has gone wrong with world economies.

In recent years he has become interested in the extraterrestrial presence and their superior technology that we have been emulating. In September 2005 he became the first person of cabinet rank in the G8 group of countries to state unequivocally "UFO's are as real as the airplanes flying overhead." He continues to take an interest in these areas and provides a bit of basic information about them in this book.